LEE DUFFY

'THE BLOOD MOON'

By Jamie Boyle

"I'd like to dedicate this book to one of the greatest men I've ever met, my father in-law Reuben 'Rob' Dickinson"

www.warcrypress.co.uk
Jamie Boyle (c)

LEE DUFFY 'THE BLOOD MOON'

ISBN: 978-1-912543-23-6

NOTE: The views and opinions expressed in this book are those of the interviewees obtained during recorded interview and do not necessarily reflect the opinions of the author.

Cover Design: Gavin Parker UK

Printed and bound in Great Britain by Clays Ltd, Elcograf S.p.A.

Find out more at: facebook.com/leeduffybook

Chapters

3.55

Follow the man in the red Mercedes
To the party at the edge of the town
The first time I saw him
He was eating chicken
Sucking it to the bone

I was driving, he pulled me over
"Take me to the blues"
So I took him and he told me
That he owned the town

Sometime later in the paper
Assassination attempt
While he ran at them
They fired a shotgun
Shotgun pellets in the legs

He used to play Russian roulette
Was Deer Hunter his favourite film?
Survived many more assassination attempts
Began to think he was invincible

3.55

There was a time in a bar
A bucket of petrol over him
But his killer couldn't strike the match
I don't know what happened to him

He had no value for his life
Like the Terminator he said he'd be back
He used to stare at the whole of the moon
It was his favourite song
By The Waterboys

On his final night he picked a fight
In the Afro-Caribbean centre
Red stripe a pound he wore his frown
He seemed to poison the atmosphere
In the car park as the moon shone down
The crowd gathered around
He was getting the better of him
As the blade went in
The crowd didn't make a sound
It was 3.55

Song from The Whole of the Moon Documentary by Charlie Thomas –
Singer/Songwriter

Contact:
chasthomasmusic@gmail.com
facebook.com/www.charliethomas.co.uk
Web: charliethomas2.bandcamp.com/releases

"No one is actually dead until the ripples they cause in the world die away."

Terry Pratchett

THE STURGEON MOON
INTRODUCTION

I suppose it was inevitable that I'd end up writing a book about Lee Duffy when I started out writing true crime books for a living. Growing up in Middlesbrough I couldn't really pretend that he wasn't a big part of Middlesbrough's true crime history. He was the main player in that genre but I have to say that I didn't think it would lead to me writing two books and bringing out a documentary about him, but people seem eager to know as much as they can about Lee Duffy.

I know other people had toyed with the idea of writing books about Lee as I've spoken to them personally, but nothing materialised. Whether that was because they weren't from Middlesbrough or not I don't know or perhaps they thought that the backlash would be too great, but I found it helped me to know who was who and people seemed comfortable talking to me because of this. There are still plenty of folk in Middlesbrough that you wouldn't want to upset!

One of the retired police officers in this book that I spoke with told me that working on Teesside always caused him more bother than when he worked in big cities like Newcastle and Liverpool so that might help you to envisage how dangerous a place Middlesbrough was and can still be! Don't get me wrong you'll find plenty of 'salt of the earth' people in Teesside but the older generation especially had a tough life.

Lee Duffy – The Whole of the Moon was released firstly on Kindle on August 3rd, 2018. The paperback edition came out on the later date of August 21st. I knew it was going to be big but I didn't realise just how big. The sales of that book on Amazon were staggering and my publishers told me it's been their most popular book to date, and they have all kinds of books on people such as the Kray Twins, Paul Sykes, Roy Shaw, Richy Horsley, James McCrory, Dominic Negus, Bobby Vanzie and Gerald McClellan on their shelves. The funny thing is the director of Warcry Publications in Pontefract had never even heard of Lee Duffy but now he can't read enough about him.

Even Waterstones in Captain Cook Square in Middlesbrough have said in the twenty years they've been there it's been the most successful book by a local author and up there in terms of sales with their monster books such as Harry Potter and Fifty Shades of Grey.

When it first came out people went in their dozens on a daily basis demanding to read this book that the whole of Teesside was talking about.

Another bookshop in Newcastle told me that it was that popular that they had to keep all The Whole of the Moon books behind the till because they were all getting half inched, in fact as many as thirty in one month went walkies. Then only a few months later I released Terry Dicko's Laughter, Madness and Mayhem and that started going missing from the shelves as well so I don't know what kind of cliental Jamie Boyle's bringing to the retail outlets these days! Saying that my publishers Warcry Press received an email from Holme House prison saying that all the Lee Duffy books keep going missing after being taken from the Library and could they have any copies that were perhaps a little damaged. They seemed surprised to learn that they had thieves in there! It was also the same with the main library in central Middlesbrough as their copies of The Whole of the Moon have been stolen too.

Middlesbrough police officers, barristers and solicitors have all told me personally they've had a snoop at it, as you can imagine many of them dealt with Lee regularly.

A Redcar solicitor told me that he'd had that much business from Lee alone that he virtually paid for his yacht.

The first book had such a huge build up that if it had flopped I probably wouldn't have been taken seriously as an author again. I suppose you could say I placed my head well and truly on the chopping block taking on a project as big as the Lee Paul Duffy story.

I said in the first book that I wanted to dig a bit deeper and bring a more balanced view to what had been written about Lee before and I think I achieved that. I did not know Lee Duffy and I had never met him but I grew up hearing the stories the same as everyone else in Middlesbrough.

It's funny because what I've read of the nasty messages I got (surprising I know) is "Ooh you're writing books about people you've never even met", well I'd guess the people who've over the years written the best sellers on Jack the Ripper or Adolf Hitler had never met them either unless they're still about and are 142 so I can never understand that comment.

The one memory I have was when the book had only been out 48 hours on the kindle, I was walking down Albert Road in Middlesbrough and a man stopped me in the street who I didn't know, he asked if I was Jamie Boyle then the guy said he'd been up all night reading the book in one day and although he grew up thinking Lee Duffy was a figure of pure evil, he now thought differently because he wasn't aware of the childhood abuse Lee had suffered at the hands of the bullies, not to mention the hard upbringing he had from his sadistic father.

For me, that book was about looking at the whole picture. I've had people criticise me because they think I'm glorifying him and they say that because they have a one-sided view of Lee, as everything that was in print about him before this book focused solely on the terrible things that Lee did. I just wanted the book to be balanced, for people to make up their own minds. In that sense they are like the Paul Sykes books that I wrote. When you tell the full truth about someone who people have strong opinions

6

about you are never going to please everyone, if you do you're doing something wrong!

Lee's best friend once told me "Jamie you could write a book alone from one day of Lee's life, you've only just scratched the surface", and that's why there is a second book as when we went to print with the first book I was still getting people coming forward wanting to speak to me about the situations they'd been in with Lee. If you were around Middlesbrough through the 80s and early 90s then maybe you have your own story about Duffy.

In this book we'll dig deeper into Lee's Newcastle connections, how his one-man crusade caused problems for the constabulary and how he was in his school years.

There's been so many expressions I've heard being used to describe Lee in the last eighteen months whilst I've researched him. I've had a lot of people contact me to speak about Lee and some of it hasn't always been pleasant but that's part and parcel of being a crime writer I suppose and I've had to learn to cope with copious amounts of abuse although it hasn't always been like that.

Towards the end of the Duffy projects, Lee's only biological son thanked me for having the balls to do the books, which I found heart-warming, he had never met his father in person so I suppose it might have given him a little insight into what he was like.

Steve Wraith, who has written books about the Kray Twins, Paul Ferris and Freddie Foreman, went on to tell me that after the huge success of Stephen Sayers book in 2015, in which Lee Duffy is mentioned, that him and co-author Stuart Wheatman seriously considered doing a book on the Duff. In the end both were put off because Lee is still such a controversial character.

Middlesbrough's boxing royalty, 2 x ABA champion and former Commonwealth Gold medallist Middleweight John Pearce told me that for someone to take on such a highly emotional project they'd need to be seriously odd or not all there, John said I am both (I'll take that as a compliment John honest).

During these two books and the documentary on Lee Duffy I've been offered all kind of projects like to sell Lee Duffy shirts but of course I've declined. At the end of the day Lee wasn't a gimmick, he was someone's son, brother, father and friend and I would never disregard those facts. The people close around me and the correct ones who were around Lee know just how respectful I've remained in doing these projects, especially considering some of the evidence I could have used and stories I had on record with people's permission to use but I never put them out there out of respect for the Duffy family.

I've had to endure people saying horrific things about my wife and kids. Another then wished cancer on me and even threatened to hurt my wife which is a hard one to take! Imagine being that sick to send someone things like that because they write books for a living eh! There was even a well-known namedropper making up ludicrous stories about me to get himself a bit of attention who then tried to blackmail my wife! It takes all sort's doesn't it?! It's a good job I've got a skin as thick as a rhino's.

It does make me laugh that people have had things to say about me writing the Lee Duffy books but the same people are ok with reading books such as Ronnie Kray, Freddie Foreman, Charlie Richardson, Joey Pyle and "Mad" Frankie Fraser because they look like nice old chaps and are old and harmless now like ya grandad is. Believe it or not folks, but those people were just as bad as Lee Duffy and actually in some cases much worse once over but it seems to be accepted because it's a part of social history. Well Lee Paul Duffy is Middlesbrough's social history people!!!!

Some people have even tried to hold it against me for the things Lee Duffy did when in actual fact I was never any older than being at primary school when Lee had his reign over the town of Middlesbrough.

If you've read any of my other seven books before this one then you'll know the last thing I do is glorify anything like that but they happened. Lee Paul Duffy happened from June 1965 – August 1991 and that's not my fault. He became infamous in the North East from 1985 – 1991 and after that he achieved a lifetime of immortality in death.

The majority have been happy with what I'm doing and some of the people who were close to Lee, when they've actually took the time to read the book, have told me "Jamie I can't fault you with what you wrote, it was all very fair". Some of the closest people to Lee have read that book and told me I got it bang on, some have told me it made them cry and that it brought back some fabulous memories that they had completely forgotten about. Others told me it was powerful and thought provoking and revealed a bigger picture that the whole of Teesside had not seen before.

In the aftermath of the first book I've had messages from all over the world such as America, Canada, Thailand and all-over Britain.

People who I've never met before saying they'd bunked the day off work and that they'd been waiting a quarter of a century for a book to come out about the Duffer and that please would I do a second one.

I suppose you could say the title of the first book, although Lee's favourite song, we used as a vehicle and boy did it serve its purpose. The messages I've had from so many different people saying that they've listened to that song every day in so many of its different versions on YouTube.

People have told me that reading that first book got them out of a bad place and one man from Scotland said it even saved him from the brink of suicide, its stories like that that make being author for a living worthwhile.

Well to be honest I didn't have any plans on writing this book that was until I received around fifty inboxes asking for another one, I had the information there, as I said, it just kept coming after I'd finished the first one so I started with the second one and thought I'd see where it went.

The first was read by all kinds of people such as famous Premier League footballers, actors, comedians, gangsters and boxers.

This is my eighth book in exactly two and a half years that I've released. I haven't accepted all the books I've been asked to write, even though some have been famous, it's soul destroying when you spend over three months writing a book then it flops so I have tried to write the ones I have an interest in myself. Now I have a feeling and a bit of a sixth sense on what will sell and what won't.

This will be my final book on the Duff's story and then I'll be walking away from it as promised to some of those that were close to Lee. Even though, as short as Lee's life was, he did that much to merit a dozen books like Charles Bronson or Chopper Reid.

I suppose the only time I would ever consider possibly even doing another Duffy is if it was somebody who had been very close to Lee like his good friend Neil Booth, Mark Hartley a very close friend and the man who held Lee as he passed away, Lee's Tyneside brother Stephen Sayers, the true love of Lee's life Lisa Stockell or his younger sister and closest sibling Louise but in my opinion they will never choose to do it so it will certainly be left alone from me and they'll be no 'Final Moon', I've also got other projects in the pipeline that I have to move on to, opportunities to write books that I wouldn't have been offered to write if it hadn't been for the Lee Duffy book such as Roy Shaw's, Charlie Richardson's (Kray's nemesis) widow Ronnie Richardson and former Kray gang member Chris Lambrianou's.

In my opinion, from researching Lee to the extent that I have, I would say he was at the top of his game in the summer of 1990. In 1990 he was fresh from all the intensive jail training and of course it was the year before someone tried to kill him with a gun. He was much more carefree than the year after when the struggle to survive on a daily basis was very real and had certainly started to take its toll.

Another thing which you've got to take into account is that Lee's drug use also went to another level in the last year of his life and maybe that had something to do with the stress of having attempts made to kill him, he seemed to be getting crazier as he got older.

Lee had always taken drugs since the days of him sniffing glue at 14 but by the time that summer of 1991 had come he had a deadly crack cocaine habit. Crack cocaine causes aggressive and paranoid behaviour and that's not something that Lee Duffy of all people needed, I mean, even the calmest of people who've used crack have been known to become highly aggressive. Lee and Neil Booth once spent three days in a crack house in Newcastle.

Lee died probably five years before he was to hit his peak so what would have happened if Lee had been allowed to get to 27,28,29,30 and so on, how many lives would he have gone on to affect, maybe he would have quietened down, we'll never know!

The same week Lee Duffy died he had walked up to Stockton's George Doneathy on The Mall Nightclub door in Stockton looking for bother and George was a 6ft 6 bodybuilder with a tremendous reputation (talk about looking for the biggest and hardest eh) as a hardman so why was Lee becoming even more and more violent as he got older? Would he have went on to kill or would he have repented for his sins and turned the other way? Can you imagine how much of a powerful message it would have been if he'd have turned his life around, how much of a deep message he could have been, he could have worked with offenders or kids and could have been going into prisons and schools with his bullet holes telling the youth of today to stay away from crime and not to make the same mistakes that he did. After all, he was the baddest of the bad so can you imagine the message of repent Lee Duffy could have given!

When I think of that question I think of James Cagney in the 1938 film 'Angels with Dirty Faces' where he played the super bad ass fearless character Rocky Sullivan. Rocky had a life like Lee's and before he was put to death a priest asked him to show he was scared to the young kids who looked up to him to show them that it was no way to live. Rocky told the priest to piss off but at the last minute changed his mind and pretended to cry before he went to the electric chair to send a powerful message to the kids.

On the other hand, Lee was far more 'radio rental' (fucking mental) at 26 than he ever was at 19 or 20 and that is a very unusual thing for a man as normally we mellow out.

We'll never know what would have happened to Lee for sure but one thing I am certain off is that if he'd not died when he did he was looking at some serious time behind doors. Lee had several criminal incidents hanging over his head such as threats to kill Islam Gull who was the partner of Ria Maria Nasir. The David Tapping/Commercial Pub incident but the most serious of them all was the Peter Wilson/Wickers World case. From my research Lee was looking at easily a six to seven-year stretch, he was due to appear in Middlesbrough Crown Court in around October 1991. For me the evidence was overwhelming and even if the jury believed Lee's side of events that Peter Wilson started on Lee first there was no way he was getting off with breaking someone's neck because he didn't like what was being said to him! Not to mention how many other violent offences appeared on Lee's record. Of the fourteen convictions against Lee Duffy eleven of them were of an incredibly violent nature. A now retired detective informed me that he was going away for a long time if found guilty. Another couple of police officers who I spoke to but didn't want to participate in this particular book both told me "Jamie, Lee Duffy wasn't what we expected when we got him in our station. We'd heard so much about him and been given pictures so we knew what he looked like but when he was in the interview room he shocked us both, he was very polite and articulate and he could hold a decent conversation and wouldn't use bad language."

I must admit I did think I was punching above my weight even asking the very likeable former Detective Ray Morton to even consider speaking to me for this book and I'm just so happy for you readers and to this final book he said yes. I'm sure you'll agree when reading the former lawman's views it merits a very deep insight to the men who were chasing him down to lock him up.

Also regarding the Peter Wilson case when Lee taxed "Ginger Maca" from Thornaby, this outraged one of Lee's friends who saw it as being bang out of order. This particular friend then said because Lee did that that he and Jamie Broderick were now not going to stand up in court and back Lee's claims with Peter Wilson as both this friend and Broderick were eyewitnesses. This was the reason Lee and this friend would fall out for the last time and if Lee hadn't have died when he did it was going to end in an almighty war between the two which, I imagine, would have ended up with some serious bloodshed.

When I interviewed former Middlesbrough boxer Peter Richardson for an earlier book he told me his early memories of being in Joe Walton's boxing club were of Lee and his mate who would always go there together. Another told me that the two of them would turn up for boxing, punch hell out of each other in sparring then leave together as best mates. This will have been when the pair were 17-18 as there was only seven months between the pair.

Middlesbrough amateur boxing coach, the legendary Ron Cave, who coached at Phil Thomas' gym told me that Lee used to turn up with his pal at the old De Niro's gym and they'd punch hell out of one another then leave as best pals. So the two were once over the best of friends before later on having their spats which was always going to be the case if you had a rep like Lee's friend did.

I remember when I interviewed Lee's uncle and godfather Rod Jones he told me that when Lee was growing up he'd often try to knock him out and he was a blood relation so it didn't matter to Lee if you were a relative or a mate, your name and what it meant was worth far more to the young Duffy, like silver to a Magpie. If you could fight you were instantly attractive to the Duff that's for sure!

Going back to the Peter Wilson trial, Lee knew without his two witnesses on his side his future was looking mighty bleak but he just couldn't stop going around doing crazy things even though he was on bail for three separate serious incidents. I don't think you will ever again see someone being on bail for three separate serious incidents like Lee was again. That's not even including the fact that Cleveland police were still looking into the three murder attempts that were made on Lee's life!

It got me to thinking of when Vince Agar said Cleveland police put Lee back out on the street and painted a target on his head and I can see why he'd say such a thing under those factual circumstances, although Ray Morton's views tell the other side to that scenario.

From that moment on in April 1991, a normal thinking man would have thought 'hang on a minute I'm going to lay low here' well not Lee, he didn't give it a second thought and if anything he just got more and more dangerous.

When he died he was just 26, two months and 2 weeks old and he showed no signs of slowing down. Lee was never the type to sit in the house and watch what Mrs Mangel was doing in Neighbours or what Alf Roberts was up to in Home and Away whilst smoking a pipe wearing his slippers.

He was the "Duff" and he was the talk of Middlesbrough, Newcastle and every prison in Northern England and he loved it and of course he had this reputation to live up to.

The Lee Duffy ride went at full pelt and when he died his legacy was cemented because of the last 16 months of his life. Lee Duffy even took Lee Duffy to another level and the town of Middlesbrough couldn't cope and then he was gone.

The people who'd stayed out of well-known establishments for several years could come back because Lee Duffy was no more. Many in Teesside were celebrating whilst others were mourning their friend Lee but regardless of their emotions, they were all in shock that he was now dead.

Middlesbrough, as a whole, was a funny place for the fortnight after until his funeral. The town seemed like it was almost having a comedown from what Lee Duffy had put it through those last eight years.

When you take a look at some of the books in the crime section in any Waterstones you'll find leading heavy crime figures such as Freddie Foreman, Arthur Thompson, Lenny McLean, Roy Shaw or Charles Bronson and they were allowed to get so much older than Lee. I think there's only ever been Lee's arch nemesis Viv Graham who died young and left such a high level of notoriety, although Viv managed to get to the grand old age of 34 outliving Lee by

8 years, Viv had predicted himself that he wouldn't get to 40!

If you want the truth, Lee Duffy wasn't even a very successful criminal in terms of assets and luxuries. That fatal morning when he died all he had on him was £60 and it was saturated in his own blood. In fact even that money was borrowed only a couple of hours before he died when he was in The Havana.

Heartbreakingly when Brenda Duffy was given her son's belongings back she actually offered the blood-soaked money back to the man Lee had borrowed it from but of course he refused. I suppose the biggest success and maybe his only success was his notoriety.

Lee's been gone 28 years this year, he's been dead two years longer than he was alive and he's still stirring up high emotions. Even after Lee was buried on September 9th, 1991 in Eston cemetery on Normanby Road people were still complaining about him. One woman went to The Gazette in protest and said she was going to have her husband's body exhumed and cremated because she didn't want his final resting place to be near such a figure of evil. I think even Lee Duffy should be forgiven on that one as I'm sure it was something that he didn't have much control over.

One well known man who I won't name but he's a bit of a celebrity in his own right told me even the nightclubs were closing down in the days after his death. The ones that were open had such an awful atmosphere that he couldn't take it anymore and left to go to Yarm with all his mates.

The same man told me "I've never seen anyone like Lee before or since. He was a total whirlwind of chaos just hell bent on destroying everybody. Whilst he was on this earth he was well and truly on a seek and destroy mission. How he never killed anyone is beyond me. He was the definition of Doctor Jekyll and Mr Hyde. Once I saw him flatten four men in Blaises and it was like a Chuck Norris movie and there was bodies everywhere. Afterwards Lee was just stood at the bar laughing his head off and smiling like a Cheshire Cat.

Whenever Lee saw me he would shout his usual OI OI, NOW THEN NOW THEN and pick me up and squeeze me to death. I liked Lee but to be truthful I couldn't ever relax around him because he had more energy than a greyhound. I saw Lee smack some big men and walk off like it was nothing. He wasn't a big mouth or bragged about anything and I don't think I ever heard him swear. He'd just walk up and punch people like it was normal and he didn't have a care in the world. He was too unpredictable for me. His knockout power, athleticism, cocaine and ecstasy were a deadly mix".

People like Lee Duffy only belong in books in this day and age but I can understand the public's interest in characters like him. I personally think the only chance Lee Duffy had of turning his life around was if he'd have spent a long long time inside. Now, that sounds crazy because prison's a violent vile world to live in but there was never any chance of him being shot, petrol poured over him and the chances of him being fatally stabbed were slim. I don't think it would have been a bad thing for Lee to have spent a stretch in prison until he'd calmed down.

One man told me how Lee would be escorted always by two of the biggest officers wherever he went in prison. He told me how Lee would walk around almost shadow boxing whilst looking around for people to pick a fight with, snorting when he'd walk up and down the landings.

Then again Lee was regarded as a god in jail by every con in Northern England so maybe he'd have played up to it and become exactly like your Charles Bronson's and Paul Sykes.'

A scary fact I did find out for this sequel and final word was what the song 'The Whole of the Moon' was written about. Mike Scott from The Waterboys first released it in October 1985 then again in April 1991. It was rumoured that song was written about the late singer Prince but that is untrue. That song itself was written and I'll quote the song writer, "It's written about a young prince who has a spectacular, meteor-like rise, that's why you can hear meteors in the song, but the young prince burns out before he reaches his full potential and dies young". You couldn't make that up could you?! When I told Lee's buddy Neil Booth the story behind those famous lyrics on the phone whilst he was in Thailand he told me he went cold and the hairs on his neck stood up, up until then he had no idea and it was just a song that Lee would put on over and over when they were off their boilers.

Once again this book will delve into the world of Lee Paul Duffy by the people who knew him and were around at that crazy time when Middlesbrough was arguably one of the roughest places in Britain to live in and violence was only an advantage to use as a social tool.

Please note that once again I've had no influence over what the various people in this book have had to say.

Lee Duffy wasn't all bad and I'm told he could be so funny without even realising it. One tale that did make me laugh I was told was by a man who agreed to be interviewed at length and then changed his mind twice so of course I respected his wishes and deleted it. It was a shame because his 10-page chapter was funny as hell and involved Lee jumping on a drug dealers car bonnet outside of the Thorntree pub but staying on the bonnet the full length of the road like a scene out of the Terminator movies. In the end Lee caught the drug dealer and tipped him upside down to take all his illegal contraband off him when they fell out of his pockets. (At least it was a drug dealer and not a law-abiding citizen in Lee's defence eh)

That same night he ended up in a pub called The Dog & Gun in Potto, or as Lee used to call it "out in the sticks".

Lee had only got in the pub because a friend of Lee's had knocked him up and Lee had had to hide around the corner because if they saw it was Lee Duffy the landlord wouldn't have let them in. After a while of Lee sat in the bar with his hood up he must have pulled it down because the landlords face dropped when he looked at Lee and said "OOH NOOO, it's you that bad man from the papers", Lee walked over to him and just said "you'll have no trouble from me old fella, you're my friend, just keep serving the drinks". That night Lee bought everyone in the "stoppy back" drinks and they were in there boozing for over three hours.

Lee did have a loving warm side to him, it's a side that has never really been documented certainly in the media because it doesn't tie in well with his image does it when the tabloids are trying to sell papers.

Apart from the violent side and the loving side there was also a crazy rather bonkers side that Lee showed everyday like it was normal, for instance the story of how Lee came about owning his beloved English Bull Terrier Bulla was down to him winning the dog in a card game from his onetime hero/friend Kev Duckling (Ducko). I'm told that he loved that dog to bits and took it everywhere with him.

Middlesbrough boxing champion John Pearce junior told me about the time he would see Lee in his gym. A woman had wandered into the gym as she was looking to take the Wellington pub over which was downstairs, Lee was in the gym and he was just coming out of the showers when he saw her Lee ran up to her and dropped his towel and stood in front of her. I'm told the rather embarrassed woman didn't know where to look but Lee just found that hilarious. John would often pop in the gym during the day and he'd see Lee working out with John Black and others. John, I think it's fair to say, knows his boxing and he told me Lee looked awesome working out.

Out of the dozens upon dozens of people I've interviewed regarding Middlesbrough's most infamous man probably the most bizarre story was from a Stockton man who had the displeasure to have been locked up with Lee for three nights in Durham Prison. He said it was the longest three days of his life as Lee made him do cell circuits a few times a day, he also ended up getting a good hiding off Lee. When I asked why he told me, "because he said I was looking at him when he was having a wank". I couldn't help but laugh when he told me Lee slapped him several times across his head with his size 10 Adidas Samba's. Now Lee is known for dishing out random acts of violence as you know, for things like taxing but I'd never heard anything like that before. I'm sure you'll agree he had some funny ways about him and if you knew Lee you'll be nodding your head in agreement reading this.

One of the most memorable arrest attempts on Duffy by Cleveland police was an early morning raid on his Eston home. Duffy who was in bed with his girlfriend, fled stark naked through a bedroom window as officers broke into the house. Detectives said they saw Duffy powering away despite it being uphill and he was off in seconds, the officers said he was moving that fast they didn't even attempt to chase him. Duffy was off and the only things he had on his body was just his tattoos, a dagger and rose, a naked woman, born to raise hell devil and a black panther saying, "watch it I bite".

Then there were the really bad stories of Lee taxing people of huge amounts of money but instead of just doing that, he punched one drug-dealer straight through a window and told him afterwards, "now I've got your lover", meaning money. That came from an eyewitness. The man who watched it told me Lee got about £1200 from that victim then went and spent the full lot on his mates or gave it all away in one night giving people £20 notes. He said

Lee woke up rough and penniless and then was back on the hunt for more of the drug dealers ill-gotten gains.

Lee, towards the end of his life, was far more into drugs than he'd ever been and I believe that was responsible for his behaviour going to another level. To give you an example of how he was in the end Lee was waking up and smoking crack pipes first thing in the morning. In fact, I spoke with someone who told me he was doing that the Monday before he died.

Lee Duffy's hours of sleep were from 6am in the morning to 1pm in the afternoon for the last year of his life. That source told me that when he went into the attic bedroom Lee shared with his partner at 6, Durham Road in Eston about 1pm Lee was asleep, when Lee woke he jumped out of his skin because he thought he was about to be shot but of course it was only a friend. He'd become paranoid, living on his nerves as you would be being the most hunted man in Teesside. Lee, at that point, trusted no-one apart from people like Buster, Boothy, Agar and his girlfriend Lisa.

Yes towards the end he was that wild and unpredictable and would often stand in pubs giving people "blow backs" from joints of wacky baccy. Lee didn't give a hoot who was watching. One of Lee's favourite pub tricks was to smoke hash on a needle through a beer mat. What he would do was burn the cannabis then put a half glass over it until it was full then he would inhale over and over. Another one of Lee's things he did was eat blocks of cannabis resin to get stoned.

Lee would always be sniffing to the point of struggling to breathe through his nose. I was told by somebody close to Lee that Lee was actually born with this condition and it had nothing to do with his fights. It's the little tweaks like that which made Lee who he was. Another one of Lee's mannerisms, and this may be hard to believe, but he always sat very lady-like with his legs crossed and his hands-on top of his legs. Lee would creak his neck in close when he was listening to somebody speaking and he never ever interrupted anyone when they were talking. Another Duff trait was he always drank out of half pint glasses.

One of Lee's favourite things was to look for reactions in people like when standing in front of them he'd put his hand up in front of them, like he was about to hit them but combed his hair with his hand instead. This done very quickly by Lee Duffy was far more frightening than it sounds. Lee used to say, "if people want to believe the stories about me rather than get to know me personally I'll put them all on edge" and he used to pretend he was going to "kick off." He used to say he respected people more if they came up and spoke with him.

Considering Lee didn't have any interest in football, believe me all the full Boro team had heard of him. Largely down to the manager at the time sitting the full squad down and warning them to watch what they were doing when they were out drinking because of Lee Duffy's extra weekend activities. A former Boro legend told me back in those days the players would drink in places like the Madison Nightclub and the Dickens Inn but were all warned about the Duff in a staff meeting. These days footballers drink out of sight but back then it was different.

Growing up in Boro I used to hear that favourite saying of his "NOW THEN NOW THEN" and it was always a reference to the Duffer. The same if I ever wore just shorts as a kid, people would say to me, "who do you think you are the Duff?"

Another term you'd hear growing up in Berwick Hills was "have you got your Ducko vest on?" It's a reference to Lee's hero Kevin Duckling who, no matter what the weather was, in wind, hail, rain or snow would wear a vest. Kevin is probably the best vest wearer the town of Middlesbrough has ever produced. Although Kevin is a very private man these days and totally changed from when he was the lad about town, it is true that once over Lee absolutely idolised Ducko. One of Kevin and Lee's close associates told me once that Lee asked him "do you think I look like Ducko?" The week later he asked the same man "do you think I sound like Ducko" maybe because Kevin Duckling is one incredible singer and has always been famous around Middlesbrough on the karaoke. I've heard Kevin myself in places like The Newcastle House in Berwick Hills and the man can sing. In fact these days when Kevin goes into pubs and sings everybody stands up in awe so I'm told. His name on the karaoke is "the singing vest"... Absolute genius!!!!

One funny story Kevin's sister Tina did tell me was once Lee came in a pub and told her he was related to his hero Ducko, now at the time Lee didn't know this was Kevin's sister so when she asked him what he called himself he said "Lee Ducko". Tina, Kevin's sister said "that's funny because I'm Kevin's sister Tina so you'll be my relation as well then and I've never heard of you! Lee was left very red faced although he was very young at the time.

One man who was in prison with Lee and Kevin told me that Lee used to follow Ducko all over and because Ducko used to wear his shirt not tucked in and outside of his prison jeans then his young apprentice followed suit.

The two had a fall out many years later but once over they were great friends and there's no doubt that in the early days Lee based himself on Kevin Duckling.

One man who did think a lot of Lee was Kevin's dad Ray who sadly passed around a year ago. Its thanks to Ray and his lovely widow Christine that I managed to retrieve the old VHS footage of Lee's news clips from his death for the upcoming The Whole of the Moon documentary. From my research and from what people have told me old Ray Duckling was a lovely fella, was quite a character and is deeply missed by all who knew him.

Ladies & Gentleman I give you the final word from me. Lee Duffy 2 - The Blood Moon is another truthful and accurate account of a young man who once upon a time owned the town of Middlesbrough!

I hope you enjoy this book as I've enjoyed researching Lee's life for the final time. He was funny, he was crazy, he was bad but don't forget he was extremely young and he was Boro's own. Middlesbrough will never have another like Lee Duffy that's for sure.

Jamie Boyle, author

P.S. Thanks go to Charlie Thomas, Steve Wraith, Warcry Publications, Boris and Floyd the Bulldogs, Terry Dicko, Gavin Parker, Middlesbrough Central Library, my father in law Rob Dickinson, for thinking of the title of this book, and most importantly my lovely Wife Shirley-Anne Boyle, without her help and support this book wouldn't have been possible.

NOTE: This book not only supports Scope, a charity which was chosen by Lee's close friend Mark Hartley and the man who held Lee in his arms the night he died but a percentage, every month, of any profit will also go towards supporting a young disabled boy who can't use his legs to make his life a little easier. I have however kept his family details private as that is what the boy's family wished.

"Those were the days, not a care in the world, just happy times, then I grew up and discovered the big bad world out there."

Lee Duffy on his childhood in a letter to his Mam Brenda

MY MATE THE DUFF
by Terry Dicko

*Wild and dangerous yes he was, there were no lies, ifs,
buts or because,*

*When angry and in doubt, Lee the Duffer always knocked
them out,*

*He then would walk off at a gentle pace, to let Teesside
know he was the real hardcase*

*He'd meet his friends with that familiar smile but then often
went missing for quite a while*

*It was usually Durham or Walton jails, in the workshops
perhaps sewing bags for the Royal mail*

*He walked the landing without fear with a big fat joint
tucked behind his ear*

*He did not care who the hell could see as all the screws
would say "it's ok it's only Lee"*

*So on the fatal night his life did drain only for a much
bigger reputation to be born again*

*Now almost 28 years draws near and the name Lee Duffy
is spoken loud and clear,*

*Now love him or loathe him, Teesside can't get enough
born 24 Keir Hardie Crescent, South Bank he was the Duff*

*Now we who've read The Whole of the moon can't wait for
the documentary and new book coming soon*

So as we wait in eager anticipation for Warcry Press' new Blood Moon publication

Now if you think you've heard it all before go buy the Blood Moon book it opens up another door

So those who know me must agree there's no doubt about my love and loyalty to my friend Lee

"Lee Duffy could fight like the Devil"

Terrence Nivens

STEPHEN SAYERS
FOREWORD

I met Lee Duffy around 1982 down the block, we had cells next door to each other in Low Newton. At first we could only talk through the crack in our windows but that's how our friendship developed.

I would often hear Lee punching walls with towels wrapped around his hands. I even heard Lee fighting with two screws once and I could hear them reeling from him banging body shots into them.

We spent three days talking through the walls before we became firm friends and as the years progressed we became extremely close, not just Lee and I, Lee became close to my brothers too.

Lee used to come to Tyneside to see us or I'd go through to Teesside and spend the weekend with him going to blues parties.

When we got together we had a scream. One weekend I'll never forget was when four bouncers tried to tell me I wasn't getting in a nightclub because I was a Sayers. So Lee went down and knocked the four bouncers spark out in as many movements as there was bouncers and before he left he shouted "tell Graham the Duffers been" of course referring to Viv Graham.

Lee had incredible speed. Lee was like a coiled spring and he could knock people out even though they were two metres away such was his agility, he'd bounce into range and unleash hell. Lee had arms on him 6-7 inches longer than everybody else and he was frighteningly quick BOOM-BOOM-BOOM in and out. Lee was really something else fighting wise and he was better than anyone I've ever seen.

The day I found out Lee had died, I was in the Bay Horse Inn, I was still rough from the night before and when the word came into Newcastle that the Duff was dead, well

I was absolutely devastated to say the least. The pub was full of my pals, about a hundred of us and the bar was overtaken with emotion. There was one guy walking around in circles screaming "LEE DUFFY LEE DUFFY" just in pure disbelief.

Lee Duffy was a one off and I loved him, I'll always love him. Even today in 2019 I've still got such fond wonderful memories of my pal. He was the biggest Geordie that never was, he was one of us.

"When you dance with the devil you wait for the music to stop before you can finish"

Lenny McLean

LEE'S BEGINNING

When you look at the life and times of Lee Paul Duffy towards the end of his life you can be bamboozled as to how he actually lived. To get a full understanding of why he behaved like that for me you have to go right back to his childhood.

Middlesbrough might actually be pound for pound the roughest place to live in Britain for its size and population. It could also be the most working-class town of them all, well South Bank, the manor in which Lee Duffy grew up in, I'd say, was the roughest/hardest place to live in the whole of Middlesbrough. Today in 2019 there's nothing much left of South Bank now and everybody from there has either been moved away by the council or they've moved on by choice. Very much like the area of Terry Dicko's birthplace St Hilda's (over the border) its long gone.

Back throughout the 1970s and 1980s South Bank High Street was a booming little place in itself. People have told me that before the local Asda opened in 1992 you didn't even have to go into Middlesbrough town centre because you could get everything in South Bank, it had everything i.e. its own market, nightclubs, clothes shops and even a football stadium but there's no doubt about it they bred them tough in South Bank. Growing up in such a rough, hostile environment you learnt at a very young age that if you wanted something you had to fight for it. In this day and age in 2019 we're all guilty, myself included, of bringing our children up a bit soft, maybe because now we have so many news sources so we hear a lot more about the scum of the earth that do harm to children, I think that's why we wrap them up in cotton wool a bit these days. It didn't mean it didn't go on all those years ago when Lee was growing up but we just weren't aware of it so much, you rarely heard about it. Kids also spend a lot more time indoors anyway now because of the gadgets they have. When Lee was a youngster, no one had anything much at all. Now I'm not saying South Bank was a poor area but it was a tough area and if you compare it to some other places in Middlesbrough you'll understand what I'm saying. Not only did Lee grow up in such a tough place but being bullied to the extent that he was for sure mentally scarred him. From my research the years of bullying Lee was subjected to, the physical and mental abuse was at its worse for him between the ages of 6 to 12 years and it was always carried out by lads a lot older than him and they were usually in gangs.

I've just finished writing Roy Shaw – Mean Machine and he suffered the exact same as did Dominic Negus whose book I wrote before this one, so there must be a pattern. In fact experts say that the worst age to endure any kind of horrific event is between the ages of 8 to 10yrs old. It's at that age that doctors say anything that happens to you has the most profound and dramatic effect on your life and in Lee's case it was certainly true.

If you look at Lee's school years he wasn't what you would call academic and he left a good two years before he was supposed to. From my research I would say things started to change when Lee became 14 years of age. That's when people started seeing what you might call "Lee Duffy the fighter" and he got involved in a lot of anti-social activities. From the age of 15, people have told me that Lee started showing the first signs of arrogance and that stayed with regarding his rivalries until his death. It was at that age when his mother Brenda sent Lee packing off to his uncle Rod's house in Hemlington away from South Bank because he was getting into too much trouble. As a teenager he began thieving and burgling with other bits of criminal activities thrown in for good measure. After leaving school he worked on a variety of government work schemes, including rewiring houses. Work like that just wasn't for Lee Duffy. Duffy then wanted to create his own empire fashioned with his enterprise and fists.

It was as a 15-year-old boy that he received his first prison sentence and he was sent to a detention centre for three months on burglary and motorbike taking charges. For Lee, at that point, violence soon started to figure in his life on a day to day basis. One attack plus another couple for good measure landed him back in the nick, this time for six months.

In his early teens Lee was into glue sniffing which was a thing a hell of a lot of kids in Middlesbrough tried at least once. In those days there was no heroin. One of Lee's friends once told me that he was sniffing glue with Lee when Lee grabbed hold of his mate and put the bag of glue over his head and his mate ended up having to get his hair shaved off. Lee thought it was hilarious.

Lee, in his early teens, started as the song say's "you climbed on the ladder" in the fighting sense in Teesside. Everybody knows what Lee Duffy the ferocious lion turned into when he was 25-26yrs old but what's not commonly known about Lee was that he did lose a couple of fights at the start of his journey. Now I'm not talking about his younger years when he was getting beaten up by the others boys on the South Bank estate, Lee came unstuck against Grangetown's Mark Johnson and Paul (Livo) Livingstone. I told you in the first book about Lee losing to one of the Johnson brothers but losing to Paul Livingstone is something only I discovered whilst researching for this book. Paul took on many people in Middlesbrough and before he had his accident Paul was the "man in the town". The young Lee went up to Paul Livo when he was maybe around 17yrs old and said "Paul, you're the hardest in this town aren't ya? Well give me a couple of years and I'm coming for you", and with that Livo stuck the head on Lee and Lee came off second best. Lee went away and licked his wounds but from that day in 1982 you could see exactly what the young cub who was not quite the king of the jungle was trying to do, he was already set on his plan of domination to take over Middlesbrough. I've listed the names of the heavyweights of Boro that Lee clashed with in this book.

Lee, by this time was now a regular on the pub and club scene and his love for sheer brutality followed.

Lee wasn't really your most avid football fan but he was once fined for threatening abusive words and behaviour at the old Sunderland football ground Roker Park in his late teens. In April 1983 aged just 18 he viciously attacked and robbed someone in the old Dragonora hotel in Middlesbrough and would go on to receive a custodial sentence of 30 months for it later on that year. On Lee's release in 1985 he was assaulting people in the Speak Easy and three separate cases against him were dropped due to a lack of people wanting to give evidence against Duffy. In July of 1986 just gone 21 he was arrested again for an assault in a Middlesbrough street but that also fell by the wayside at court.

I don't think Lee Duffy could have ever sat back and let others do his dirty work like maybe he should have done if he'd have used his brain. Lee liked to be involved because it wasn't about the money for him, it was the power and being the No.1. This was also the downfall of the Kray Twins, the pair were the same as Lee and got involved even when they didn't need to.

Over the last twenty odd years in Middlesbrough how many people have we seen open up highly successful security companies? People whose name on a sign was enough to keep the would-be-intruders out. Yes it might only be a 60-year-old potbellied security guard working for the national minimum wage on site but on the sign it said somewhere Graeme O'Malley (ex-professional boxer), Brian Cockerill, Mark Debrick or Mark Johnson, their name's on a sign screamed out "come on this site and you're getting it" to the would-be burglars of Teesside. Other more prominent names have done the same across the UK, not only in Teesside but major names across Britain such as Glasgow's Paul Ferris or the Noonan family in Manchester, so can you imagine what weight the name Lee Duffy would have carried! Lee could have quite easily become a very wealthy man in his life if he'd had a plan but he quite clearly didn't. All Lee ever wanted to do was find hard men to knock out, then when he'd done that he'd find more and do the same with them.

Lee's cousin, Daren Collins, used to try and tell him to calm down a bit all the time but he would never take any notice of anyone. All Lee ever cared about was living for today or maybe at a push tomorrows Havana bash then blues parties in the heart of Teesside's underworld. The blues parties were like jungles and maybe you would have been safer in the actual jungle with the snakes and tigers roaming freely than inside a blues party in Middlesbrough but Lee didn't care. He went on to become the undisputed king of the blues parties and the only thing which could have ever challenged his title were guns and bullets, which is why they were brought in to stop him and he was shot at two different blues parties in the space of just five weeks!

In the putting together of this second book I again spent a bit of time with Lee's childhood saviour the lovely Lorna Lancaster. In the first book I told you how she first met Lee when he was being beaten up at only 6 years of age by boys who were the same age as Lorna and at that time she was 13. Whenever Lorna was about the little Lee would be safe from the bullies. Lorna told me that even when Lorna would walk around the South Bank estate infant Lee would follow her shouting "LANGY LANGY LANGY!" Lorna would have to say, "Go home Lee and I'll come and take you out tomorrow", then he'd hide around a corner and then follow her some more.

Being bullied by the much older boys wasn't the only thing that the young Lee had to endure, it was his home life as well. In this day and age in 2019 it's all very different and some of the treatment he had to endure from his strict alcoholic father would not be allowed today. Their next-door neighbours of many years told me they would often hear little Lee and his siblings screaming from the good hidings Lawrie Senior dished out. It's a reason so many people in the area would see little Lee on the streets well away from his home like on Redcar Road and Pym Street, South Bank basically anywhere but his own end.

Lee's father Lawrie Senior was a very articulate man and from my sources "incredibly well read". Lee's mother would be out working seven nights a week doing what she did and when she came in she'd have to bring him in all the big papers like The Guardian and The Telegraph. Lawrie senior would never dream of reading papers like The Sun and The Star because he classed himself "above that crap" intellectually. Lee's father was what you would call a 'kept man' and he didn't go out to work although his wife Brenda did and mostly every night.

Brenda was very house proud. She made sure her kids were provided for and tried to give them the best of what she could. Although Lawrie Senior would spend his days drinking in the Albion Club in South Bank with his papers and a pouch of Drum baccy he was an intelligent man. The people who knew Lee's old fella told me he'd have been ideal if you were on the programme 'Who Wants to be a Millionaire' for a phone a friend because that man knew everything.

The young Brenda Duffy met Lawrie Senior in the late 1950's when she already had three children from another relationship. Brenda very quickly became smitten with the extremely handsome Lawrie who was a man of Irish descent and who was well-dressed. Lawrie knew how much Brenda had fallen for him and he allegedly gave her an ultimatum, if Brenda wanted to get with Lawrie then he wasn't interested in the three children she already had. In the end Brenda's three children were brought up by her parents or put into care. Brenda and Lawrie would go on to have four children themselves, two girls and two boys and all their names started with the letter L, Lee being the second oldest.

Rod Jones, Brenda's brother, told me he would often have to keep Lawrie Senior in line because the fact of the matter is he didn't treat his sister nicely. To quote Lee's uncle and godfather, "some days old Lawrie Senior would be in the pub and he'd come home and beat hell out of our Brenda for nothing". There's no doubt about it there was a big issue with domestic violence in the Duffy household when little Lee was growing up. At times he'd be sat in his front room watching cartoons when all of a sudden he'd see his uncle Rod burst in and start bouncing his father all-over the front room because of the way he was treating his sister Brenda. Little Lee grew up seeing this kind of violence a lot and it became the norm for him to witness things like that. Not only did Lee grow up watching violence at home but he would watch it on the telly, he was only at a young and impressionable age when he started watching Bruce Lee films and practising his moves in the front room as a boy. Brenda Duffy used to say that Lee had far too much energy as a young boy and it was exactly just how he was as an adult.

When you look at the pictures of Lee when he got older he had the same kind of definition as his hero but a far bigger version, he had big legs, small waist and from his waist he filled out like a wedge, almost like a spitting Cobra when it's annoyed. One of the reasons that Lee was always wearing shorts was because he couldn't get jeans to fit him on his thighs. Every pair of jeans he wore they were tight on his legs and massive around the waist because his waist was very lean. Lee would pinch his waist daily to check if he was getting fat, that was something he was obsessed about. He ended up with the physique any film star would have been pleased to have attained.

Lee Paul Duffy was brought up tough and I don't think he could have had a harder start to his life. There's an old saying, "tough times breed tough people" and in little Lee's case it was most certainly true. Lee was as streetwise as they came and when you look at his background of growing up on the hardened streets of South Bank you can understand why. Lee's arch-rival Viv Graham was quite naïve in that respect maybe because he grew up in the countryside.

You've probably all heard of the upbringing the young Mike Tyson had growing up in Brooklyn, New York, well Lee Duffy was raised as rough and tough as he could be in Great Britain in the 1970s. The early beatings by older gangs, having nothing and coming from a large family all contributed to make him exactly what he turned out to be.

As Lee got older he wanted the world and everything in it just like Tony Montana in the movie Scarface, he had the reputation but wasn't any good with money, it was spent as soon as he had it, and after death his reputation has helped him to achieve immortality in a way, certainly in Teesside at least.

He paid the ultimate price and boy what a huge price that was, it was something more priceless than anything in the world...he paid with his life! So, when some shout out that Lee is being glorified they would do well to remember that there is no glory in losing your life at only 26!

"All Lee Duffy was, was just a big strong boisterous youth who could punch hard. He wasn't like these skilled MMA fighters today. Duffy's main assets were youth, power and being completely fearless"

Lee's close friend

ANONYMOUS – SCHOOL FRIEND

I'm from Eston and I'm 56 years old now I went to Stapleton school with Lee Duffy in Eston. I was two years older than Lee so out of the five years you do in secondary school I spent three in the same playground as Lee.

I first clapped eyes on Lee when he'll have been 11 and I was 13 years old. I would say even back then Lee Duffy was really distinctive and stood out in the crowd but for very different reasons that he did as an adult. What I remember about Lee was he always had an incredibly snotty nose, almost like candle wicks coming down to his mouth. Kids in junior school often have snotty noses but don't usually in secondary school so he used to get picked on for that. He seemed to have this big buffoon hairstyle and a pair of big lips on him. Lee also seemed hunched over like a monkey like he had no neck as well. Lee was never really big in them early school years I'd say he was average to smallish size and he also used to carry a lot of weight on him. Quite chunky if you like.

Early on I wouldn't have said Lee Duffy was a fighter, certainly not in the years I knew him in 1976, 77 and 78 although Lee was very mouthy. My main memory about Lee is when I was 15, so Lee will have been 13, and he grassed me up to the teachers for something I'd never done. What happened was that I'd been given a job to do with the dinner queues. I think, looking back the reason I was asked was because I was a big lad but Lee turned up with a couple of his mates and started pushing in which I had seen. I told him to get to the back and Lee started to get mouthy with me, he didn't get violent or anything but he was telling me no basically. In the end I've walked over and lifted him up physically and plonked him at the back of the queue. I didn't think anything of it because Lee Duffy had no reputation at school whatsoever. It was the other kids in the school who had the reps like the Hoes, Paul

Bryan or the Grangetown lot. The next thing is that Lee's come back for more and barged into me which took me back a little, so I walked towards him and Lee shit himself and stepped back but as he did so he tripped over a fence below knee height and fell flat on his back. Well everybody turned around and started laughing at Lee. Most people there who hadn't seen it must have thought I'd hit him but that was never the case. Lee literally fell over because he was retreating so much from me. The next thing I know I'm called into the teachers office for bullying Lee Duffy. In the end I found out that Lee had got up off the floor and ran and told the teachers of me so when he got older and became the Lee Duffy we all now know, it always lived with me because when I used to see him in Eston I always thought he would come for me because of that day.

It's funny because I'd left school when I was 16, so that would have made Lee 14, but that little kid who I left at 14 just seemed to shoot up. In the years that came later when Lee Duffy got this massive reputation for going around knocking people out I thought to myself, hang on a minute, this can't be the same lad who ran off crying and grassed me up to the teachers but it was. When I found out this same kid had turned into some kind of mechanical robot my initial reaction was, "fucking hell I hope he doesn't remember what happened back in that dinner line"! I don't mind saying I lived in fear of it for many years after that.

Lee, in reality started out operating in South Bank, Eston and Normanby but then he moved on into the town centre of Middlesbrough. After Boro centre Lee started venturing into Redcar and eventually to Newcastle and onwards. Back on the domestic front, particularly in Eston, the Hoe family were the big thing around my old area and everybody in it knew that there was tension between the Hoes and Lee Duffy (ironically Robbie Hoe who passed in February 2019 is buried in the next plot to Lee 28 years on).

In my adult life, if truth be known, I feared Lee and I avoided him like the black death because it was well known he was going around clipping people who bullied him in the past. Even though I didn't and I never professed to have done anything to Lee I always thought he was going to come for me, particularly as there was so many witnesses who were there and thought I knocked him out. I probably could have dined out on that story alone back in a time when Lee's name got so well known in the late 1980s. I never ever wanted it to get back to Lee that I was the guy who knocked Lee Duffy flying in the dinner line so I never told anybody about it until now. I did used to see Lee walking around Eston Square in just his shorts and trainers but every time I did I would do a U-turn. I wasn't interested in hanging around in case he recognised me from back in 1977. I actually lost my hair as soon as I left school so I think maybe that is the reason Lee never recognised me and never tried to exact revenge. If I ever went into a pub in Middlesbrough I'd hear things like, "oh Duffy's just been in here" and I'd think, 'SHIT he's out somewhere'.

Let me tell you something now, back in the Duff's reign the town of Boro was rife with talk of him daily. Back in Eston people used to talk about him all the time seriously. Let me give you an example, Peter Hoe used to have an outside gym at his house on Jubilee Road in Eston and when they saw Peter training those people would walk into a boozer and say, "its gonna kick off with Duffy this week because Peter's been training every night!"

A lot of the lads from South Bank used to drink in Eston, particularly on bank holidays because Eston used to be the place to come with The George, Oscars, The Foundry, The Talbot because all those places were known for fights basically. I know one story I heard from one of my best mates who was there once in The Miners Arms in Eston. Now my friend who told me is the most honest man

I've ever met in my life and I don't think he'd tell me any lies. He told me that one of the Hoes walked into the pub with a massive overcoat on and it was a boiling hot day. Well the Hoe family were incredibly feared around Eston so if he wanted to wear a big overcoat on the hottest day of the year nobody was going to tell him any different. The next thing is Mr Hoe pulled this sawn-off shotgun out of his coat and blasted a bar stool, then he turned to the watching drinkers and said, "tell Duffy when he comes in that if he'd have been sat there I'd have done exactly the same thing" then he left!

There was a genuine fear of Lee Duffy from about 1985 - 1991 and as those years went by there was a rise in fear. Even a "straight goer" like me heard about Lee Duffy's every move it was unbelievable. Even my fellow mates who were the same as me all used to say, "have you heard about that snotty-nosed kid from school", it was bonkers.

I'll never forget seeing Lee not long before he died in his trademark shorts when I was in my work van outside of Yorkshire Bank in Eston Square and thinking to myself how much of an impressive physique Lee had. He was literally unrecognisable to the person I knew at school.

When Lee died I'd been away for the weekend and I'd just come back on the train. It wasn't until I was in a taxi going past the James Cook hospital when it came on the news on the radio about a stabbing in Middlesbrough. Well before it even said the name I'm not kidding you that in my mind about five seconds before it said Lee's name I was thinking, 'I bet its Duffy!' When it was confirmed I was almost numb and couldn't speak for the last two miles of my journey. If you want me to sum up my emotions then I'd say I was in utter disbelief but at the same time not surprised.

Looking back on it now it was inevitable that Lee Duffy was going to die young at some point but he had an air of invincibility about him. When you heard about him surviving the four attempts on his life that I know of then you even start to think, hang on a minute, this guy can't be killed! Then again, if anybody in Teesside was going to be killed in the early hours at a blues party in that style it had to be Lee didn't it?!

Lee's funeral was massive. There was a lot of respect there for him but at the time in Eston, in the fortnight beforehand, there was a lot of apprehension because Eston was a big drinking place and many were expecting trouble. If you can imagine it, every villain, would be villain or wannabe villain from the North East was going to be there so the best thing to do was to stay indoors and not go out if you weren't involved.

The crowds in Eston that day can only be likened to crowds I've only ever seen at football matches. You'd have thought Winston Churchill was being buried again. I was at Middlesbrough's greatest ever footballer and fellow South Banker Wilf Mannion's funeral in 2000. They even drove Wilf past the old Ayresome Park route but I'd say Lee's was far bigger than Wilf's. Wilf is also buried not far away from Lee's grave today.

After Lee's funeral there were a lot of rumours around Eston that people were going to dig Lee's body up and hang it on a tree. Some saying people were going to cut his head off and place it on The Havana roof. I'm not sure if these rumours were true but I certainly know the police put a guard on his grave for a few weeks after. If you have a look at the back of Eston cemetery were Lee's buried you'll see a tall pole with a camera pointing in the direction of Lee's grave. That was especially put in place for Lee alone.

I would say even up to 2-3 years after Lee died he was spoken of so so much in Eston. Even though he was no longer here he was very much a big story. After Lee's death someone very close to Lee started doing a lot of crazy things and trying to emulate Lee. Allegedly he'd even go around saying, "THE DUFF IS BACK" but he could never get away with it and carry it off like Lee did. For a start its commonly known that this person got himself in bother with a well-known Grangetown hardman and was kidnapped in a van and beaten up. In my opinion Lee just was a different animal and he wouldn't have allowed himself to have been kidnapped in the first place. I'm happy to say that since then the guy has changed his ways now and is doing very well in life.

These days Eston's died now. It's no longer the big vibrant place where everybody came to drink. A lot of the main players like Duffy and even three of the five Hoes are no longer here. There's still a few of the old characters though in their 60s and some older who often sit in the pubs talking about the Lee Duffy days reminiscing. Lee's become a kind of legend who's spoken of a lot and he's the nearest thing Middlesbrough will ever have to the Krays I suppose.

The same people who sit in the pubs telling stories about 30 years ago talk about the Eston legend called Nipper the tramp. It was rumoured he lived on Eston Hills like the troll who lived under the bridge in the story The Billy Goats Gruff. Nipper was a right character and once went and had a shit in the Eston dole office because they never paid him his money. I'm in the pubs in my area maybe three or four times a week and people like Nipper and the Duff are brought up all the time. You know something as well, I don't think it's going to go away any time soon.

"CLATTER-BANG-BOSH....You've just met The Duffer"

Lee Duffy

MARTY TURNER

Marty Turner is a name I knew of myself from around the Middlesbrough amateur boxing scene in the 1990's. Marty was the founder of the old Grangetown ABC which produced several boxing champions such as Michael Gibbons, Anthony Hoe, James Hunter, Peter Richardson, and Middlesbrough's most successful professional ever Middlesbrough middleweight world champion challenger Cornelius Carr.

Marty was one of the old school most well-known trainers alongside John Dryden, Ronnie Cave and Richie Cosgrove.

The good that Marty did for the youth of Middlesbrough through the 80s/90s can only be commended and I take my hat off to him. After all, you don't get paid in that game and it's a big commitment to deal with stroppy teenagers three or four times a week.

Marty spared me a little time on how he found Lee from when he first met him as a 12-year-old chubby kid, until a month before he passed. Marty said:-

"I ran the famous old Grangetown boxing club for almost twenty years. I used to be sent all the misbehaving lads by the local authorities to try and straighten them out if you like. Lee Duffy first came to me in 1978 when he was around 12-13 years of age. Lee got into his training and stayed with me for around 12 months. The reason Lee came to the gym was because he was being bullied at the time. It was a bad time for Lee because he was getting knocked from pillow to post on a daily basis by much older lads around the South Bank and Grangetown estates.

Lee used to knock around with Billy Foster, Johnny Morrow, Dave Tankey and Lee Jameson (now sadly passed) and he was a canny kid.

Lee became quite good pals with another kid in our gym named Anthony Hoe who was a top schoolboy champion boxer. Those two for a good while became inseparable then Anthony's brother Peter came on the scene also.

I trained all my boxers the same way I trained Lee, they were nice stylish boxers but Lee was interested in being more of a banger than listening to what I was telling him to do. I'll say one thing about Lee though, he could hit hard. Even at 13-14 years of age he could punch, he would get bored easily though I found. If he didn't fancy doing something I was telling him he'd go hiding behind the bags like some boxers do and I'd have to pull him and say, "what you playing at?"

I would, at times after training, go and drop Lee off at his house on Keir Hardie Crescent and most of the time they'd be nobody in so he'd be locked out. Then Lee would have to stand about on the street corners looking for his Mam Brenda or his Dad Lol. I remember swearing at Brenda once saying "we're not a fucking babysitting service you know" but she just walked off, no apology or anything like that.

His Dad Lol was a tough guy as well. He had real capabilities when he lost his temper shall we say. Old Lol loved a drink most days. If the kids used to batter the young Lee, which they did quite often then old Lol used to force the young Lee back outside there to have a go or he'd belt him. They were many times that Lee used to run in that house crying. I often used to sit the young Lee down and say, 'who's been bullying you son?' Lee would say it was the older lads on the streets of South Bank and sometimes even at school. It was a shame because that kid was knocked around a lot and there was nobody there to help him. I tried to intervene a couple of times, even suggested I go up the school and have a word but I couldn't be there 24/7 for him. I suppose I was a father figure type to Lee for the time he was in my gym but he went the other way as he got older. He went the way I didn't want him to go!

As a boxer Lee did get his medical at my gym but he never had a bout. He was matched up a couple of times but he just wouldn't turn up which was a shame because he was more than ready to fight. Lee would drift away from boxing and as good as he was I knew I couldn't put a lad in the ring who'd not trained or even been near the gym in over a week.

I had Lee fixed up for his first bout at a show in Scarborough on Tommy Johnson's show but Lee didn't show up. When I took my other lads to the show Tommy said, "I thought you were bringing that Lee Duffy for my lad?" I had to tell him the truth and could only apologise. Then the week after I had him matched up and Lee promised me he'd turn up this time but he failed to turn up again. 'I thought what's going on here' but then he never ever came to my gym ever again after that. In fact that was when I heard that Lee had started training down Maxi Smith's gym above The Albert Hotel on Newport Road with Jimmy Teasdale (Lee's brother-in-law) and a few more of them.

There's no doubt in my mind that Lee could have made it in boxing if he'd have shown the dedication. He was up there with regards to his potential, up there with anyone I'd ever seen, lads like Peter, Tommy, and Anthony Hoe, Paul and Peter Millington, Dave Tankey, Alan Spencer, Cornelius Carr, Brian Reid, Brian and John Graham he was as good as any of them potential wise but he never stuck it like those lads did.

In the years after Lee finished my gym I would often see him and he always acknowledged me. When he was on the rise and the talk of the town he would always come over to me and say, "Hello Mr Turner how you keeping?" Of course I knew what he was about by then and I used to say to him, "Lee keep your hands in your pockets son!" I would tell him that all the time. I knew what he was up to because I was told about it daily. People used to say, "Marty do you remember Lee that tall skinny kid, well he's doing so and so or he's hit that person the other night" etc etc... I used to ask the lads in the gym what was going on too.

At that point Middlesbrough and in particularly Eston was getting worse daily with the likes of Lee and the Hoe's and the Jennings all fighting each other wanting to be the top man. Peter Hoe in particular was in almost touching distance of Duffy for being the No.1, for some reason Lee wouldn't fight Anthony as he had such a soft spot for him.

One of my memories of Lee in his later life was when I saw him at one of Cornelius Carr's fights at the Thornaby Pavilion. All the lads were there with Lee such as Brian and Molly Jaffray, Terry Dicko and John Graham. Lee shouted me over and said, "look at that Marty" and he's lifted up his shirt to show me his 6-pack. I said that's not a 6-pack Lee that's an 8-pack, he was completely chiselled like one of those statue's. Then in front of all his mates he's said, "I could have made it Marty couldn't I?" I said, "yes Lee you could have" and I wasn't lying. Then Lee said, "but look where I am now!", but I never answered. I knew what he was meaning but what do you do? I just said to Lee what would be would be and I left it at that.

Lee was always respectful towards me and I'd like to think it was because of the respect he learnt when he was with me in my gym. Sometimes I would take Lee all-over in the van going to boxing shows in the late 70s.

In his adult life Lee Duffy's name was that big in the town because everyone was scared of him. To give you an example of how scared of him, I was in the Erimus pub in South Bank one night, I was only in there to see Peter Kearns who'd been helping us at the gym with the kids, I only went for one pint to be polite. Anyway, I was in there and the place was full with people like Derek Beatty,

Donny and Dougie Reid. Lee then came in in just a pair of shorts, walks around, he looked to be almost in a daze and then he walked straight out the fire door. Now I'm not saying anything but I thought what the fucks he doing and I know everyone in the bar was thinking the same. Then about 30 seconds later Lee reappears in the bar and stands still just staring at the pool table for maybe a minute. Then after this he walks back out again. It then suddenly dawns on me that Lee's high as a kite. This happened a couple of times that night but the committee men daren't say anything to him so he was allowed to act daft and not a thing was said. The attitude was if Lee wants to come in and stare at pool tables then he could crack on and be left to it. People knew that if they said the slightest thing they were getting a clip because Lee just hit everybody.

It is true that at the end of Lee's life he was just getting worse. This was, in my opinion, because there were certain people of an older generation who were just using him daily to do all their dirty work for them. Lee was used and abused.

One night I was actually turned away from the Bongo Nightclub door by old Abdillahi, you know what his reason for knocking me back was? He said I was a friend of Duffy's! Lee had got to that stage of naughtiness where people didn't even want Lee's associates in pubs and clubs.

The last time I ever saw Lee was about a month before his death, it was outside the Shell garage in Eston. We were just talking in general. Lee was asking me how I was but I told him never mind me, I wasn't the one who people were out shooting at. Lee just laughed saying he had to do what he had to do but I told him it wasn't worth it. I told him that having a reputation only leads to one thing and I asked him if he knew what it goes with? Lee told me of course he knew and that was the reason everyone was coming after him. I clearly remember talking to Lee that day telling him he should end this feud he had going with Allo, I said to him "just shake hands and have it over with", that's what we used to do. I knew Davey and his Dad because we were all working on the same building site in Middlesbrough, that's where I first heard about the ongoing battle between the pair of them.

The month after when I heard the news he'd been killed I felt sick. Sick. I knew him well and I still pass his grave to this day in Eston. I think he should be remembered for what he was and not what the media say he was. He lived life to the full didn't he?! Deep down he was a good kid and didn't deserve the tragic ending he got.

"I know it's only a matter of time before something happens to me. I'm not long for this world and I know I'm going to kop for it sooner or later".

Lee Duffy, April 1991

GLEN METCALFE

Glen Metcalfe is 54 and now lives in Grimsby but originally he came from the South Bank estate. It suddenly dawned on me whilst typing Glen's chapter out that he gets a mention in the first book, The Whole of the Moon, on page 88.

I spoke to Glen about his memories of Lee and here is what he said:-

I spent most of my life living next door to Lee with my sister. I was only two weeks older than Lee and I spent a lot of time with him when we were growing up.

My early memories of Lee were of his dad having him on the punch bag in the wash house trying to get him to stand up for himself. Lee's old fella was a big man as well but I would often sit with my sister and watch little Lee training out of the back window.

When we were kids Lee was bullied terribly by a family from Keir Hardie Crescent the Hoare's. It would be mainly Jeff and Peter Hoare who tortured Lee. The pair of them used to work on the fair at Eston Rec behind the baths when it came. Whenever they saw Lee at the fair they'd run over and give him a clip. If I remember rightly, both had about 4 or 5 years on Lee, but I do know for a fact that when Lee got older he sorted them both out in one go in the street.

I grew up with Lee so take it from someone that saw it happen, I'm telling you that the reason Lee turned out the way he did was because of what happened to him when he was just a young kid. Lee was a good lad before he turned the wrong way and became a different person.

I first started going out drinking with Lee in Rumours nightclub and meeting people like Terry Dicko when we were just young lads of maybe 17. It was around that time when Lee had just started getting a name for himself.

As I got older I had even more wheeling's and dealings with Lee as I started dealing drugs before Lee did and of course he took an interest in me when I started working with Kevin O'Keefe (beefy). I first met Kevin when we were both doing community service and we both came up with this great idea to start selling drugs. At that time in my life I had been out of work for 12 years and I did 7 of those years in jail for doing things that I'm not proud of these days.

Being involved with drugs got me into a lot of bad scrapes like my jaw being fractured in five places by Brian Cockerill for dealing on his patch in Redcar. When Brian was in jail in 1991 he caused a riot because he wanted boiled potatoes and I was sneaking him stuff down the block when I was cleaning. After Brian hit me I was eating through a straw for three months. I was getting taxed by Anthony and Peter Hoe if ever I went in The Miners Arms. Those two were my biggest nightmares in Eston. Then I got kidnapped and took up the hills in a car by Paddy Moloney (The Altar Boy) for something which was totally my fault. I even ended up getting filled in by Lee Duffy himself because of drugs. Even though I'd known Lee all my life once you're in that game there's no loyalty to anyone.

I was never scared of Lee Duffy though and I had no need to fear him until I started dealing drugs. That's when he changed from the young kid I knew, when others got him involved in the drugs world.

The reason Lee turned on me in the end was because he told me he was going to supply me from now on and the obvious followed when Lee caught me trying to deal for 'Beefy' at the same time. That's what caused the conflict between Lee and Beefy and it went on for weeks, it always surprised me though that whenever those two met it never came to blows and I could never understand that. There were times when Lee would come to mine and say

"I'm gonna put Beefy to kip good and proper", then Beefy would come round and say he was going to do all sorts to Lee but nothing ever happened. I'd sometimes stand watching Lee and Beefy stood talking and I'd think, 'I thought you were going to kill him Lee'.

In those days I was only nine and a half stone so I was a little man in a big bad evil world. I wasn't only out around Lee Duffy in South Bank but I was in jail with Lee in April 1991 not long after he gave me and Pauly Tapping a good beating. I was on the servery on remand when I heard a rumour that the Duffer had just come in and I thought 'SHIT', this wasn't long after he battered me. My main thoughts were that I had got nowhere to hide like I had on the out. In fact, I was probably going to have to serve him his food like three times a day. I was serving the sausages so I thought maybe if I give him six he'll like leave me alone. Anyway, it wasn't just a rumour anymore because I saw Lee's gigantic wide frame walking down the stairs and as he was getting towards me he was just getting bigger and bigger. Lee had his trademark hair slicked back like the Krays used to have and I thought that always made him look even more intimidating. My only thoughts were, 'FUCK ME I'M DEAD'! Lee came over to me and grabbed my wrist and said, "look what's going on outside doesn't matter when we're in here". Then he gave me a lump of blow and said, "we're both Boro lads and from the same area of South Bank so we look after each other in here so don't worry about it", and off he went. I was like 'PHEEEWWWWW FUCKING HELL'!

Pauly Tapping got a beating from Lee for the same reason I did. It's funny because I ended up in prison with my best mate Dave Tapping who came in with all his jaw wired from the beating he took when he'd tried to set Lee Duffy alight in The Commercial. Basically the story behind that was that Dave wasn't happy that Lee had bashed their Pauly and Dave tried to take matters into his own hands.

When Dave did that to Lee he was very drunk and Lee was sober as a judge because he didn't drink in pubs, only half a lager now and again. So, when Dave poured the petrol over Lee, instantaneously Lee ran outside and took all his clothes off then ran back in, at that point David had got the matches wet but Lee ran in and took him to the floor and made a mess of him. When David Tapping came in my cell after Lee had beat him up I didn't recognise him, I actually had to pause and say 'is that you Dave' because of the state he was in.

I'll never forget I was on community service once with four big men and I'm not kidding you, Lee had battered every one of them on separate occasions. You can't fail to give Lee his due because he was good at what he did. My best mates at the time in early 1991 were Paul Bryan and Kevin O'Keefe and it was them and a few others who were all arrested for conspiracy to murder Lee. I wasn't involved but I knew what was being planned against him before it happened. Ria Maria Nazir was also behind it all telling the hitman where Lee was but it all got flung out of court after Lee had died. I was also in jail with the two lads from Birmingham, Leroy Fischer and John Leroy Thomas who'd tried to kill Lee. It was Nazir, Bryan and O'Keefe who had allegedly all chipped in for the contract to put an end to Lee's life.

I was actually in Durham jail when Allo came in on remand for killing Lee. I've got to say if you want the truth that when the news came into the jail that Duffy had been murdered the full prison was happy. Even though Lee had done me in, I had extremely sad emotions that he had passed.

There was an 'awkward moment' shall we say, about six months before Lee died, it was after he had beat me up and I'll never forget Beefy coming round and saying to me, "if he comes round again shoot him" and he gave me a sawn-off shotgun. Now that was something I didn't want to do so instead I just kept away from my house as much as I could because I didn't really want to shoot Lee like they did. I was just a drug-dealer I wasn't a mercenary like those lot were.

It was all getting too much for me, I was getting out of my depth, Duffy was wanting me to set up a deal between Mark Miller and Beefy, then Lee was going to turn up and do the pair of them in. I told Beefy what Lee was asking me to do and they stayed away, then Lee was after me again because I hadn't followed his orders!

When Lee Duffy died it was a dream come true for all of the drug dealers in Teesside.

Only quite recently Lee's right hand man Neil Booth got in touch with me. He said it was because I'd written something along the lines of R.I.P Lee on social media and Neil told me that he had a lot of respect for me for doing that because of what Lee had done to me and he'd like a drink with me to talk about the crazy times from back then.

When you got Lee on his own he was totally different from what you read about him. Lee was such a generous bloke and he'd often come around my house at 5am and supply me and my mates with free blow and other drugs. Lee used to say he was making my home like his private blues party and he'd whack the reggae up.

At the end of Lee's life he was losing his own head. Often Lee would come round telling me I owed him for the 3 kilo of blow but I'd be thinking, 'hang on a minute, it was 4 kilo'!

For the last six months of Lee's life he was majorly under pressure with people out to kill him left, right and centre in Teesside. There were times towards the end of his life that Lee told me he knew everybody in Middlesbrough hated him. He used to show me the bullet wounds when we'd sit having a smoke together, when he wasn't after me that was. I'd never seen a bullet wound before and here was someone showing me two on the same leg and laughing like it was normal. He'd had part of his foot blown off but it just didn't seem to register with Lee like it would have your normal man.

A lot has been said about the punishment Lee Duffy could give out but what doesn't get spoken about is that he could take it also. I was there in The Speak Easy when Lee was fighting with a load of men from Leeds (this is the fight which Lee received four years for) and I saw Lee not even budging when he had a chair smashed over his head from behind. Lee just turned around without even flinching and tore into them.

I got out of jail on the 8th of September, the day before Lee's funeral and I saw all the rows of fences and bollards which had been put in place for that day. I could hear The Whole of the Moon song from outside the church when I was passing and the carriages of everybody in bits.

When I look back at the bad things Lee Duffy did to me I just see it as my own fault. I brought it on myself by being involved in his world. I was knocking that much gear out that I would employ people to cut it up for me and this was never going to go down well with Lee Duffy was it. These days the majority of people in South Bank who've got money are the ones who sell drugs so it's still the same.

At the end of Lee's life when he was bad on the crack he even taxed me of all my gold and he gave it to his Mam Brenda. I then had to go around his Mam's on Keir Hardie Crescent and I had to pay Brenda money to get my own stuff back.

If you look at things like that then I probably had reasons to hate him than anyone did, but I didn't. These days I look at the full picture and because of the way he was it cost him his life didn't it?!

It wasn't all bad times with me and Lee Duffy. It just went a bit Pete Tong in the end. We were all involved in doing bad things at that time so I don't want to curse about anyone.

The people who thought Lee was rolling in it couldn't be further away from the truth. He wasn't making anywhere near as much as me that's for sure. Sometimes Lee used to come in pubs without a wrap to his name, Boothy would admit that if you ask him! I don't ever remember Lee Duffy ever owning his own car. There's no way Lee Duffy was a rich man in his life. He would stop lads in South Bank who were successful shoplifters and take things off them or nick their cars. I've actually been in taxi's with Lee and he's told the taxi driver to get in the passenger side and he drove. He used to do that to all A1's drivers on Normanby Road. He was a devil for doing it to Malcolm all the time. I know A1 taxi's had this unwritten rule to all drivers that if Lee Duffy got in your cab you had to let him go where he wanted and NEVER ask him for payment at any cost. This was just accepted.

I just wish I hadn't gone down that road and I wish Lee hadn't either!

Lee Duffy was a better man than people these days say he was. He didn't deserve to die the way he did and in my opinion he was led down the wrong path by certain people in Middlesbrough who used him because of the way he could fight. Yes Lee Duffy did do bad to me and a hell of a lot of others and caused a tremendous amount of suffering but I'm still here. I'm only the same age he would have been but I'm now sat this very minute with my own son and my grandkids. He's not.

Lee Duffy was a complete bastard but so was I by ruining society but I had the chance to change and Lee didn't. If I hadn't done what I did back then I wouldn't be the good person I am now. Some of the stuff I did back then like messing around with dangerous people, I'm lucky to be still here. These days I have a good job as a steel erecter and I'm working in Liverpool at the minute.

Sometimes I sit down with my son and he says, "dad how come all these big names have done bad things to you", but I tell him not to make the same mistakes I did. He's 27 years old now and wasn't even alive when Lee Duffy was about but he's totally intrigued with his story like the thousands of others in Britain in 2019.

"He was unbalanced. The bigger and harder the person, the more attractive they were in the eyes of Duffy to have a fight with. It didn't matter if they were the hardest in Liverpool, Newcastle, Leeds or Manchester. I know personally from my time around Lee that he was carelessly building a reputation for not paying bills among them, 'big boys'. Lee didn't care and he thought he just had to be meaner, badder and more vicious than ever and believe me, he was just that".

Anonymous - Middlesbrough

COURT RECORDS
Thomas & Anor v Cleveland Chief

England and Wales Court of Appeal (Civil Division) 2001

October

Thomas & Anor v Cleveland Chief

Information Source:

https://www.casemine.com>judgement

1. LORD JUSTICE KENNEDY: This is a claimant's appeal from a decision of Judge Michael Taylor who, on 9th December 1999 at Middlesbrough, dismissed the claimant's action against the defendant. Permission to appeal was granted by the single Lord Justice in relation to one head of claim only, namely the allegation of misfeasance.

Background

2. The background to this civil action is a criminal investigation which resulted in the acquittal of the two claimants. The offences which gave rise to the investigation were committed on 31st January 1991. At 2 am there was an armed robbery at the home of Lisa Stockell at Eston, Teesside. At 3 am her boyfriend Lee Paul Duffy was shot in the leg at a blues party nearby. He was well known locally to be involved in drugs, dishonesty and violence but contract shooting was not then a feature of Teesside crime so the incident caused the police considerable concern.

3. Statements were obtained from the eyewitnesses at Eston and from Duffy. The descriptions of the offenders were not particularly consistent but one-woman Ria Maria Nazir was thought to be able to help. Duffy, armed with a gun, had recently visited her and, together with his henchmen, tried to recruit her as a drugs dealer. On 2nd February 1991 she was brought by two police officers to the police station. After a time she was seen alone by Inspector Mallon, who has subsequently become a well-known name. There were no tape-recording facilities at the police station at that time. No contemporaneous note was made. It was the Crown case that whilst alone with the inspector Nazir admitted involvement in the attempted murder and immediately afterwards the inspector instructed the two police officers who had brought her to the police station to arrest her on that charge. That was done. She was then interviewed by the two officers. The judge found that interview to have been properly conducted and in it the admissions were repeated. For that interview she did not have the services of a solicitor, but after she had seen a solicitor she attempted, as the judge found, to backtrack. She also tried to create a diversion. She said that she had miscarried at the police station and was removed to hospital where it became clear that she had not even been pregnant. There was a suggestion that in hospital she made some attempt at suicide but there was no real support for that suggestion.

4. While she was in hospital her home was searched. The police found nothing to link her with the offences of 31st January 1991 but they did find the paraphernalia of a drugs dealer and 900 in cash.

5. On 5th February 1991, whilst still in hospital, Nazir asked to speak to a senior police officer. Superintendent Miller and Inspector Leonard went to see her. They were in charge of the investigation into the attempted murder, as it was then believed to be, and the robbery and the burglary. She wanted to do a deal. If not prosecuted she would give information about the crimes committed on 31st January 1991. Superintendent Miller

discussed the proposal with Keith Simpson, a senior local Crown Prosecution Service Crown Prosecutor, and with Keith Leigh, Nazir's solicitor. The police officer wanted to get at the men who had used weapons and Mr Simpson agreed. The solicitor was naturally anxious that his client be free. On 6th February 1991, after she was returned from hospital to police custody, the deal was done and she made a long statement in the presence of two women police officers and her solicitor or his representative with occasional visits from Superintendent Miller. At 4 pm her extended custody time limit expired and she was bailed, but she remained to complete the statement.

6. At 6 pm her solicitor, Mr Leigh, came in and found her drinking brandy from a small brandy bottle. He did not intervene or express concern. Superintendent Miller never saw her drinking but one of the women police officers recalled that she did so. The brandy, as the judge found, was hers. It was with the property restored to her when she was granted bail. She was a known alcoholic, but on the evidence the judge found that she had her senses about her and was able to give information. At that stage she did not identify the men involved on 31st January beyond indicating a link with Birmingham, saying that she had turned to Birmingham for help to sort out Duffy. No doubt to try to prompt some identification she was shown photographs. The judge was caused, as he put it, "a degree of disquiet" by the fact that no proper record was made of the use of photographs.

7. The police had or later acquired some other evidence to link Teesside and Birmingham. There was a white BMW motor car which had been seen locally and in company with Nazir's Honda Civic. There were also telephone records that linked Nazir and her brother in law John Leroy Thomas in Birmingham and also linked these two claimants.

8. Nazir was taken to Birmingham and there she gave police officers the names of John Leroy Thomas and the two claimants.

9. John Leroy Thomas was a notorious local fence specialising in jewellery. Jewellery had been taken at the time of the robbery. His appearance was such that he could have been the third man described by witnesses and he owned a white BMW.

10. The two claimants had criminal records and had been involved with robberies and, in the case of the second claimant, with firearms. All three were arrested and taken to Teesside. John Leroy Thomas was arrested on 27th February 1991 and at that time had on him some 940. They all three denied involvement and the two claimants offered at that stage to take part in an identification parade.

11. Off the record John Leroy Thomas gave some information and Nazir tried to broker a deal for him. Her solicitor - who also became his, Mr Leigh - saw Superintendent Miller who, as the judge found, was less anxious to do a deal than he had been in the case of Nazir. He was prepared to consider what charge should be preferred and, if he received co-operation, to say so to the court. But, in the event, John Leroy Thomas was charged with conspiracy to murder. As Mr Lally, who has appeared before us for the appellants, points out, he was never charged with robbery or burglary.

12. On 25th April 1991 the senior police officers involved in the investigation and the representative of the Crown Prosecution Service met counsel in conference and amongst other things the question of an identification parade was discussed.

13. Inspector Beech, who had been appointed identification officer, asked the two claimants if they would take part and they refused to do so. Therefore the police photographed the two claimants and separately photographed a number of volunteers, everyone being photographed at the charge office. Thus the police were in a position to create a video film which they showed to potential identification witnesses in the presence of

the claimant's solicitors. The second claimant's solicitor objected to the procedure but Inspector Beech decided to go ahead, nevertheless.

14. The second claimant was positively identified by Wendy Stockell and Nicola Richardson in relation to the burglary or robbery. Nazir did not at first identify him. She indicated a desire to say something different and was allowed to see the film again in the presence of the first claimant's solicitor. She then identified the second claimant on both matters.

15. Committal proceedings followed at which Nazir gave evidence confirming the involvement of John Leroy Thomas and both claimants and others. The case was committed for trial. In October 1992, shortly before the hearing in the Crown Court was due, the indictment was amended on the advice of leading counsel. The allegation of conspiracy to murder was abandoned. In its place there was substituted an allegation of conspiracy to cause grievous bodily harm which reflected the evidence which at that stage Nazir was expected to give. However when the case reached the Crown Court in that same month Nazir refused to give evidence and the prosecution offered no evidence in relation to either matter; so the claimants were acquitted.

Civil Proceedings

16. These civil proceedings were commenced three years later in 1995 with allegations of malicious prosecution and misfeasance in public office. Shortly before the trial began in late 1999 an attempt was made to add allegations of negligence and breach of statutory duty but the trial judge refused to allow the late amendments. He did however allow the claimants to expand the factual basis of their case. In his judgment he rejected the allegations of malicious prosecution and that is no longer a live issue before us. He also rejected the allegations of misfeasance.

General Thrust of Case

17. As Mr Robert Smith QC for the respondent points out in his skeleton argument, it is instructive to see how this case was presented in the pleadings and in the court below. It was presented as a case of dishonesty where the police had acted with corrupt and improper motives and had dishonestly abused their power with the intention of injuring the claimants by getting them convicted at any cost. That case was, in effect, destroyed by the factual findings of the trial judge which I have attempted to summarise. But nevertheless it is contended that there is something left of the allegation of misfeasance which is worthy of further consideration by this court. I turn therefore to the grounds of appeal.

Ground 1

18. In Ground 1 it is asserted that the trial judge erred in law in respect of misfeasance.

19. The judge gave judgment on 9th December 1999, five months before the House of Lords gave judgment in Three Rivers District Council and Others v Governor and Company of the Bank of England [2000] 2 WLR 1220 which is now the leading authority in relation to this branch of the law. Counsel for the appellants and the trial judge did have the benefit of the judgment of Mr Justice Clarke in Three Rivers. That judgment, which was approved by the House of Lords, was reflected in written submissions placed before the judge by leading counsel for the appellants. The judge adopted counsel's formulation, saying at page 19 of the transcript:

"As far as misfeasance is concerned, again no great dispute taken by the defendant as to how misfeasance is committed. Misfeasance or malicious abuse is committed by a public officer in one of two of the following ways. Firstly, where a public officer

69

does something for a malicious motive which causes damage for the plaintiff and secondly where damage is caused by a police officer knowingly doing something which he has no power to do."

20. That means that Mr Lally in this court can only submit that the judge erred if he was misled by counsel in the court below (which is not contended) or if, as a result of the decision of the House of Lords, it is clear that the law is not as the judge believed it to be. But in my judgment the decision of the House of Lords as applied to the facts of this case, shows that the judge was right.

21. The leading speech was that of Lord Steyn who at page 1230 onwards set out the ingredients of the tort. At page 1231B, under the heading "The third requirement concerns the state of mind of the defendant", he said:

"The case law reveals two different forms of liability for misfeasance in public office. First there is the case of targeted malice by a public officer, i.e. conduct specifically intended to injure a person or persons. This type of case involves bad faith in the sense of the exercise of public power for an improper or ulterior motive. The second form is where a public officer acts knowing that he has no power to do the act complained of and that the act will probably injure the plaintiff. It involves bad faith inasmuch as the public officer does not have an honest belief that his act is lawful."

22. At 1231G he continued:

" ..... there are not too separate torts. On the other hand, the ingredients of the two forms of the tort cannot be exactly the same because if that were so there would be no sense in the twofold classification. Undoubtedly, there are unifying features, namely the special nature of the tort, as directed against the conduct of public officers only, and the element of an abuse of public power in bad faith. But there are differences between the alternative forms of the tort and it is conducive to clarity to recognise this."

23. Pausing there, it is worth noting that in the present case it was the first form of the tort - targeted malice - which was alleged. But either way bad faith was, as the House of Lords makes clear, an essential ingredient.

24. Lord Hope agreed with Lord Steyn and Lord Hutton in relation to this aspect of the case, as did Lord Millett. So I turn to Lord Hutton who, at page 1266F, said:

"My Lords, I consider that dishonesty is a necessary ingredient of the tort, and it is clear from the authorities that in this context dishonesty means acting in bad faith. In some cases the term `dishonesty' is not used and the term `in bad faith' or acting from `a corrupt motive' or `an improper motive' is used, or the term `in bad faith' is used together with the term `dishonesty'."

25. He gives some examples and continues:

"However, as the term `dishonesty' in some contexts implies a financial motive, I consider that the term `in bad faith' is a preferable term to use and, as I have stated, I consider that it is an essential ingredient in the tort."

26. Mr Lally invited our attention to parts of the speech of Lord Hobhouse. I do not myself believe that those passages are at odds with the passages I have cited. If I am wrong as to that the passages cited still represent the decision of the House and, as Mr Lally in the end accepted, they do not demonstrate error on the part of the trial judge.

Ground 2

27. I move therefore to Ground 2. In paragraph 17.1 of their amended particulars of claim the appellants give ten particulars of alleged misfeasance and they now complain that the judge failed in his judgment to address three of those particulars, namely those numbered (ii), (iii) and (x). There is a misprint in the notice of appeal in relation to the last number. Paragraph 17.1 (ii) of the amended particulars reads:

"Allowing the charges against John Leroy Thomas for robbery of the Stockells to be dropped and reducing down the offence of attempted murder to that of attempted assault when there was sufficient evidence to suggest that he was involved in the attempted murder or alternatively the conspiracy to murder or to cause grievous bodily harm and the robbery."

28. In fact John Leroy Thomas never was charged with robbery and, as I have already indicated, the charge of conspiracy to murder was reduced to conspiracy to cause grievous bodily harm in respect of all defendants on leading counsel's advice. Why he was not charged with robbery or burglary is not clear to me at this stage, but even if the charge was withheld in order to encourage him to give information about his co-accused I do not see how that could possibly amount to misfeasance.

29. The next particular of misfeasance referred to in Ground 2 of the grounds of appeal is paragraph 17.1 (iii) of the amended particulars which reads:

"Allowing Ms Nasir to administer brandy whilst being detained and questioned in the investigation at the police station."

30. This apparently relates to the incident at about 6 pm on 6th February 1991, to which I have already referred. But, as is clear from the narrative, Nazir was not then in custody. The police officers who saw her drinking could perhaps have discouraged her from doing so, but apparently neither they nor her solicitor

did discourage her. The reality is that the police wanted the statement that she was then giving. To my mind the judge was right not to regard this as any evidence of misfeasance.

31. The final particular of misfeasance referred to in Ground 2 of the grounds of appeal is paragraph 17.1 (x) of the amended particulars of claim. It reads:

"Allowing Ms Nasir to induce John Leroy Thomas to give evidence by administering him with brandy."

32. The incident is not referred to in the judgment. It seems that on 2nd March 1991 when John Leroy Thomas was in police custody he was visited by his sister in law Nazir who was allowed to speak to him in private with a police officer outside the room. When her solicitor entered he found her pouring brandy from a bottle in her possession into John Leroy Thomas's soft drink container. Apparently, she was also trying to persuade him to co-operate with the police. There was, as Mr Smith points out, no evidence that the police knew what was going on. The judge, clearly, at least by inference, rejected the suggestion that the police were trying by improper means to induce John Leroy Thomas to give evidence against his co-accused. Furthermore the reality is that he never did so, or even agreed to do so, from which it follows that his access to brandy had no effect at all on the appellants, even assuming he was allowed to continue to have it, and it cannot possibly amount to misfeasance.

Ground 3

33. Ground 3 begins with these words:

"The learned trial judge was plainly wrong in not establishing that the defendants had acted in misfeasance, given the following;"

there followed eight particulars. The first relates to the decision not to prosecute Nazir. Mr Simpson of the Crown Prosecution Service, in reliance on a file note made some several days later, said when he gave evidence in the present proceedings that when that decision, that is to say the decision not to prosecute Nazir was taken, he was only aware of her admissions to Detective Inspector Mallon, those being admissions which it would be very difficult to adduce in evidence. Clearly he should also have been informed of her admissions to the two interviewing officers. The assertion now is that Superintendent Miller deliberately or recklessly withheld that information.

34. This is not an allegation that was ever pleaded and so it was not fully explored with Mr Simpson. Furthermore it was never even put to Superintendent Miller beyond an assertion that he "downplayed" the effect of the evidence. The point was not developed in argument in the court below. In the circumstances the judge could not safely have found that Mr Simpson was not fully informed. In any event, it is clear from the rest of his findings that he could find no bad faith and no dishonesty.

35. The second particular relates to the immunity granted to Nazir. It reads:

"(ii) in granting a local immunity in not prosecuting Ria Maria Nazir for the attempted murder causing grievous bodily harm and/or drug offences rather than going to the DPP."

36. There was no evidence that procedurally the question of immunity should have gone to the Director of Public Prosecutions. The judge found (at least if Mr Simpson was properly informed) that there was no irregularity.

37. *Particulars (iii) and (iv) relate to the consumption of brandy at the police station by Nazir and John Leroy Thomas. I have already dealt with those matters.*

38. *Particular (v) deals with the failure to charge John Leroy Thomas in respect of the robbery. Again, I dealt with that matter earlier in this judgment*

39. *Particular (vi) deals with the return of money to Nazir and to John Leroy Thomas and the judge did, not surprisingly, express some concern about this. The fact is that (1) Nazir got her 900 back on 15th February 1999, nine days after she made her statement on 6th February 1999; (2) John Leroy Thomas got back his 940 on 26th March 1999, just under four weeks after his arrest.*

40. *As a result of what seems to have been an administrative error, both were repaid for a second time after the conclusion of proceedings int he Crown Court, but, as Mr Lally accepts, nothing can now turn on that. Mr Lally's submission is that the earlier repayments are indicative of misfeasance because of the weight of evidence against Nazir and John Leroy Thomas. But, as it seems to me, once it was decided not to proceed against Nazir she had a right to her money. She could have been charged with drugs offences, but for obvious reasons the decision was taken not to follow that course. Similarly, as Superintendent Miller made clear when giving evidence, he had in his judgment no good grounds for holding on to the 940. He could not show that it was part of the fee for the attack on Duffy committed 27 days before John Leroy Thomas was arrested. So, in my judgment, the judge was right to find in the end that the repayments did not amount to evidence of misfeasance. Certainly, there was no real room for the inference that the evidence of Nazir and John Leroy Thomas was being bought with their own money.*

41. At particular (vii) there is complaint of the handling of the identification procedure. The trial judge expressed disquiet about two matters: (1) the fact that the identification parades were not held soon after the two claimants were arrested, and (2) the fact that Inspector Beech, the identification officer, did not see the descriptions given by witnesses of the attackers.

42. As to the first, the failure was unfortunate but it has nothing to do with the tort alleged given that the two claimants, as the judge found later, refused to take part in an identification parade at all.

43. As to the second matter, Code D of the Codes to the Police and Criminal Evidence Act, only requires that the identification officer should be aware of the first description given. He does not need to be aware of all other descriptions, and I do not share the judge's disquiet.

44. The eighth particular given in support of Ground 3 in the notice of appeal relates to the handling of Nazir and John Leroy Thomas generally and adds nothing to the particulars which precede it.

45. At the end of the day what, in my judgment, makes this appeal virtually unarguable is that the judge - for what I conceive to be good reasons which he gave - rejected the allegation of bad faith. That, as the House of Lords has made clear, was an essential ingredient of the tort. I would therefore dismiss this appeal.

46. LORD JUSTICE MUMMERY: I agree.

47. LORD JUSTICE LAWS: I also agree.

"Lee Duffy was a Rottweiler in a world of Poodles".
Stephen Sayers

PETER KING

I'm now 47 years old and I grew up in Grangetown which is the next estate to Lee's manor of South Bank. South Bank and Grangetown have always had a big rivalry and I think that's why Lee started going into Grangetown, he was looking for bother.

I first heard of Lee Duffy in the early 80s when he used to come over the pubs in Grangetown whilst still a teenager looking for big names so he could put them on their arses. Lee's name was feared at the time of course because he was the new kid on the block who everybody was talking about. There used to be a gang of football hooligans named "The Boro boot boys", I forget just how many of them Lee put away. One lad even moved away after the hiding Lee gave him to save face.

Lee would just be causing mayhem wherever he went like in The Kings Head pub on Bolckow Road. What happened was that Lee walked over to two lads playing pool and put his dog on the table and said "the dog will play the winner next" completely ruining the game of course. I think it was Roy Stonehouse who was a big lad but not really a handy bloke that said to Lee "what the fuck you playing at?" and Lee just mullered him. He was doing things like that all the time, his reputation rocketed and he made his mark in and around Grangetown.

When I was growing up I wasn't a bad lad but at times I used to get myself into all sorts with drugs. I was always into my music and DJing, which in those days seemed to go hand in hand with taking ecstasy tablets.

I used to work down South during the week but at the weekend I'd usually come back to the Boro and the party lifestyle.

When I got involved with drugs I was going to run into the Duffer sooner or later. Yes I'd been in parties with him a few times but he never really took an interest in me until he found out I was selling drugs.

What I found with Lee was that he had a real presence about him, you knew he'd entered the building within seconds of him arriving. You'd see his rather intimidating figure with his trademark hairstyle and he would clear rooms faster than police raids. One memory I'll always have of Lee was walking in the Blaises toilets and seeing him smashing some guys face into the sinks, I just gathered Lee was taxing some young drug dealer. His good friend Boothy was there but I just turned and got the fuck out of there ASAP.

I did have a kind of run in with the Duff myself and probably the only reason I got away lightly was because I knew his best mate Neil Booth. I think if I didn't know Boothy so well I'm sure I'd have been like that kid getting his face smashed into the sinks in Blaises.

Now my tale about Lee Duffy happened around 1991 and it was at the height of the rave scene in Teesside. I was a face around Grangetown doing things with Kev Harland on the rave scene but because I worked down South I had the best of both worlds, that was until Lee Duffy found out I was selling Doves (E's) and got interested in me. Now Lee at the time was going around all the dealers in the area and taxing them so really Lee just saw this as his right to get something from me.

When I'd gone back done South, Lee must have got wind of this "Kingy" and became very interested in me for obvious reasons. When I was working away Lee had already started his search for me and it was Davie Sharp who told my dad that Lee Duffy was trying to find me which really dropped me in the shit because firstly, my dad clocked what I'd been doing and two, my dad didn't want Lee Duffy coming to our door!

Now I'd become aware that he was after me and I was sure I was going to get a pounding off the Duffer, it became like a game of cat and mouse between me and Lee for about 7-8 weeks. At the time I didn't think I was doing anything wrong but looking back with hindsight I was.

I was taking too much of what Lee Duffy was entitled to, or so he thought. Now Lee didn't catch up with me for ages, in fact it was the week before he died when he eventually did catch up with me and I went into the Lion's den, Lee Duffy's playground (Ramsey's blues) on Princess Road. How I remember it was that I was already in there when and Duffy and Boothy came in and I thought FUCK what am I going to do? I knew it was Lee when I heard someone shout in a soft Boro accent "OI OI... NOW THEN NOW THEN KIDS, LEE DUFFY IS IN THE BUILDING" on his arrival.

To tell you the truth I was trying to hide but nothing got past the Duffer and he found me within seconds. He was so aware of everything that was around him, like he had eyes in the back of his head, or in my case that he knew I was in another room. I'm sure he had the Terminator vision from the movies where it told him all who were in his surroundings.

I'd clicked on I was now in major shit so I tried to quickly and quietly walk past him when all of a sudden he blocked the doorway. I gulped, because I knew what was coming. With that, Lee then smiled and give me a wink and walked towards me. He then ruffles my hair and picked me up by my ears like he was lifting the F.A cup whilst shaking me about saying "so you're this fucking Kingy eh, I've been looking for you lad"!!!! To this day I don't know how he even knew it was me. I wasn't even aware that he knew what I looked like.

Well I'm not going to lie my whole life flashed before me and I've never felt fear like it before or since in my life but then thankfully Boothy had a word with Lee and told him I was alright. As quick as he had picked me up he then plonked me back down on my arse, didn't hit me but said "you stay there sunshine, I'm coming back to see you shortly." Well you'd have thought someone had poured concrete on my feet because even though I was dying for a piss I did not move for the next three hours.

The drugs I'd been on were wearing off and my comedown had trebled because I'd been caught in Lee Duffy's net. I was sat there until broad daylight and the birds were chirping and even Lee had left, he must have forgotten all about me because he'd got too stoned. Eventually I saw Boothy who told me I'd got off lightly and that Lee had gone. I'd never been so relieved in my life. I always found Neil Booth and Lee Duffy to be extremely close, almost like brothers.

A week later Lee was killed outside the Afro Caribbean centre and I was there that night as well. Before it kicked off with him and Allo you could sense something was going to happen.

I went back to a party in Grangetown afterwards and when the news came through Lee had died it was as though it was nothing because everyone expected it to happen. A won't mention names but a few people there were happy about it but even though he'd picked me up by my ears the week before I wasn't. Now this might sound fucking crazy but I viewed Lee Duffy as a gentleman at what he did and I know he let me off lightly compared to the horror stories of what he'd done to other people.

I've even been over to his grave and paid my respects because even though at the time I was mixed up in my own life, by rights he should have flattened me but for some reason he never and maybe I had some kind of strange respect for him.

"He was like the Terminator, he kept saying 'I'll be back' and that's just what he did after the shootings. Lee used to like to be seen in busy places after the attempts on his life, even if it meant he was on crutches and bandaged up. The people in the town used to see him and think 'bloody hell, what's he doing out'. I think the people of Teesside started to believe he was invincible and he couldn't be killed before he died. That's why the town was in such disbelief when it happened because he'd always managed to come back. Well he won't be coming back this time".

Anonymous, 1991

The Evening Gazette

DENIS LOWE

Denis Lowe grew up in Saltersgill, Middlesbrough and is 57 years old now. Him and his brother John "Topsy" Lowe, who'd fought against former world champion, Alan Minter, not to mention a good few around Middlesbrough, are known as, "The fighting Lowe brothers." Denis didn't turn pro but he was one hell of an amateur boxer with an outstanding winning record. Denis was also a tremendous footballer and was once on Middlesbrough's books so he was very sporty.

Not only was Denis known as a sporty man he was also known as one of the staunchest doormen in Middlesbrough around the time of Lee Duffy's reign. Denis mainly worked on the old De Niro's doors (now Liquor Vaults) and that's where he boxed from the ages of 16 to 30 where his brother coached in Phil Thomas ABC upstairs.

Denis and his dog/horse Samson (all 12 ½st of him) were mine and Neil Jackson's (cameraman) favourite to interview when filming the Lee Duffy documentary. Even the bits that weren't used for the documentary were so enthralling. I liked Denis a lot and I could have spoken to him all day that Sunday afternoon in his garden in Coulby Newham.

Denis said: –

When I worked the De Niro's door through the 80s and 90s it used to be nicknamed, "the O.K Corral", because there was always something going off back then in that place on Friday and Saturday nights. At that time Dave Stanwick was the head doorman he was a big powerful lad himself.

When I got the job the two people who he warned me of were Lee Duffy and Brian Cockerill. Dave told me that the latter was so strong with his legs that it was unbelievable.

I went on to have a long career on the doors at such places such as The Cornerhouse, The Arena, The Theatre then lastly the Aqua Bar (formerly The Havana), I used to own that in the end. When I owned that place it brought a boatload of memories back for me. Back when the Havana was open you could have a fight in those days and that was it sorted, they didn't phone the bobbies.

With me being a Middlesbrough lad I knew all the bad lads but hadn't clashed with them because I wasn't the type of person to be mixed in their world until I started the doors. Before then the only fighting I'd done and really still preferred was in a boxing ring. Of course when you're a doorman though you're going to get into situations aren't you at some point.

Now, with me working on the doors for a living around Middlesbrough through the late 80s and early 90s it was inevitable that I was going to hear of Lee Duffy. I knew who Lee was for many years before that and I'd even got locked up with him in South Bank police station regarding a load of stolen goods in the mid-eighties. Before we parted, Lee shouted to me, "tell em nothing Den and I won't either."

Lee, in all the time I knew him was wild, from punching people for fun to even banging his mates mothers. For all the crazy things you heard about Lee, 99.99% there was always some kind of violence involved. I myself had one sort of incident where I thought we might have come to blows in 1983. I was working one night in the Spacey (arcade centre in South Bank) that I used to own. I was locking up when I heard a rumour that Lee Duffy was planning on robbing me at the end of the night. Shaun Day was there that night and I told him to give me a shout when he saw Lee. This was before Lee had gotten a name for himself. In the end I was that wound up with what I'd heard that I went looking for Lee in my car, at that point he wasn't as feared as he went on to become. I found him on the streets of South Bank and I jumped out of my car, "is that right you're going to rob me Lee?" I lunged forward and tried to punch him but missed. Lee, who was startled just jumped 10 yards back and genuinely looked surprised at what I'd just asked him. I'm maybe punch drunk these days but I'm sure Lee was with some of the Massey's from South Bank. Lee totally denied that anything of the sort was ever going to take place and I believed him because of how surprised he looked. Me and Lee never ever had a crossed word from that day on but in truth you could never really trust him.

I would hear of all the mad things he was doing like pouring glue over his mates head for his own entertainment, he was always doing that to people.

All these crazy stories around 1983 when he was still a teenager was the start of the 'Lee Duffy journey' when I look back with hindsight. You only can say things like that at the end of something.

I know one of the maddest things I ever saw Lee do in his early years in a pub was wanting to play a game, well the game that he wanted to play was where he and his six mates stood in a circle, then he said he'd punch the man next to him, then that man punches the other and so on and the winner was the one left standing. I'm not lying I watched the young Lee doing that, he was around 3 ½ years younger than me and I thought, 'you're off your fucking rocker mate' because his idea of a good time was just stood punching people and then taking punches. He was like a pig in shit!

Lee looked like a boxer because of his features but to tell you the truth I don't think he ever boxed. He did look the part though and he was well cut up in a physical sense even then, long before he put all that muscle on years later.

When I saw Lee sparring in Joe Walton's gym he never took a backward step. He wasn't your skilful fighter he was just 100mph, knock your head off with everything thrown, kind of boxer. I don't think there was a lot of thinking behind his boxing style it was just sheer brutality with power and speed in abundance. In fact Lee came one day in 1983 with one of his close friends who was the other name in the town at the time. Both sparred and Lee dropped him, then his mate got up and flattened Lee then they both cuddled and were happy with it and off they went! Maybe Lee was testing his mate out which was probably more than likely considering Lee was around 17 then and that was about the age he was feeling everyone out.

When I was on the door in De Niro's around 1990, as bad as it sounds, we had around six lads in total who also worked there and they all did a sweep stake on Lee and at what age he was going to die. It was 25 to 30 because the attacks on his life were that regular. Of course whoever had 26 must have won that.

Like I said after that time when I tried to lay one on Lee we never ever had a crossed word, but one-man Lee was bad with every time he saw him was big Paul Salter. I was told Lee whacked him a few times and one of them was for no apparent reason whatsoever. That time they were in a room full of people and all of a sudden 'WALLOP' and he hit Paul. That was the kind of thing Lee did to pass the time of day. That was Lee's favourite party game literally.

Several times when Lee was about, a bar would be flourishing and bouncing with a happy vibe then Duffy would turn up, not even take his jacket off and you just heard two almighty noises one was Lee thumping someone and the other was them hitting the deck, you'd turn around and Lee had hit someone within the first ten minutes of being in the place. Then that bar's attendance would literally fall from 60 to single figures within one minute. Lee used to clear bars that effectively they'd be tumbleweeds blowing about. A lot of the time you could tell

Duffy had been in before seeing him because there would be no one in there. I used to say that I didn't even think Lee used to care who it was, he'd just hit them so he could relax. It was like he needed this fix before he could even begin to chill out. I don't care who says that's not true, that's just what Lee Duffy did.

I heard that Lee had been killed on the morning of August 25th, 1991. There was a lot of relief in the town for some people but for me I was very sad. It was after Lee had died when I was told by a lot of his close friends just what he'd been up to in his last year like going chasing Viv Graham up in Newcastle for a fight to put Boro on the map and I was like, good on ya. To me, that was just Lee on his game if you know what I mean!

He didn't deserve to die because he hadn't yet fulfilled what he'd set out to do. If he hadn't been killed then in 1991 and he'd have been allowed to have seen the years 1992/93/94/95 that would have made the Lee Duffy story even bigger. Don't forget the fact that he'd have still been only 30 in 1995! That thought is absolutely frightening isn't it when you take a minute to think about it.

If you want me to sum Lee Duffy up to you from my experiences then I'd say he was a man before his time. Although it may have been short, sharp and bloodied to most, Lee Duffy made his mark in this world. He died far too early when he was only just becoming the kingpin.

When I sit here now and talk to you in May 2019 I just couldn't begin to imagine how rich Lee Duffy could have become if only he'd have stayed alive! Especially when you see who's gone on to rule since his demise because nobody in the area was a patch on Lee in that field. Today he'd have only been 54 years old and he should have been a wealthy man.

For as long as I live I'll never forget the feeling in the Boro after he died. The town of Middlesbrough just went solemn. It was as if the town of Middlesbrough was crying out in its thousands, yes he was a bastard, but why's he gone?

"Lee Duffy was like marmite, you either loved him or you hated him. He was a one-punch fighter and no matter how many times you hit him, you were gone in one. He certainly wasn't what you'd see every day and there was no middle ground to him".

Stephen Sayers

FIGHTING PROWESS

Lee Duffy's fighting prowess was awesome it really was. Lee was raised on the toughest estate of them all, South Bank, so he'd done his apprenticeship for the big bad world. The difference between Lee and the other hard men of Teesside was that Lee was an athlete. One of Lee's best friends told me Lee was like "the blackest white man" that ever lived and what I mean by that is he had such incredible bone structure. Have you ever noticed that all the top boxers in the world are mostly black Americans. A boxing trainer and ex-heavyweight pro that I know, calls it "nigga slick" and it seemed that Lee had whatever that meant! When Lee was young climbing up the ladder as an 17-18-year-old he would go running up Eston Hills with logs tied to him as well as heavy rucksacks on his back. He was the ultimate athlete. I'm told by the people who saw Lee ripping into the heavy bags in the gym that he had more power than what was necessary.

Even if he wasn't training he was always in good shape all year round regardless of what drugs he was taking, how late he was staying out or whatever he was eating he was forever in shape.

From the age of 17 years old Lee Duffy's name was a major force to be reckoned with in South Bank. When he was just that age landlords like Barry Suggett, who had a couple of pubs, told me that if he ever had any problems he would "go give the Duff a shout" and Lee would sort it out for Barry. Lee was extremely close to Barry's younger brother Robert at the time. Most of the time Lee was up against fully mature men when Lee himself was still a skinny beanpole of a lad. Lee used to also do the same for Stu Stamp in his pub in South Bank.

After a year or so of honing his fighting skills around South Bank's High Street, which was an incredibly busy place in the 1980s with pubs galore, Lee decided he would venture into the town of Middlesbrough and wreak havoc in his own special kind of way, a way that only Lee Duffy could. Back in 1982/83 the city centre had absolutely no idea what was laid ahead at that time but even in those early years whenever Lee Duffy was out of prison the town as a whole braced itself.

I told you all in the first book that Lee wasn't the trained boxer the media had made him out to be for the last twenty-eight years. I have a little knowledge myself regarding boxing because I myself boxed as a kid and helped out coaching kids in Middlesbrough at various gyms over the years. I don't believe until you've maybe had a dozen fights of so, that you can really understand the logics of boxing. I mean, if you can't stand with your feet correctly you can't throw a punch with any force, nor can you receive one with any chance of staying on your feet. You need strong foundations just like building a house and if your foundations are all wrong then you're wasting your time and you can't shift the power from your legs, a punch doesn't come from your arms it comes from your shoulders, legs and hips, well Lee I'm told by the people around him was different, he was a freak of nature! He'd never had one amateur contest for that matter but he was unique in that aspect.

He mastered the very basics of boxing and moulded it into his own style along with ferocious speed and bad intentions.

Mastering the basics of pugilism can be deadly effective although so simple. Just look at Wladimir Klitschko who ruled the heavyweight division for a decade. When you watch his style it's very basic although incredibly effective with his one-two and grab. If you look at all the best Kazakhstan's and other Eastern Europeans it's all very basic but effective.

All Lee Duffy ever had boxing ability wise was the basics but it was all he ever needed fortunately for him or rather unfortunately for others.

Not only did Lee have the boxing side of things but he was an out and out streetfighter, although I'm told it rarely reached that point because he was so so heavy-handed and one punch was usually all it ever took.

Lee when in fighting mode had pure bad intentions to the core. Lee used to say he would always go out to damage someone that extra bit because they wouldn't be coming back for revenge in a hurry. When I say that, I think of the Middlesbrough boxer Lee really did a number on. The boxer, Lee and a few others had been drinking together all day. Lee himself stayed more or less sober but Lee's future target maybe should have known a bit better then to let his guard down with Duffy and of course Lee turned on him and broke his jaw with a sneak-shot, which is something he was a master at. Not only that but Lee kicked him all over the floor then went on to kidnap him in his own car and took him up the hills to dish out more damage.

When I did a bit of digging on that story I was told the full lot, although the victim wouldn't speak with me I did get the full facts. I was told that when Lee had finished beating the man up that he turned to Ducko, who was there, and said "will you tell everyone I knocked him out with one punch rather than kicked him all over?" When I asked Ducko about this he confirmed it to me but he wouldn't speak to me regarding doing his own chapter about Lee and I completely understand why.

When you look at Lee's 6ft 4 physique in some of the old pictures on our Facebook page you can see for yourself that Lee had a natural fighters body. Rather than be rigid, slow and stiff like your former heavyweight champions like Frank Bruno and James "Bonecrusher" Smith who were just "top heavy" and full of muscle, Lee was built more like Thomas "Hitman" Hearns, Gerald McClellan and Deontay Wilder. Lee, although a big unit, was rangier and wirier. Hearns and McClellan were ferocious, murderous, thunderous punchers who could knock men into next week and that's where Lee's strengths over your average man on the street laid. I remember chatting with Middlesbrough's most famous boxing promoter not long back and I quote my good friend John Spensley, "people think it's these little squat muscular guys who can punch but it's not, it's these big skinny lean, beanpole fuckers who can bang!" Well Duffy was very much your "big lean, beanpole fucker wasn't he?!" until he went in Durham prison in March 1988. That's where he did all his training and came out weighing seventeen and a half stone and then caused mayhem in the town before his death. Even when Lee went on 'the juice' and was given courses of steroids by Craig Howard he did very well on them. Rather than just become massive like a weightlifter Lee still looked natural on it just a lot bigger.

Craig Howard got into bodybuilding from taking steroids as a fifteen-year-old boy who needed them for fighting stomach cancer. Lee was quite close to Craig although I'm told he did the dirty on Lee a few times. Craig liked the idea of hanging around with Duffy but sometimes it would get too much because of all the mad things that Lee was doing, then Craig would give Lee a wide berth. One of the reasons they fell out was because when Craig took Lee and a couple of others to the Kenton bar in Newcastle Lee's friend Michael Sayers told Craig that he recognised him but couldn't think where from, only a couple of minutes later Michael told Craig, "you're that grass from D-wing in Durham jail"!!!! Craig ran out like he was carrying carpets because he was that muscular and Lee was on the floor crying with laughter. That was until he went to find Craig twenty minutes later and he realised that he'd driven back to Boro leaving Lee, Boothy & co foaming at the mouths.

Lee would have been a natural boxer had he chosen a different path and today we could have all been reading about a very different Lee Paul Duffy than the one you're reading about at this very moment. A lot of boxers have skill but lack a nasty streak, then some don't have any skill but are bad to the core, Lee Duffy, I'm told was like a shark who could smell blood from four miles away and had both nastiness and skill in equal measures. Not only that, but he was an expert in violence literally and could be quite sadistic with it. No other example is needed than when he made a former best friend of his beg for Lee not to hit him whilst on all fours in the Cleveland pub in Linthorpe Village. He liked to be flamboyant with it because all 6ft 4 of him oozed confidence of the highest order.

It's not commonly known but Lee did have a couple of arranged fights for big money like the one time a group of men came up to meet Lee and a close friend in The Masham pub (now a sports shop) outside of the Hillstreet Centre. These fella's came up from Nottingham and one of them was said to be the hardest man from their city. The arrangement was that Lee and the man from Notts would fight bare-knuckle and the winner would collect £1,000 which was a substantial amount back in 1990. Before the men arrived from down South, Lee's friend turned to him and said "how much have you got in ya pocket Lee? Lee told him £12, Lee's mate had £36, Lee's mate told him "well ya best not lose then eh" and Lee just replied, "as if". The men turned up and Duffy and his opponent left the Masham and walked around the back of the Hill Street Centre and the crowd followed. The fight got underway and Lee led with a huge right hand which I'm told by Lee's buddy was "utterly embarrassing" and he thought we are "MEGA FUCKED" here thinking Lee was gonna lose and all they had was £48 of the £1,000 they'd have to pay. At the time Lee had been taking all sorts and it's not the sort of preparation you'd want going into a big money fight with your rep as the baddest man in Britain on the line. The rep alone was worth far more than the £1,000 ever was to Duffy. After Lee missed wildly with the first he threw his second which was a right hand that second punch caught the man from Notts square on the jaw and down he went like shit off a stick and was out cold before he hit the floor. Lee had only hit him once and the fight was over. After the fight the man was brought to his senses by the gang from Nottingham and they all went back into the Masham with Lee and friend for a pint. Things like that are a far cry from today's society, these days, it's sad to say that you would probably get shot or stabbed rather than go for a pint together afterwards.

Lee now had a grand in his pocket and he partied the weekend away in The Havana and then the blues parties without a mark on him, apart from his knuckles of course. When you think about stories like that it's staggering to think he was doing things like that without even training. Can you imagine what Lee Duffy could have done if he'd taken up boxing as a serious sport? Lee had just flattened a serious "face" from the Nottingham underworld whilst being off his box so imagine what he'd have done if he'd have been focused? When you look at the Duff's last tango against former friend David Allison, Lee hadn't been to bed for two days and was winning the fight until a knuckle-duster and a knife was used. That's staggering in my opinion because people in Middlesbrough who know Lee's last opponent will know just how much of a hard man David Allison is. Not to mention that Lee had been shot in the knee and foot only months before and wasn't as quick on his feet as he may once might have been.

If Lee hadn't of died that morning at 3.55am on August 25th, 1991 the plan was that him and his close pal Lee

Harrison were planning on driving to Edinburgh the next day at 1pm to be at some all-night rave. That just goes to show the level of burning the candles at both ends that Lee Duffy did. Everything was 100mph. In fact the day before Lee died (Lee died in early hours of Sunday morning but technically to him it was a Saturday) Lee had partied that much and that was the reason his best mate Boothy wasn't with him when he died was because he was still in bed wrote off from the night before. Lee must have done some partying if Neil Booth was a write off I know that much, but Lee Duffy didn't do hangovers or comedowns so I'm told. When I did the first book Lee Duffy – The Whole of the Moon, one of Lee's best friends Rob Suggett told me that the song by The Specials 'You've Done too Much, Much Too Young' perfectly sums Lee Duffy's life up to a tee. I think that's a very fitting analysis.

For all of the fights that Lee Duffy ever had in his life, and believe me there was a lot, he would say that the toughest man he'd ever faced was David Allison, who of course was also the last man Lee ever fought with.

Over the last year I've read all kinds of things on social media saying Lee Duffy was killed by a junkie or just some little guy, which goes to show that what people don't know they just make up. I can assure you that this is very far from the case in regards to David Allison. David was certainly one big powerful man and as game as they come. Allo, if you speak to most Middlesbrough F.C supporters, was their main man and General in battle. He became a legend in his own right because he never backed down from anyone when fighting with the Boro Frontline (soccer casuals) and he is known all over the country even without his association to Lee Duffy. If you pick any football hooligan book up the Boro Frontline will always get a mention, even from sets of fans such as Chelsea, Everton and Sheffield United because I've read some of them myself. Those books say that although they couldn't stand the Boro lot, they were always one of the hardest set of supporters they'd ever faced. Apart from Duffy, Allo was the other name in the town with maybe another handful of men when Middlesbrough was undoubtably at its most ruthless and roughest. David deep down liked Lee but what he couldn't abide was the way he would just overpower all the Boro lads but then kiss all the Geordie lads arses. David Allison was a proper Boro lad and I'm told this gave him the needle.

Maybe it's something in the water in Teesside or the parmo's, maybe it's what is in the smog but Teesside certainly bred it's fair share of tough men.

Every hard man or would-be hardman Teesside's ever produced from that era such as George Doneathy, Davey Fields, Allo, Paul and Micky Salter, Paul Debrick, Mark Johnson, Brian Cockerill, Ducko, the Hoes brothers, Jonka Teasdale, Dave Bishop, the Wood brothers, Dale Henderson-Thynne, Elvis Thomo, Kevin O'Keefe (Beefy), Paul Bryan, the Smith brothers, Molly Jaffray, John and Mick Shellard, Milton Spanswick, Billy and Dave Woodier, Kev Auer, Kev Hawkes, Brian Andrews, Podgey Foreman, and Terrance Nivens. Of course there were many others but I was asked not to mention them in this book. Lee clashed with or was supposed to clash with all of these men. I know some of the men named above from growing up in Middlesbrough and with a lot of them their reputation goes before them, but Lee Duffy was never bothered about things like that. In fact, the better and harder the man was the more appealing he would have been in the eyes of the Duff to go sniff them out and bring hell.

I won't name him but I sat down with one well known Teesside hard man and I asked him if Lee Duffy was really that much of a handful? His response was a funny one, he told me that even though he was at times at loggerheads with Duffy and couldn't be seen to have been scared of him, but the fact is, in his opinion, Lee would have beat him and his business partner (another hard man) in one go. To quote my source "he was just that much of a machine he had it all, barring using weapons and guns you couldn't win and even if you did, well I'm still not sure".

Even though there's some extremely tough men named who could hold their own in any city across Britain, most had to do as they were told when Lee told them. He also told me that Lee used to say to him that he knew he was going to die young, but also that was all part of Lee Duffy's front, the act if you like of 'oh I'm that mad I don't give a fuck if I die'. He said deep down it was a persona that Lee Duffy had to put on but after ten years of knowing him extremely well he said he was really a different person behind closed doors. Deep down, the real beef between Duffy and Allison wasn't anything to do with drugs going missing, yes it happened, but in my opinion from my meticulous research, I would say that in the whole of Middlesbrough at that time, Allison was the only man in the town who publicly wouldn't bow down to Duffy, and that seriously fucked Duffy off! Lee viewed himself as national and when people with big names for being hard men like Viv Graham were running scared of him then Allo wasn't worthy to be in the same league as he was. Maybe that's true or maybe it's not, but one thing is for sure David Allison would have got stuck into Duffy every single day of the week and twice on Sundays if he had to, win, lose or draw. That's just the type of person he was I was told by some people close to him.

When I've sat in the Northern Echo and Gazette archives and read some of the articles from Lee's family and partner I have to say it seems to back up my sources claims that behind closed doors Lee Duffy was a very different man indeed.

Only three weeks before he died Lee did go to see a man of the cloth about changing his ways, the Priest wrote down some things for Lee to think about and told Lee that although he was doing some very bad things, overall he was a good man. Brenda Duffy kept that letter for years and even showed it to Lee's close buddy Lorna Lancaster.

Going back to the lovely Lorna it's as clear as the day is long that her and Lee had a very close bond right up until the day he died. On the day of Lee's funeral Lawrie Duffy Senior told Lorna just how he remembered her carrying his little son all over the tough South Bank estate on her shoulders like a mother bird cradling her baby chicks. Lorna told me that if she went into the Duffy household Lee's dad would jump up and make her something to eat, even using other people's steaks in the fridge because he loved how she doted on his young son who was having troublesome times in the early seventies.

I sat with one of Lee Duffy's close friends one day and he explained the difference to me between Lee and Brian Cockerill who he also knew extremely well. He said "Brian could fight don't you worry about that, but overall he was a nice man, whereas the Duff was just out and out bad to the core. Lee had a nasty streak in him big Bri never really had. If I had to choose two doors to walk into and one being to fight Cockerill and the other to fight Duffy I'd have walked in to fight Brian any day of the week. The reason being was that Brian was the nicer man, Duffy always wanted to really hurt you bad if he was fighting you. Brian might have felt sorry for you eventually, but Lee wouldn't have. I've never known anyone to cause as much trouble wherever he went like Lee did. I think with Lee, and I knew him very well, was that all he had was his reputation and he knew it. Without that, he was a nobody. I feel Lee's early life left him a bit disturbed."

Overall Lee Duffy was a gutsy young man and violence was his answer to everything. The only time in the 18 months of researching Lee's life have I ever been told that he was genuinely scared of something was from

Middlesbrough boxing royalty John Dryden. John told me about a time when Lee was out the back of the Welly gym and there was a big Alsatian barking at him. Lee was that scared he ran and stood on the roof of someone's car to escape it shouting, "GET THAT DOG AWAY FROM ME" almost in tears. Although he was just a teenager at the time and wasn't the fiery lion he would go on to become.

Maybe Lee had an undiagnosed mental illness, back in the 1970/80s these things weren't spoken of like they are in 2019. Of course, now we'll never truly know will we but in my humble opinion it's far from normal to feel like you need to hurt someone every time you go out.

I've read 56 of the 63 books on The Krays Twins and the only other person I've heard of who was exactly like Lee was Ronnie Kray and he was diagnosed as having paranoid schizophrenia.

"If you said you weren't scared of the Duffer you are a fucking liar. I don't care how hard you were or how much of a name you had in Boro. Everybody I ever met was scared of Lee. It's easy to sit in a pub almost 30 years on and tell lies."

Lee's close friend.

MANNY BURGO

Manny Burgo is someone I'd have loved to have spoken with for the first book although I did try to get hold of him at the time Manny is a very private person and doesn't use social media and I ran out of time. Luckily, through Steve Wraith, I did manage to get hold of Manny this time.

Manny is 58 years old and from North Shields, he's 6ft 1 and was a former heavyweight professional boxer. I knew him and Lee Duffy were close before I got in touch with Manny from the research that I had done for the first book so, I was thrilled when big Manny spared me a little time to talk with me for this book and also when he agreed to be featured in 'The Whole of the Moon' documentary. Manny said :–

I'd never heard of Lee Duffy and had no idea who he was until I met him in Durham prison in 1986 when he was just 21. At the time Lee was only on remand but he had a load of charges against him but a lot of them were dropped.

Lee was really angry that the authorities were hitting him with charge after charge after charge. Lee told me that the police in Boro were just doing anything to keep him off the streets.

I'm sure, if I remember rightly, that he got convicted on the last charge which is when he spent a bit of time in jail.

I found Lee Duffy to be a lovely lad and could only speak well of him as a person. I saw a different side to Lee that not many people speak about. On his own Lee was very soft-hearted you know!

What Lee used to like doing when he was in his cell was that fancy writing that's all joined up, calligraphy I think they call it. He'd often sit there for hours writing pages and pages of super neat fancy joined up handwriting. He would also write poems. I'd often walk past his cell and say to him, "who's taught you to do that?"

Another thing that doesn't get spoken about regarding Lee Duffy was that he was incredibly generous to a fault. I've been in taxi's were he's given the driver £20 and told them to take me wherever I want to go.

It was only when I got out of prison in 1987 that I started to hear all these bad things about him which didn't add up to me. I was convinced there must have been two Lee Duffy's, a goodie and a baddie because the lad I knew wasn't like that. It was that same year that I was at a rave at The Mayfair in Newcastle that I bumped into Lee Duffy once again. Lee came over to me telling me he couldn't believe he's bumped into me again. Then saying he couldn't thank me enough for what I did for him, I said, "what do you mean Lee, you can't thank me enough?", but he kept saying how I'd took him under my wing and showed him the ropes if you like. Maybe he was on drugs at the time but all night he was saying I was like a big brother to him in jail. I was just being a friend to him.

When I look back at it and what he could have meant, I suppose it could be that Lee was very angry in prison and wanted to fight with the screws on a daily basis but I just tried talking to him and said he'd never get out if he didn't calm down. I told him that they were just doing their jobs.

From that night at The Mayfair in 1987 until he died I kept in contact with him over the four years and would often come down to Middlesbrough to see him and meet his Mam. Lee would then come to Newcastle and stay with my family or we'd go out for food with my brother.

The stories regarding Lee coming to Newcastle looking for Viv Graham are true because Lee told me. Lee told me from his own mouth that he was out down the Bigg Market with a couple of the Sayers family. He said the trouble happened in Macey's Bar and Viv had all the doors there. Lee told me that Viv had barred all the Sayers for no reason and when they stopped the Sayers from getting in one of them put their hands-on Duffy so Lee chinned the full squad of them there and then. The next day Viv Graham rang Lee up to tell him he wasn't happy with Duffy wiping out his door crew. Lee then tells Viv that he'd come to fight him now and to give him an hour and he'd be in Newcastle. Viv then turned around and told Lee it was a warning and if he did it again they'd be serious repercussions and put the phone down.

Now, Lee Duffy was a dead honest kid you know with things like that, Lee even told me, he said, "actually Manny when I first spoke with Viv I was a bit nervous because I was out my area, then I thought fuck it I'll come up and have a fight with him but then he put the phone down." I totally believe Lee when he told me that because in the years I was close to Duffy I never knew him to lie about anything in a fighting sense, he didn't need to he could walk the walk and talk the talk in his Boro accent better than anyone.

When I heard Lee had been stabbed I was out in Whitley Bay. Heartbroken is not the word and I cried like a baby. When I heard who did it I wasn't surprised because Lee used to tell me he fought with the guy all the time.

I went to Lee's funeral and it was the biggest send off I've ever seen in my life.

Today in 2019 he's still loved and spoken of in Newcastle. If I ever hear people bad mouth him I won't have it in my company and I tell them straight. The Lee I knew was a lovely person. Even today I think about him all the time and often his name pops up where I live. People often have asked me in the last 28 years if I knew Lee Duffy and I tell them that I didn't just know him, I was one of the few who was close to him. Lee was a big big part of my life and I loved the man.

"I had flashes… but you saw the plan".

Mike Scott

LEE DUFFY'S PLAYGROUND

The Havana was probably Lee Duffy's favourite place in the world when he was at the top of his game. Today on Linthorpe Road at the spot The Havana was stands an empty waste land. When it was still going back in the day it had several names such as The Speak Easy, The Belmont, Club Toxsin and Aqua Bar. It was Lee's playground and it provided easy prey for him with the young and upcoming drug dealers to tax. Every single dealer in Boro knew that if you went into that place dealing drugs you were getting taxed and knocked out by the Duffer and the experienced ones stayed away, but because of the huge success of the club, it meant people travelled from all over such as Sunderland, Sheffield and even Scotland, particularly when massive acts like Guru Josh and others came to play there live.

Like in the animal kingdom, the experienced Jackals would keep a safe distance away from Lee Duffy's domain, they'd seen him bare his teeth once too often but the inexperienced ones, well they were the easy pickings for the man who considered himself to be king of the jungle. Some of them knew the score and with them many times Lee wouldn't even have to use violence he'd just hold out his hand like a mother to a toddler, retrieving something it shouldn't have in its mouth. Those that didn't know the score were given a lesson on who was the boss.

One guy I spoke to but wouldn't be interviewed for this book told me about how Lee cornered him in the Havana toilets only weeks before his death. Lee thought he had drugs but it turned out to just be chewing gum, Lee made the 16-year-old lad (he'd got in using fake i.d.) hand over his chewing gum and walked off laughing. He told me Lee was literally robbing kids of their sweets. In fact two of my personal friends in their fifties told me similar stories of their experiences with Lee. One told me how he was cornered in The Havana and forced to give him £2, the other literally had the shirt stolen off his back. Lee had previously asked for the lads Fred Perry shirt and Lee told my friend that he wanted that shirt. The very next time Lee saw him wearing it he punched the living daylights out of the well-known Middlesbrough man and stole his top from his back.

Its little tales like that which prove to me it's true that Lee was much more volatile and unpredictable in his last year compared to the year before. Little stories like that may upset some of the people close to Lee but I'm afraid Lee was what he was and there's some things that can't be sugar coated.

One of Lee's best friends told me when Lee used to be in The Havana he'd usually be stood right next to the DJ box usually with Lee's friend Lee Harrison, Alan Appleton or Craig Dickson banging out the latest dance tunes. One guy from Sunderland told me just how Lee cleared the whole dance floor when he took to the floor dancing to Shades of Rhythm by Sound of Eden in just a pair of shorts. Even if he wasn't dancing Lee would stand in the place rocking back and forth with a bottle of water in his hand, enjoying himself but at the same time staying alert for drug dealers and potential people to batter before going off to finish the night in the blues parties he frequented.

The inside of the Havana wasn't a massive place holding a capacity of around 200 people maybe. It was an incredibly hot little nightclub and often the walls would be dripping with the condensation. Afterall, it's fair to say people only went there to take drugs and dance the night away until 2am!

"It was all to do with drugs it was all about Lee Paul Duffy involved in the drug scene approaching people and taking money off them unlawfully. It was different fractions who were attempting to get back at him and obviously the two where guns were used were obviously attempted murders, they weren't warnings they were attempted murders there's no doubt about that".

Detective sergeant Ray Morton on the attempts on Lee's life in 1993.

VINCE AGAR

There's not many people as close to the Duff as Vince Agar was, he knew Lee for most of Lee's life. Vince now resides on the other side of the world but I was thrilled that he granted me an interview over the phone for this book as even Neil Booth told me they didn't come closer to Lee than Vince. Vince's house was open 24/7 for Duffy and Boothy because they knew no matter what time of day it was, Vince would be sat in the corner smoking a joint. Like the alias Reuben in the first book, in my opinion Vince's account alone makes reading this book worthwhile.

Vince said: –

I'm 74 years old and I spent a lot of my time in Eastern Asia but originally I was an over the border lad growing up in St Hilda's on Stockton Street, Terry Dicko country near where the old Steam Packet pub was.

I knew Lee Duffy's mam Brenda and his uncle Rod Jones and their parents well before I knew who Lee was. I knew Lee's father Lawrie Snr quite well but I wouldn't class old Lawrie as a hard man. Lawrie senior was a bully and I saw poor Brenda in some terrible states with black eyes and more. What I found was a lot of people never liked old Lawrie but they could never say anything to him or answer back, especially as Lee got older because they knew what would have happened. I know Lee's uncle Rod gave old Lawrie a good few hidings because of how he treated Brenda. Lawrie Snr was often kind of cranky which used to get him into a lot of arguments, he was a very clever man though so he would use his brain to talk his way out of situations. A very intellectual man was Lee's father although one of his favourite sayings was, "god damn it Brenda!" Lee would always mimic his dad behind his back taking the mick.

In fact the first time I ever clapped eyes on Lee was when he was just a baby. I suppose I never really took any notice of Lee Duffy until the first time I ever saw him fight when he was just 16-17 years of age. Lee was stood in a queue outside a nightclub on Newport Road, the place has had that many names over the years and I forgot what it used to be called back in 1981/82ish but it used to be called The Arena when John Graham and Billy Woodier had it, anyway there was a big burly hard man named Milton Spanswick (Spanny) and he could look after himself. Spanny had been a bit of a doorman and instead of queuing he walked straight past maybe 30-40 people waiting in line to get in. So, as Spanny was walking into the entrance door you heard this voice shout "OI OI, GET TO THE BACK OF THE FUCKING QUEUE YOU!" Spanny turned around and said, "who the fucking hell are you talking to?" to this big skinny kid in the line. Well it was the young Duff waiting like a tiger in the grass ready to pounce. I didn't know it was Lee until the next day because I hadn't seen him for years. Now Spanny was a handy lad himself so he walked over and stood right in front of this mouthy youth in the queue. Lee was just a big skinny lad at the time, possibly around 12 stone and he didn't yet have the power in his punch that he would go on to have but he fucking boxed the hell out of Spanny 'BANG BANG BANG' Spanny didn't know where the punches were coming from he really didn't. Lee's speed and ferocity was beating this bloke, Lee really was something else and at one-point Lee was bouncing him off cars! Well I was watching in fucking amazement! Poor Spanny thought he was surrounded and I don't think he managed to lay a punch on this young kid he was facing. I was thinking 'who's that fucking lad?' because I'd never seen anything like it. Anyway a hoard of bouncers came out and stopped it and they wouldn't let Lee in the club then because he was only a young kid at maybe 16-17 yrs old and nobody had heard of him. Well I ended up going in the club with Spanny and I took him to the toilets to clean him up. "Fucking hell Vince who was that outside"? he asked. I told him I had no idea "but he didn't half give you it Spanny" I told him. Spanny was a total mess with blood all over his face. The next day I got a phone call out of the blue from Brenda Duffy, Lee's mam, "Can I have a word with you Vince"? she's asked, I said of course Brenda what's the matter? She wouldn't talk to me over the phone but she asked me to go to the family home 24, Keir Hardie Crescent, South Bank. Brenda confirmed to me it was Lee who'd given Spanny the hiding and that naturally she was worried about him because he was still only a teenager. Brenda asked me if there was going to be any repercussions. Lee was really still a kid compared to Spanny who was a mature man by that point and she was convinced Lee was gonna be jumped. I told Brenda not to worry and to leave it to me, I assured her I'd sort it out as I used to knock about with Spanny at the time. So, when I next saw Spanny I told him that the kid who'd given him a pasting was Brenda Duffy's son young Lee. Spanny said "Ooh tell her from me its forgotten about, I don't want a fucking rematch with that kid," which made me laugh. I told Brenda that there was going to be no comebacks but that was the first time I would witness Lee Duffy the fighter. I was always good to Lee from then on and he never ever forgot that over the next 10 years.

Lee used to get mad with bullies and he'd put it on everyone's toes if he saw them bully people. I never saw Lee hit a little lad, ever! What I will say on the Duff was he always was able to fight from being 16 years old with Spanny, but when he was around 19-20 he got that punch power which was like a whirlwind in itself. It was like you see in these cartoons where the superhero uses its special powers and 'BOSH' it was goodnight. That was with either hand as well. Whatever he hit he destroyed.

Lee would walk all-over by himself, he was never one to be in a gang. Lee would come in clubs & pubs by himself and he never looked for trouble, but trouble used to come to him. All of a sudden Lee was the talk of the town from 1985 and by then he was knocking everyone out and it took him to another level.

When Lee had the fight with Brian Cockerill what happened was Lee saw Brian in Redcar but they'd been some kind of ongoing feud between the pair for weeks before that. Brian told me this himself. He said that Lee was with John Fail and when he saw Brian, Lee walked up to him and said, "You're a big lad aren't ya"? Before Brian got chance to answer Lee walloped him. Brian told me that he's never been hit so fucking hard in his life and he was seeing stars. Brian, at the time, had a splinter on his finger as it had recently been broken. Brian told me Lee had put him on one knee then Brian picked Lee up and rammed him into a door then John Fail jumped on Brian's back. John actually told me he said "Vince, Brian shook me off like a fucking fly". People think Brian won and it was a big fight but that's all that really happened, it wasn't really a fight as such it was more of a scuffle. Lee told me afterwards that when he left hooked Cockerill he made the mistake of standing still and he couldn't escape Brian's grip when he had hold of him. Lee said what he should have done is after he'd walloped him he should have stayed on the move like a boxer and he'd know that for the next time he bumped into Brian.

Lee didn't have to wait too long as from what I heard Brian was at Lee's house the next day wanting to be friends and they then became partners.

I was with Brian once when he saw the heavyweight boxer from Hartlepool Dave Garside on Newport Road. Brian walked up and offered Garside out, I thought fucking hell! Garside didn't wanna know because he was with his wife. I told Brian to leave it that day.

From about 1985 to 1991 Lee owned the town. When he was locked up I was always running up the jails to see him and I would take his girlfriend along with me. I was loyal to him and went to all kinds of jails to see him. One visit I was on with his girlfriend in Durham prison in April 1991 and two screws walked in and said, "this now has to be a closed visit". I thought what the hell's going on here, of course I had contraband on me to give Lee so we waited and waited, then two more screws came in and said, "it's too dangerous for you both to be in here so we'll have to take you to see him in the block". Now I'd been in Durham jail many times from as far back as 1964 when the last hanging took place. Back in those days when I was a young prisoner on D-wing I would have to go and clean the room after the hangings. Boy it was scary, I could see the trap that opened and when I finished the screws would give me two cigarettes. Why I got the cigarettes I'll never know but I was only 18 at the time. Maybe it was to calm my nerves. I knew Durham prison inside out and I knew what went on but I'd never heard of anything like this before the Duff, maybe the reason was that there was a load of men in that prison at that exact time plotting to murder Lee. As we sat down during the visit on the special wing another couple of screws came in and said "get ya stuff packed Duffy you have just got your judge and chambers". Absolutely crazy!

In June 1986 Lee had his 21st birthday party in the old Empire upstairs. I went along with the video camera and videoed the full lot. The next day I took the tape to his mam's and she was over the moon with it. At the time I had a camcorder and I used to video things, not many people had video recorders in them days. Lee was dancing to his favourite song The Whole of the Moon by The Waterboys which came out in 1985.

Believe it or not but Lee Duffy didn't really have a bad temper considering he used to fight all the time. If he wanted to do something to someone he just did it, he didn't harp on about it. It was just BANG then it was forgot

113

about. The only time I ever saw Lee really annoyed and taking something personal was with big Mac the undertaker. Now big Mac was about 6ft 6 and he even moved to Guisborough to get out of the way but Lee would be constantly out trying to track him down. Lee was determined to find him and was always asking about him. Lee and big Mac were once good friends but fell out and whatever it was over it was the only thing I ever saw Lee Duffy get bad tempered about. I once caught big Mac coming out of a house and he was a bag of nerves because he knew I was good friends with Lee. To be quite honest I liked the lad. Every time he saw me he'd put his arms round me but that day I saw him he said, "please don't tell Lee Vince, it's the first time I've been out the house in months I'm only popping out to the shop for a few things". Big Mac, at the time, had seemed to vanish off the face of the earth and nobody had seen him in months. I kept my word to him and I didn't tell Lee for the simple reason I'd never seen Lee go on about somebody as much as he did about big Mac. I thought if I tell Lee where he was I thought Lee would have got fucking lifed off! I don't think it would have stopped. Lee never ever caught up with his intended victim because Lee was killed.

I was there when Lee was shot for the second time. What happened was that we'd been out around town me, Lee and Boothy, when we decided to go to the Blues party above an old boutique shop on Hartington Road but you entered it at the back of the property.

As we went in we paid £1 to get in, got a drink and Lee said to Boothy can you go get some ganja so we can have a few joints. I was stood with Lee and he had such a sixth sense when something was about to happen, I've never known anything like it. God he was so streetwise it was unbelievable but I noticed Lee became quite edgy. The next thing that happened was this big black man with a Brummie accent came bursting through the door pulling

114

something out of his jacket. Another man was with him also, Now I thought it was an iron bar but of course it was a shot gun so Lee flew for him and grabbed the gun. So Lee and the gunman are wrestling but it was almost pitch black, if Lee had got the gun off him he'd have shot him dead. All of a sudden I heard this big bang with a blue flash. God the stench it left it was like ammonia, I've never smelt anything like it and it reeked the place out. I knew by then it was a gun but after it went off the gun snapped with the strength of them both wrestling. Just before the gun snapped the gunman had his finger on the trigger and its went off on Lee's left foot. I didn't know this at the time because the blues only ever had such very dim lighting so I never saw any blood. When Lee was shot it was towards the end of the struggle and everybody had made for the doors as you would when you know there's a gunman on the loose. When everyone ran out I ran back in to try and empty the till because I knew it was full of money but I couldn't. Afterwards when I went to visit Lee in the hospital I told Lee and he was laughing his head off. Within minutes the police turned up with their torches because I think the place only had 2-watt lights in it. The police took everybody outside and questioned everybody in the place. The police questioned me because they knew I was Lee's friend. I didn't know then where Boothy had went to but Boothy had went off with Lee and two police officers had found them outside Rooney's Bar (now The Oak) only quarter of a mile away. Boothy said that as Lee was hobbling off he was shouting "white heat white heat" to Boothy. Lee told Neil Booth he daren't look as he thought his foot had been completely blown off as they were running away. Neil told Lee his foot was fine but it was far from fine although not blown off as Lee first thought. Lee's foot used to smell for ages when it was healing.

Yes I heard the gun going off but the first I heard of Lee being shot was from the police. The old bill ended up taking me to the general hospital to see Lee and as I went in Brenda was by his bed. Lee's foot was all bandaged up and the Duff was just laughing his head off and he'd been smoking dope. In the months after Lee was shot in the foot he would take his shoe off and say, "watch this" and he'd move his foot and you could see the tendons in it. It was as if a hole around two inches deep had dug into his foot.

A story was printed in the Evening Gazette on February 1st, 1991 with the headline:

'POLICE WAIT TO INTERVIEW PARTY SHOOTING VICTIM'

Detectives were hoping to interview blues party shooting victim Lee Duffy in his hospital bed today. The 25-year-old was blasted in the left foot at close range by two West Indians at an empty Middlesbrough town centre shop the venue for the illegal party. He underwent surgery to remove pellets from his foot and was heavily sedated yesterday. His condition is described as "comfortable". Mr Duffy was shot minutes after arriving at an illegal blues party in the former wedding boutique in Hartington Road at about 3am yesterday morning. Detectives believe the hitman used a shotgun.

"We are hoping to talk to Mr Duffy today about what happened," said Detective Inspector John Kelly, who is heading the hunt.

Yesterday we managed to have a brief chat with Mr Duffy, of Durham Road, Eston, before the victim went into the operating theatre.

The police are not making a direct link between yesterday's shooting and the incident two days after Christmas, when Mr Duffy was shot in central Middlesbrough.'

Lee was actually in the same hospital as his girlfriend Lisa at the same time, although she'd just given birth and he was in for four days nursing a shotgun wound. There's a picture of Lee holding his new-born baby daughter from that time in February 1991. If you look at his wrist you can see the hospital band on him.

When Lee was in the General hospital, me and Boothy got a pair of ladders put up to the second floor and sneaked in his room when he was still under armed guard. Lee used to hobble over to the window and smoke everything he could get hold of and blow the smoke out of the windows. Lee loved his drugs but he was never into psychedelic drugs like acids or magic mushrooms, Lee's things were blow, E and cocaine.

Lee told me that when he'd recovered David Woodier would be "getting it" from him because he saw him get shot and did nothing to help. A few weeks later I went into Rumours nightclub with Lee on his crutches. The first person he saw was David, he turned to me and smiled and said, "Vince look who's here", he told me to mind his crutches then hobbled over and banged David out cold, David was then flat out for half an hour. David said in court at David Allison's trial that he'd been punched senseless by Duffy for no good reason, although I'm sure Lee thought he had a good enough reason. It was at the same point in the trial that QC David Robson who was defending Allison was describing Lee as an, "evil supremo who had terrorised many in Middlesbrough". It was a shame because Lee and David must have been good friends once because I personally took him to prisons such as

117

Durham, Armley and Acklington to see Lee. Not only David but his family also.

Going back to being at Lee's bedside, I asked Lee what the fuck happened there but that's when we found out that an hour or two before that the Birmingham men went to Lee's house 6, Durham Road, Eston and while we were out partying they'd threatened Lee's girlfriend, who was nine months pregnant at the time and her sister and held them in the house whilst ransacking the place and taking all their gold off their fingers.

Authors note - The Evening Gazette also ran this story on February 2nd 1991 with the headline:

WOMAN IN GUN TERROR ORDEAL

The terror-stricken pregnant girlfriend of a gunshot victim was threatened by an armed duo, police confirmed today. An hour before former bouncer Lee Duffy was blasted in the left foot two masked men burst in to the Eston house of the mum-to-be. They were armed with a shotgun and an iron bar. Inside the house with the girlfriend was her mother, sister and a man friend.

During the terror ordeal the men savagely yanked gold jewellery off the fingers of the girlfriend. "They were all threatened with a shotgun and an iron bar," said Detective Inspector John Kelly. "This incident was not immediately reported to the police and only came to light after the shooting incident. "No-one was hurt although they were shaken by the incident. "The men demanded to know where Mr Duffy was and had similar descriptions to those who later attacked him at a party in Middlesbrough," he added. Dad-to-be Mr Duffy is recovering from an operation to remove gun pellets from his left foot. Detectives say the former amateur boxer is recovering and assisting as best he can. Mr Duffy was shot shortly after he arrived at a blues party in the former Wedding Boutique shop on Hartington Road, Middlesbrough.

Anyone who can help with the shooting should contact the incident room on Middlesbrough 248184.'

At the end of the day and even though there was witnesses these people didn't even get convicted of it! When Lee got killed those men were still on remand but because he died nobody went down for it. I think that was a conspiracy because Cleveland police wanted Duffy out of the way. I mean you've only got to look at David Tapping who poured the petrol over Lee in The Commercial. Now he went in that pub and started talking to Lee all nicey nicey and goes out to get a bucket of petrol and pours it over Lee and tries to BBQ him alive. Lee's only lucky he used matches and he got them wet because if he'd used a lighter he'd have been fucked. It was not only Lee that got the petrol on him but he also got a woman named Debbie Lucas there in a wheelchair that couldn't walk and over a few others. Now what happened next just shows you how clever Lee was because rather than grab him there and then, he ran out of the pub, stripped down to his underpants then came back in to get him. If that had been me I'd have tried to grab him and probably be set alight but that's what I mean about having such a sixth sense. After he'd wiped all the petrol off himself he went back in the pub and he got hold of Tapping whilst he was trying to get out of the back door. Well nobody could get Lee off him in the end. I've never seen Lee use his fists so much in his fucking life BANG BANG BANG BANG. Afterwards David Tapping was in a right state you'd have thought he'd been hit by a train, he had a shattered jaw, lost several teeth and had multiple other facial injuries. What happens then? Well the police and ambulances come and take David Tapping to hospital. When he was in the hospital he barely managed to move the side of his mouth but managed it just enough to say two words "Lee Duffy" and then they go and arrest Lee and take him to court the next day and he gets remanded for it. Fucking staggering!!!! A man tries to set fire to him and Lee Duffy gets remanded. The forensics actually went and cut a chair cushion out of the Commercial pub the next day and they said it's a good job it didn't get set alight because it would have took the full pub up in flames because the liquid was that potent. That seat in The Commercial remained like that long after Lee's death. The worst thing about it was that David Tapping had actually been drinking with Duffy and it was Lee who'd gave him the £3 to buy the petrol because he'd asked for it but of course for a very different reason. When Lee had brayed him at the back door he then turned to Boothy and said, "aren't you gonna do anything?" meaning get stuck into him as well because Lee had half killed him. I know someone's theory behind that was he wanted to share the blame with someone if he ended up on a murder charge. It was Neil who dragged Lee off him otherwise I think David Tapping would have been killed

The Gazette printed this story on April 30th, 1991

MAN IS DOUSED IN PETROL IN PUB

A man was doused in petrol as an attacker tried to set him on fire in a Cleveland pub, police said today.

The attack was the third alleged murder bid on a 25-year old Lee Duffy in the space of four months.

Police said the nightclub bouncer was uninjured in the incident, which happened in the Commercial pub in South Bank last Friday. A police spokeswoman added: Mr Duffy was in the pub when a male poured petrol over him and tried to ignite it with a match, "without success."

A man has been charged with attempted murder and was due to appear before Teesside magistrates today. Cleveland police appealed for anyone who was in the pub between noon and 5.30pm on Friday to contact South Bank CID on 452323 if they have not already been interviewed.

Duffy, of Durham Road, Eston, has been a victim of two shooting incidents in December of last year and in January. Three Northumberland men have been charged with attempted murder in connection with the December incident in Princess Road, Middlesbrough.

They are Raymond Palmer 38, of Ingram Drive, Robert Charlton, 29, and Anthony Cole, 27, both of Hortondale Road, all Blyth. They are at present in custody.

And seven men have been charged with conspiring to murder Mr Duffy as a result of the January incident in Hartington Road, Middlesbrough. They are Shaun Thomas Harrison, 24, of Kingsley Close, Grangetown; Paul James Bryan, 30, of Church Lane, Eston; Leroy Vincent Fischer, 30, of Nelson Road, Aston, Birmingham; Marnon Clive Thomas, 30, of Alexandra Drive, Birmingham; Kevin James O'Keefe, 31, of Lyne Road, Teesville; Peter Corner, 22, of Barmouth Road, Eston; and John Leroy

Thomas, 35, of Wadhurst Road, Birmingham. They are also in custody.

Duffy himself was given bail by a judge in chambers last week. He faces charges of causing grievous bodily harm with intent to Peter Wilson and attempting to pervert the course of justice by offering him £2,500 in cash to withdraw his complaint. He is also charged with causing actual bodily harm to Islam Gull and threatening to kill him.

I went to see Lee in Durham's A-wing and that's when he got his judge in chambers whilst I was there, I mentioned it earlier.

That day I went to see Lee there was already 9 (not 18 as reported in Stephen Richards book) different men on remand for attempted murder or plotting to murder Lee Duffy, not only the Brummie fella's but a few Blyth men from the first shooting on Lee's life and Paul Bryan's gang. The first time was outside Ramsey's blues on Princess Road. I only lived around the corner and every time he'd come out of Ramsey's he'd come to my house for a sleep. Lee was forever knocking me up. As soon as Lee was dead everybody was let off, no charges whatsoever. I don't think that would happen today do you? That to me just proves they wanted Lee dead doesn't it to let four separate parties off!

How Lee received his four-year sentence in March 1988 was another dubious one and I'll tell you why. Now there was a Middlesbrough v Leeds Utd game on during the day on Saturday September 19th, 1987 and a lot of the Leeds lot came down just to fight the Boro Frontline (Middlesbrough FC hooligan firm).

On Monday, 21st September the Gazette ran this story with the headline:

'YOBS EMBARRESSMENT FOR BORO.'

A police chief has slammed the "moronic minority" of Cleveland soccer yobs who brought shame to Boro. Gangs of up to 200 Boro thugs hurling stones and missiles clashed violently with police outside Ayresome Park after the match with Leeds. And a councillor representing terrified people living in the shadow of the soccer ground today called for the club to introduce a full identity card system for supporters. Middlesbrough Councillor Edmund Pearson, who is campaigning for the relocation of the club, said: "The people in this area are absolutely desperate. "On this occasion the threatening attitude of the hooligans created a situation where people were suffering from shock, fearing their homes were going to be attacked."

A total of sixteen people were arrested on Saturday, mainly for public order offences.

Chief Supt Alan Bruce said: "Our moronic minority are determined to turn football matches into attempts to confront visiting supporters. If they fail to manage that, they confront police officers."

He said their behaviour was to be deplored. "Without them football matches at Ayresome Park would be a peaceful family occasion," he said. Mr Bruce said the behaviour of the Leeds supporters by comparison was responsible.

Trouble flared in Ayresome Park Road near the junction with St Barnabas' Road when the gangs of up to 200 youths began throwing stones and missiles at police barriers. Mrs Rene Porteous, 52, from nearby Clive Road, said: "they were like animals. We were absolutely petrified. We are living under siege conditions."

Now I'd been drinking during the day with the Duff and we went on to go into The Speakeasy (before The Havana) and many of the Leeds firm where in there. I know many of the Boro lads who were expecting an almighty rumble with the West Yorkshire lot became very excited when they knew the Duffer was in the building, all asking for his help in battle. I told Lee straight I said leave them fucking to it, it's nothing to do with you but so many of these so-called hard men were asking Lee to stand by them which I always knew he was going to. Lee liked to help people and although he was never into the fighting at the matches he viewed the Middlesbrough lads as one of his own against the Leeds firm. Afterall, they were in Lee Duffy's town and he owned the lot. Well eventually the inevitable happened and bottles, glasses and chairs were flying on the dance floor. There must have been twenty men going for it hammer and tong and I noticed one of the Leeds lot hitting people with a bottle. Lee's fighting away but he's just punching and knocking bodies flying left, right and centre, Lee was just in his element happy knocking people out all-over. It was like watching something like a Bruce Lee film where just one guy is going through a load of men it was something else. I saw a guy walking towards Lee with a bottle raised up but Lee had his back towards this man. Well I jumped in and I put my elbow up to shield the blow from crashing on Lee's head. It didn't half hurt my fucking arm as well, it was black for weeks.

I didn't see Lee actually hit that guy but the next day I learnt that one of the Leeds lads, Martin Clark, was in a bad way and it was down to the Duffer. After the almighty rumble the crowd started making for the back doors and me and Lee went off to the blues. Lee didn't even talk about the mass fight that had just went on he was like that, he never needed to brag he just went and did it.

The following day the police came to arrest me and I went to the old Middlesbrough police station and they took me in the interview room… "We know you were in The Speakeasy last night Vince" but see me, when I'm being interviewed I'm a very funny man. Normally people give 'no reply' but I don't, I just sit silent. Now there wasn't tapes that day the old bill were just writing it down but they were trying to say I intervened but all I did was try to stop a man from putting a bottle over my friends head. Then they basically said "looka Vince, do you wanna walk out of here?" I told them of course I did but then they've said this man Martin Clark was in the operating theatre and he could die! At a different point they told me he'd lost an eye and it was all Lee Duffy's fault. In fact it was touch and go as to whether or not he would even survive which made my arse completely go then but I remained silent throughout. Then the police said "who do you think told us all about it from last night anyway Vince? Basically trying to blame the Duff but I thought naaaah Lee wouldn't say nothing he wasn't like that so I just sat it out. Anyway the two C.I.D check off their shift so they fetch Lee from downstairs with his handcuffs on and he comes up laughing his head off. Lee then tells me to tell the truth that we were together last night and it wouldn't be detrimental to his case so I say alright I will so I explained the full case to the Middlesbrough police and again they've asked that same question again of "do you wanna walk out of here Vince?" so I knew something was up. Basically what the police wanted me to say was that it was Lee Duffy who had the bottle, not Martin Clark which was utter bullshit by the way. Then they said they were going to charge Lee

Duffy with a section 18 which was Wounding with Intent and I've just said, "FUCK THIS, I WANT A SOLICITOR" and straight away my legal representative said to me "you're in a bit of a predicament aren't you Vince because you intervened!" I couldn't acknowledge this because all I did at the time was stop Lee being hit across the back of his head with a Millers bottle. To cut a long story short I was told I'd be let go if I told them it was Lee Duffy who hit the man with the bottle but I told them to fuck off and I'd be sticking by my story. They charged Lee with section 18 (wounding with intent) and another lad, who's since sadly passed, and remanded them both whilst bailing me for 6 weeks. After I reported back to Cleveland police they told me there was no charges being brought against me and it had all been dropped.

Now, since the time when we were first brought in, there were a few more coming forward giving statements for Lee Duffy backing him up but the police were threatening them the same as me i.e. a man could die etc.... so their bottle went and the police let them back out without anything recorded because all they wanted to do was take Lee Paul Duffy off the streets so bad and that was the reason why Lee got the 4-year sentence doing 26 months of it. When Lee was on remand I went up to see him the next day. Lee should have been found not guilty on that charge but he never was and that was such a real injustice because he was innocent. I was loyal, I stood by the man.

When I used to go in Rumours Molly and Brian Jaffray used to come up to me saying "aah Vince I'm glad you're here because Lee's upstairs". To cut a long story short all the door lads were panicking and asked me if I could take him out! So, I used to go find Lee and I'd say come on Lee we'll go to the Bongo (Lee was only ever allowed in with me). Lee used to love the Bongo, he loved the music and the Rumours lads were happy as fuck then because the

Duff was out of their hair for a few hours. One night me and Lee were in Rumours. It must have been around last orders because we were stood with the door lads like Brian Duckling and Molly Jaffray when two coppers came busting in looking for Lee. They shouted "Get up Duffy you're coming with us" without explaining what for. I asked the pair of them what they wanted him for and they said, "we'll tell him down the station". Lee stood up and told them that if they wouldn't tell him now the pair of them can fuck off, well the two bobbies didn't know what to do and a nosey crowd was gathering so they radioed for back up. About 2-3 minutes passed when half the shift from the Middlesbrough police station and the top inspector came and told Lee he was under arrest which really pissed Lee off, Lee jumped straight up and stood in a fighting pose and told them all to come ahead and who wants it first! I'm not exaggerating but this must have went on for a good 15 minutes but none of the coppers wanted to make a move and be the first one to kop it from the Duff. In the end I stood up and told Lee just to go with them. I told him to go get it over and done with and then he could come back and I'd get him a pint for a stoppy back. Lee just laughed and said, "come on then gentlemen lead the way" and off he went. Literally around half an hour later the Duff came lumbering back in on his tod and I said to him "that was quick", he said that there was nobody there to interview him so he was asked to go back tomorrow. When I asked him are you going? He just said, "am I fuck" and carried on drinking with a scowl on his face.

I know the law inside out and if that had been anyone else but the Duff they'd have been dragged out and put in cuffs.

There were a good few incidents like this regarding Lee in Rumours Nightclub so that told me that the bobbies were constantly watching Rumours because they knew Lee was in there all the time.

Another situation me and Lee were in was upon leaving Rumours and it was after 1am and we were going to the Speak Easy Nightclub. Anyway as I was driving I saw a police car following us and I told Lee he's gonna stop us here. Back in them days I was always getting stopped and I put many complaints in against Cleveland police, but to no avail. If they weren't stopping me for me they were certainly stopping me because I had Lee Duffy in the car. I just kept driving and Lee told me the Old Bill had now put their lights on but I never stopped. I thought I'll stop when we both get to outside the Speak Easy on Linthorpe Road because I knew they'd be witnesses. When we arrived outside the club I told Lee to let me do the talking and for him and to just be quiet. When the officer came over he asked me if I hadn't seen the flashing lights and I told him I hadn't. The copper told us that he wanted to search the car for stolen goods! When I asked the officer where he'd got that from he said he'd seen me driving from an industrial estate over the border, which was an outright lie as we'd come from Rumours so I told the P.C that he was a fucking liar. Lee was really pissed off not only was this police constable now telling lies Lee had started kicking off because it was a cold night and Lee was saying he was fucking freezing and his cock had shrivelled up. I told the copper again to fuck off and there was no way he was searching my car and as soon as I told him that a lorry load of police turned up with the top Chief Inspector again. As soon as the Chief seen Lee he was nice as pie trying to butter him up. I was so annoyed that this copper was lying and I was stood there arguing with them for maybe 20 minutes and by that point Lee was going blue with frost and said, "Vince just let them look in the car I'm going inside for a drink". In the end I agreed but I told Lee to stay with me as if he'd have went inside the club I was sure they were going to nick me but I knew it was going to be more trouble than what it was worth if the Duff was by my side. In the end I parked the car over the road from the Empire pub and gave them the keys. Then me and Lee went in the club and when we were at the bar Lee said, "by Vince, you're one stubborn old bastard" and we laughed. Up until then we hadn't had a drink put we downed four pints in 25 minutes. The next day Lee rang me up and asked if everything was ok? I told him not really as when I went to pick the car back up it was covered in fine tickets and someone had let the full four tyres down. Lee burst out laughing.

Lee, until he was about 19, was a bit of a brawler but then he developed that special one hit punch and it was goodnight Vienna. Where he got that fucking power from I don't know because the Duff would go out days on end drinking and didn't do any training.

I used to travel all over the country playing poker with a fella called Rudi Khan and a few others. At times I would go to Liverpool, Manchester, Birmingham and many more places. Lee was always asking me to take him with me and once I did take him to Sheffield. It was an illegal gambling den and when I introduced him and said this is my friend Lee Duffy all the Sheffield lads were in amazement because they'd all heard of him from prison. For the rest of the night when I was playing cards people were forever knocking on the door just to shake hands with Lee and telling stories of how he looked after their mate inside.

One thing about Lee was that he had such an incredible memory and he remembered all these stories of when he looked after people inside. That night in Sheffield was the only time I ever saw Lee drunk as a few of the Jamaicans plied Lee with this expensive potent white rum and got him hammered. When we left Sheffield, by god did Lee get a good send off and all the Jamaicans were begging him to come back. That night Lee lost £150 in Kalooki but he said he'd had the best night of his whole life. On the way home Lee said to me "oh well Vince, back to reality and people gunning for me". The same happened when I took Lee to Moss Side, people loved him and all wanted to know him.

I used to go to a gambling house for many years on Woodlands Road in Middlesbrough. The game I used to play was called Kalooki. Mainly it was full of Jamaican's and West Indians who would come from all over. Freeman Nelson from Leeds and Clive Ramsey were always in there. I used to make a good living from the card schools. It was £5 a game usually but I used to have £50 - £100 side bets as well. Lee asked me if I would take him and funnily enough considering what he was, the Jamaican's used to ask me to bring him because they'd all heard so much about Lee. Well when I took him he was in his element and there never was a spot of trouble out of him. Lee loved to just sit there smoking dope with them all. I took him and Boothy there several times. I would sit there playing cards and Lee would just sit there eating huge portions of chicken curry and rice and by god could he eat. Lee would usually eat two or three portions in one go. In fact, once he had four and all the African men were looking at him in amazement thinking were the fuck is he putting it all just astounded! Lee used to say to me "Vince when I'm in here with you I can relax, I don't need to look over my shoulder and I can just be myself". One night in there I can see Lee was itching to join in playing Kalooki but it's a very difficult game to pick up so I told him to sit next to me and watch because you can lose a lot of money if you get caught napping. I told Lee to stick to playing snap and he just laughed. I wasn't comfortable with letting Lee play but we both put £100 in and I played and we both came away with double our money that night and Lee was well happy. Over the next few weeks when he became more familiar with the fella's in there he started going in himself and he lost a few quid. Lee wasn't much cop playing cards and sometimes he'd even put the wrong sets down or the other men would know what Lee had in his hand and all the Jamaicans would be in stitches at him but there was never any threat of violence from him, even if he lost. Lee never ever caused any hassle in there and he loved the company of the Africans at Woodlands Road card school.

I used to also go through to Jimmy Murrays blues in Newcastle on a Sunday night. Many lads from Middlesbrough used to go and Lee asked me one day why I was always going up Newcastle on a Sunday. Lee asked me to take him the next time I went and I agreed. That was until I told him they used to be a big card game with about six lads playing and a load of money with many gangsters going through like fatty Dave Glover there most weekends playing £10 blind cards, now I'm a very good card player, ask John Fail or Ducko, I showed them to shuffle they'll tell you. Anyway I was telling Lee about this blues that had major money there every Sunday and the Duff asked me to take him along because he wanted to "rob it". He certainly didn't show this lot the same love as the Woodlands Road lot. I said I'm fucking sure you won't Lee! Lee said, "ooh please take us Vince I won't rob it." but I knew the Duff did what he wanted to do and he wouldn't listen to me once he'd made his mind up. Anyway I ended up taking Lee up one Sunday night and as soon as we got there he said where's this card game Vince? As soon as he seen all the money he was getting ideas so I had to pull him to one side and say for fuck sake please leave it Lee, this is Jimmy's place so please leave it and he did. He wanted to do it and for the rest of the night I was a bag of fucking nerves because he wanted to do it! There was at least six big blokes playing and he wanted to go in knocking them all out whilst stealing the purse money. That's what he was like. That was the first time he'd ever been to Newcastle then after that he met all the Sayers who I think he knew from jail and Manny Burgo from Tyneside so he was in Newcastle most weekends.

Boothy used to borrow my car to go visit Lee in jail but one weekend I myself was going up to see Lee in Durham jail and I was taking Lee's girlfriend up at the time when I was set up by a Middlesbrough man called Paddy for taking an ounce of speed up, So the night before he hid it in his garden and when I knocked on his fucking door the C.I.D jumped on me in their dozens. Well considering I had nothing in my pockets I got eighteen months jail because they said they'd seen me shot an ounce into the garden. So I went in Durham nick on D wing and I saw Viv Graham and he came up to me saying that he'd heard that a well-known Middlesbrough hard man was going queens evidence, I told him he wasn't getting it second hand, that I was there in the public gallery and that the guy had made a deal with the police to do a man in with a load of blow to get a lighter sentence. Well Viv Graham didn't believe me and just walked out of my cell shaking his head. I found that Viv Graham was wary speaking to me anyway because he knew I was close to the Duff. The rumour I heard in prison at the time was if Lee had come into Durham jail then Viv Graham and another hardcase were going to call into Lee's cell and give him it. Lucky for them two he never because Lee would have done the pair of them.

Now another Geordie I was very close friends with was Freddie Mills AKA Fred the Head. I was in borstal with Fred and he was a proper face in jail who could really have a fight, Fred fought the likes of Roy Shaw and had a few punch up's with Sykesy in Durham nick. Sadly Fred died only a couple of years ago but he was once up there in Northern England jails in terms of hard men.

Lee did love the blues parties he would go to and he went to them all like one on Kensington Road, Shaggy's, Noels, Sadu's, Salvano's or his favourite Ramsey's. There was a fella named 'Nosha White' who used to run his own blues. Well this one night a load of lads turned up from Leeds and locked Nosha and Lee out of the party. Nosha was locked out of his own place and him and Lee had to fight the whole lot of them to get back in and then get them all out. Blues parties were the twilight world in which Lee spent his final years. All these places were really was terraced houses and disguised shops. Inside them alcohol was sold illegally and wads of cash was exchanged in these card schools with lethal cocktails of drugs going about to the sounds of reggae beats listened to by the pimps and prostitutes in attendance. Violence was never far away in places like that.

If Lee ever hit anyone in the blues it always led to the poor fella being carried out, Lee always treat me ok though, he had a lot of respect for me.

In the early hours of the morning when the Duff died I got a big bang on the door and I look out to see that it was Neil Booth who was sheet white by then, "I've got some bad news for you Vince, Lee died about half an hour ago". So it was Boothy who came and told me. It should never ever have happened because once over Lee and David were friends, I know because I've sat in both their company at the same time. I don't know what went on and why they fell out but what I do know was Lee wanted to fight Allo every time he saw him. What Lee didn't like I think was that David wouldn't ever back down from him and boy could Allo fight! David was like a bulldog and no matter what punishment he ever took from anybody he just kept coming and coming. He seemed to always have this ability to get up and give more back. Trust me, back in those days in Middlesbrough David Allison was one man you didn't want to fight with but Lee thought otherwise. After I heard the news of what had just happened I didn't go back to bed I just sat up smoking joints thinking about everything we'd done together and listening to the reggae beats we used to listen to. The Duff loved Neil more than anybody else he knew in my opinion. If Lee ever shouted at Neil I used to shout back at him and say don't be fucking having a go at Boothy. They were like brothers. It's funny because when Lee was down London with all the gangsters all he ever talked about was getting Boothy down. If anybody else would talk to the Duff like that he'd have just banged them but when I used to tell him to leave Boothy alone he never reacted. Lee did tell me a few times that if anything should happen to him could I make sure young Boothy was ok. Well over the years I've kept my promise to Lee and I've loved Neil like a son but believe me he's took some looking after because he was wild as well.

You can see why Lee and Neil clicked because both knew no boundaries for doing crazy things. One funny story I'll never forget about the Duff was when he came sprinting in my house laughing his head off like Jack in The Shining. Anyway after a minute of calming him down and him laughing like a hyena he managed to tell me what had just happened. Lee said he'd been walking along Acklam Road in Middlesbrough just by himself when this nosey young copper pulled up beside him. When Lee turned round the bobby shouted "Duffy you're going to have to come with me to the station so Lee nodded his head in agreement and went to get in the car. Just before he got in he saw that there was a cemetery with a tall fence all the way up and the gates were locked, Well Lee told me he saw the coppers car door still open and the keys were still in the ignition so what he did was to pretend to get in the car but then at the last second he reached in, snatched the keys and flung them over the cemetery wall then he legged it like a rat up a drain pipe. Lee then started his laughter again saying, "you should have seen the coppers face Vince". There was no catching the Duff he was some runner and he never stopped running until he got to my house. Then we both stood laughing together for such a long time and had a joint, which then set Lee off in giggles and we laughed even more. He said his belly was hurting him in the end from all the laughing and he said he was in pain. Lee had such a funny side to him and he wondered how the fuck that young P.C plod was going to explain what had just happened to his boss back at the station. Lee said he threw the keys in between hundreds of headstones.

To give you an idea of the random shit Lee used to get up to I'll tell you a story about his good mate John Fail. Now, John lived near me on Princess Road at the time and I went round to see him. As I went in he said "I'm glad you've come Vince" all stressed. I said why, what's the matter John? He said Lee had left four kilos of cannabis at his house. In fact he didn't leave it with John, he just knocked on the door and gave it to John's girlfriend and said, "mind that" and that he'd be back but John couldn't get hold of him because he'd been in Newcastle for three days. John asked me what he should do with it! I told him first that we'll have a few joints of it but John said "this isn't funny Vince" so in the end I got Lee to come and shift it. He just did things like that all the time and thought nothing of it.

One time I was in the old Speedway pub off West Lane with Lee, John Fail and Boothy. Lee spotted a man named 'McKenna', I don't know what he'd done but the two went outside then less than a minute later Lee came walking in on his own. When I asked him what had happened Lee said he punched him once. Well the god's honest truth is that man was laid out cold outside for over an hour. Everybody in the pub thought he was dead outside but nobody would go outside to see if he was ok because they were all scared of Lee's reaction. In the end I went outside to give him a shake and slap his face but he wasn't moving. Then I checked if he was breathing because I thought he was dead. He was just about alive but I couldn't wake him. I went back in the pub and told Lee he needed to do something because the guy didn't look too clever so he did. In the end I don't know how he managed it but he got him up and off he walked in a dazed state.

Lee used to bring all kinds of characters through to my house on Princess Road, one guy he used to bring was the original body builder from Eston called Craig Howard. Craig was one fantastic specimen of a man who's arms measured at least a good 20 inches when flexed although he was only around 5ft 8. Lee brought Craig around the first time and said, "papa Vince I'd like you to meet my good friend Craig Howard" and before he could finish Craig come over and said, "long time no see Vince", well Lee was amazed we knew each other and asked how. I told him we'd met on a beach in Malta a good few years ago! Lee then said, "hang on a minute Vince, Craig's from Eston so how did you meet him abroad?" I told him that I was sunning myself on a beach once and this big cunt who everybody was staring at was working out then he came over to me and we started chatting because we were both from Middlesbrough. When we both got back me and Craig kept in touch for a few years and went for a couple of drinks together before losing touch. The reason Craig used to go over to Malta was to get all his steroids over there because they were legal in that country. I could tell that Lee used to be quite impressed with Craig and he would often bring him all-over, even up to Newcastle sometimes. Lee even used to wear Craig's body building shirts to go into night clubs. Although Lee wasn't really a bodybuilder like Craig, Lee had just as much if not a more impressive physique but Lee was wirier and leaner if you like. Lee's body was built for fighting and that's the advantage he had over every other man in the town. Not to mention arms far longer than anyone I've ever met in my life. He was like an orangutan.

There wasn't just that side to him though Lee had a heart, like the time somebody had stolen a load of mountain bikes from outside The Empire pub on Linthorpe Road. Lee had heard the story and he got told that these bikes were for the underprivileged kids and had been organised by the local bike shop in Boro named 'Bobbie's Cycles'. The story was in the local paper The Gazette and when Lee found out he put the word out and within 24 hours he'd retrieved the lot. The paper never printed that Lee was the hero in getting them back though. I'd like people to know that there was such a good side to Lee but the media weren't interested in reporting that were they?!

The famous picture you can see of Lee Duffy with Kevin McBride Snr, Tabba Taylor and Lee Harrison was taken at John Graham's wedding and was only a few months before he died. I was the one that took him and his girlfriend. Trouble was brewing between him and Allo that day and Lee asked me to take him home because he didn't want to spoil John's day. The first fight Duffy and Allison had was just after Lee was released from prison outside the Magistrates looking down to Grange Road. Davey was with a group of Parkend lads but he'd been drinking all day when the fresh Duffy came over to him for a fight. Lee, I'm told did a real number on Davey that day and he was unrecognisable the next day. It was from that day Davey was given the knuckle duster by a family member with Duffy in mind and he carried it for over a year afterwards. Their second skirmish as I told you was in Blaises only weeks before their final clash. People have told me that Allo was on top of Duffy in the altercation on the stairs and had got the better of Lee before it was broken up. The bad feelings between the pair only escalated and the inevitable happened weeks later on Marton Road.

Over the years in Middlesbrough people think the times Duffy and Allison clashed were into double figures but in reality I have it on good authority that it was only the three times. Although the bad blood between them was very real and things happened even when they never came to blows. Like the time Lee fired a gun in the Butterloggie in Newcastle to intimidate David Allison and Lee King. Somebody close to Davey told me that Davey thought Lee was going to shoot him that night.

One thing that did fuck me off was when Lee's murder went to court, the amount of lie's that were blatantly told were unbelievable. For instance, like Lee had a gun on him that night and a gun was found inside a jacket near the DJ box in the Afro-Caribbean Centre. This was a blatant setup by a name I won't mention but it worked and the jury believed it. A man told me that he was made to put the gun inside a jacket because the person behind it couldn't get inside the club. The man who told me was crying at the time and said, "Vince I'm so sorry but what could I do, I was being threatened as well as my family so I went along with it." I only found this out after the trial but I told the crying man don't worry, Lee would have understood. In the trial it said that there were screams from the crowd that Lee had a gun. Total crap, it was made up by people to build the picture for the final outcome.

(Authors note – when Lee's body was examined by the coroner it was found that he had not come into contact with any firearm in the last 48 hours before his death).

I used to have a one-armed bandit in my house and I used to know this scam were I'd get all the free credits put on without paying, so what I used to do is get Ducko and the Duffer out and get them playing them and we'd go halves. Ducko and Duffer were very good at those machines and even if people suspected them of fiddling nobody was gonna tell the pair of them that they had their suspicions.

Lee Duffy and Kevin Duckling were once over the best of friends but there was one time I'll never forget when Lee went to the Brambles Farm pub saying he was gonna give Ducko it. This was when he was at his most powerful so maybe about 1990, but when Lee saw Ducko he turned to me and John Fail and said, "come on lets go, I can't hit him looking like that can I". This wasn't long after Kevin had come out of prison for the manslaughter of that young lad outside the blues. Kevin had lost a lot of weight and his face was really sunken in. Ducko didn't have any idea what was about to happen but I'll give the Duff some respect because as soon as he seen Ducko he couldn't do it because he was too frail looking. Ducko was a hard man but Lee couldn't do it and had mercy on his one-time hero.

What I'll always remember about Lee when I look back was how he used to go by himself to meets, not like Viv Graham who always took a team to be safe. You've only got to look at when Viv went to meet that bouncer Stu Watson with his group of hangers on. You can see on camera Viv hit the poor guy over a dozen times and didn't put him down. Lee Duffy wouldn't have needed to have hit him like that all them times it'd have been a one-shot job then game over!!!!

One of Lee's favourite things to do was to get cars off people. If there were no car's about he'd jump on a train or bus that's what he used to do. Him and Cockerill did that so many times. Cockerill told me this he said "Vince you're the only man who tells Lee straight" because Lee couldn't drive and I'd tell him so, he was useless behind a wheel. Lee had that much respect for me he wouldn't take my car off me even though he'd pester me for it. I think I was the only man in the town who told Lee "fucking no chance" when he asked if he could borrow my car!

What I didn't like about Lee was he used to borrow people's cars and drive them until they ran out of petrol then he'd just dump them by the side of the road and get a bus. He did it to Shaun Day once and he told him he was only going to be a couple of hours, in fact Lee had a smash in it then done a runner from the scene. All Lee had to do was phone Shaun up and tell him what had happened but Lee dropped him in the shit. In the end the police went to his door and arrested him but Shaun couldn't say, "ooh it wasn't me it was Lee Duffy". Shaun was lost for words and I know he was totally sickened by Lee's actions because he was going to be charged as well. I felt proper sorry for Shaun over that, Lee shouldn't have done what he did. I'm not sure how Shaun got out of that situation but he never ended up getting charged. Shaun was always very good to Lee and would arrive whenever and wherever Lee called him to to drop another car off. I'll never forget one day that Lee lent a ringer to Heathy Randell then Heathy went missing for two days solid. After Lee had given Heathy the car he walked in the old Empire pub and said to Neil Booth, "have you got that money?" It turned out that Boothy had left seven grand in the glove compartment and Heathy had driven off. Heathy went missing for two days in that car and Lee was sending messages to him to get back to him ASAP!!!! The funny thing is when Heathy brought the car back to Lee he hadn't even checked the glove compartment and the money was laying there untouched and unnoticed.

I think the only time I ever saw Lee put petrol in a car was once on the A19 when I bumped into him on the motorway by total chance. I was driving past and I saw this big bastard carrying a petrol can and I thought it looked like Lee, as I got past I realised it was the Duffer and I pulled over because it was in the early hours. I said, "where the fuck have you been?" and he told me Newcastle and he'd ran out of fuel so he was jogging up the hard shoulder to get a fill up whilst still off his box.

One thing Lee used to do is pay his bills. People have said he'd get things for free but what he really used to do is go get the bill, if it was for food he'd maybe go in the kitchen and pay and also leave a good tip. Lee was crafty like that you never saw him pay for the bill but he'd already paid on the sly. So if people were watching they'd be thinking "FUCKING HELL he really does own the town here".

Lee's turnout for his funeral was full of the top Middlesbrough C.I.D taking pictures. The man who led Lee's murder investigation big Brian Leonard was a proper copper though, he always did a great job. One time I got arrested by him and ended up buying his car off him.

My memories on Lee Duffy were only all very good, purely good. He was good to his girlfriend Lisa. If he was your friend he'd have done anything for you and if he didn't like you well, you were fucked! I never remember a little lad who couldn't fight come up to me saying that Lee Duffy had hit them for nothing. The people that he hit were hard cases themselves.

That man didn't fear anybody on this planet. I went to Newcastle with him once and at the door they said £5 each which totals £15 to you guys! So I got the money out and these three bouncers come to the foyer arguing with Lee when all of a sudden BANG – BANG – BANG ones flat out, another was dazed and the other rang a bell to call for back up and all of a sudden another seven bouncers have come running down the stairs then I heard one of them shout "OOH FOR FUCKS SAKE IT'S THE DUFF"! two of them fell over when they put their brakes on. Lee turned to the seven bouncers and said, "Where's Graham"? now I didn't know anything about this by the way! If he'd have told me what he was intending to do I'd have said sod this Lee you can leave me well out of it. I thought we were just having a night out then all of a sudden he's hunting his arch enemy down. Yes I'm drinking but I'm not enjoying it and here's Lee dancing all over talking to the bouncers. Lee loved the fact he'd made a good impression and we both went back to the blues.

Mind you, Abdillahi Warsama made a good statement on Lee Duffy when he barred Lee Duffy out of his club The Bongo. Lee was always allowed in the Bongo with me if I promised Abdillahi he was going to behave. I worked the Bongo for ten years. At that time Abdillahi was in his 70s but he didn't give a fuck about anyone. He used to drink a large bottle of whiskey a day and was forever barring people out. Abdillahi didn't take shit from anyone and he proved that when he barred the Duff out all those times he did. The only time I ever remember Lee Duffy ever being in The Bongo was with me because Abdillahi knew I could control him. Anyway I sat down one day with Lee and I asked him why Abdillahi disliked him so much and Lee told me he didn't know. Then I said "don't fucking lie Lee tell me the truth" but he couldn't tell me and just shrugged his shoulders with a schoolboy scowl across his face. Lee asked me to go to Abdillahi's house for him, I used to go on many occasions anyway. Well Abdillahi was a funny man and he had to be approached in the correct way. To cut a long story short I purposely brought up Lee in hope he would tell me what Lee had done to upset him so. It turned out that the Duff was actually telling the truth and he hadn't done anything to old Abdillahi but he'd heard too many rumours about him and that he wasn't standing for any shit from him in his club. In the end I give Abdillahi my word that Lee would be well behaved and that's why he was only ever allowed in with me and if there was ever a time he wasn't with me then he wouldn't get in. Another rule Abdillahi insisted on was that Lee had to pay into his club and I told Abdillahi that he would. So that's how I became Lee Duffy's babysitter in places like The Bongo and Rumours. Lee promised me he wouldn't fuck it up but I hadn't told him that he had to pay in yet, I mean how was I going to hit him with that one I thought! In the end I told

Lee, look mate you're allowed in but you've got to pay! Lee just looked at me for a minute, shrugged his shoulders and said, "ok Vince". When we went in The Bongo Abdillahi was there with his crew of men such as Podgey Foreman, Peter and Danny Wood, little Alan and Camelot they expected a war but they never got one. Lee paid his £2 and walked straight over to the DJ 'One-eyed Maurice' and asked him to play his favourite reggae songs whilst he had a dance. Lee was as good as gold that night and when Lee was at the toilet Abdillahi came over to me and said "ere Vince man, give that to your friend" in his broad Somali accent and gave me Lee's £2 entrance fee back. Well old Abdillahi was just making a statement that night of, I'm the boss we do things on my terms. Me and Lee stayed until 2am before going to the Ramsey's blues which was only a 2-bedroom terraced house. The sad thing about it all was that Lee started going without me and he fucked it up for himself and caused a war which would go on for years even after he died. The feud that Terry Dicko and others had with the Bongo was all started by Lee Duffy.

One day Lee hit David Fields and he fell into this full glass window and it shook. This was outside of The Speak Easy. I don't know how it never smashed, if it had have done it would have went down on his fucking neck and David would have been dead. In the end I told Lee that's enough but Lee didn't put David Fields down. Fieldsy was an extremely handy man himself who's just done a 20-year life sentence himself. As game as Fieldsy was, as soon as he got that punch from the Duff I think he knew he couldn't have taken Teesside's Terminator on. The only people who witnessed that incident were me and my son Gary who was good mates with Davey.

Lee Duffy was a fucking whirlwind. I used to say to Lee anything that comes in your path you wipe out... Doesn't matter left or right anything he hits he destroys like Ivan

Drago in the Rocky films. Lee was also very good at knowing where to hit as well. A lot of people when they saw Lee Duffy in the club could relax because they knew they'd be no trouble because Lee would stand up for them.

One-night Lee got me on drugs, now I wasn't against them but I'd just never got round to taking them. Anyway a half hour goes by and I'm up on the dance floor doing back flips whilst Lee's laughing his head off. A couple of hours later the tablet was dying off and I went up and said, "ere Lee, give us another half of that thing".

The one man in Middlesbrough Lee Duffy absolutely loved was little Terry Dicko. People in Teesside used to make a beeline for Lee, well the only man who Lee ever made a beeline for was Terry Dicko. Lee used to go looking for little Terry and when he found him he'd pick him up, swing him around and they'd be doing all kind of kung fu kicks together. Lee absolutely adored Terry. The last time I ever saw little Terry was inside Holme House prison but I've had some great times with him as well. Everybody loves Terry.

People think the Duff was close to one of his mates fathers but that man used the Duff and he knew that towards the end. The elderly guy I'm on about used Lee and before that used another hardman from Berwick Hills Kev Ducko. The fella bought people's friendship and many people in Teesside these days know him for what he is, just a user. When he had recruited the young Duffy he got rid of Ducko and I used to tell Lee a few things about him. Lee would just smile and say "ere Vince I'm not fucking daft you know. I know what he is. Lee used to say, "I'm getting good money off him so I'm not the only one who's using someone". Lee used to say that the fella in question was a police informer.

I was forever winding the Duff up though, one day I was acting a bit sketchy on purpose as I picked Lee and Boothy up from Newcastle. I was in a 2litre Cortina GL and they'd been to Newcastle to drop ounces of ganja off. Anyway as we were going up Linthorpe Road past the old Empire pub Boothy opened the glove compartment to find a dictaphone on record. Both turned to me and said, "WHAT ARE YOU DOING YOU OLD CUNT?" If that was anybody else I would have been murdered on the spot right there! Boothy and the Duff questioned me for what must have been an hour but in the end both knew I was taking the piss, I wanted them to find it, that was part of the joke.

Lee and Boothy once got to Newcastle in less than 30 minutes. The two used to time themselves doing it maybe 60 times after being up for a few days on end utterly off their barnets still at maybe 2,3,4,5am in the morning. Lee would drive 90mph all the way home and would never ever stop on Redcar Road/Normanby Road junction.

What you've got to remember was those two had many cars at their disposal and they'd fly, they'd leave the car running with the music blazing and its alleged Eston's Paul Bryan had written LEE DUFFY GRASS and other obscenities on the motorway so the pair would have to get out and spray over it still off their nuts. The two when they were together used to get up to a million things a day and nobody knew the Duff better in the last two years of his life than Boothy. I'd love one day for Neil to sit down and write a book on his best friend. Boothy was there when Lee turned up and massacred Viv's doormen at Macey's Nightclub the lot. By god could that lad tell you some tales about Lee Duffy I tell you.

I've had some funny times with the Duff and Boothy and when they were both in jail I would send them mucky mags in (laughs). Lee used to get his and the Sunday papers I used to send in but when I used to send them to Neil I had the governor ring me up once telling me they are not allowed them kind of magazines. When I asked if Neil was allowed mucky pictures from his girlfriend instead he

145

put the phone down on me. When Neil got out we had a good laugh about it.

Me, Lee and Neil would often have a smoke and just spend the night laughing. Lee used to always wanna hear my stories about what Durham prison was like back in the sixties. Him and Boothy would make me tell them these stories and Lee would always sit there laughing his head off. He used to say I was like Uncle Albert in Only Fools and Horses telling him about his war stories. He had me telling him all sorts from when I was first at court from 9 years old to progressing and getting 28 days on remand then approved schools in 1958. Lee wanted to know about my time in Medomsley detention centre and other borstals, he was always very inquisitive with things like that and you could see when I told him he was taking it all in.

Lee often used to ask me what his uncle Rod was like as a lad, Lee grew up idolising his uncle who I first met in Northallerton prison. Back in his day Rod was a very handy lad who was always fighting and we became very good friends. In fact I had my 21st birthday locked up with Rod in jail and we were forever winding each other up. When I got out and Rod was still in he asked me to go see his mam and dad (Lee's grandparents). I told Lee his nana and grandad used to treat me like a son and I would go see them every week until they died. Lee's grandparents on his Mum's side (Brenda Duffy's parents) bought a house on Leven Bank but the house was built on the corner. Lee's grandparents bought that house thinking they were buying their dream home but in actual fact it turned into a nightmare because a good few vehicles came crashing into their home when it was icy. How them two were never killed I don't know and in the end they had to live in their kitchen and boycott the front room because the council refused to put protective barriers up even though they'd been hit with several cars over the years in their house. I went a few times to the council with Lee's

146

grandparents but nothing was ever done about it which is fucking scandalous isn't it? When I told Lee that story he had a tear in his eye and he said he'd wished he'd have been around to have helped them. I'd often seen Lee cry at sad stories like that but he would never show them feelings to anyone else. It didn't match his image did it!

I think it is fair to say that Lee did look up to his uncle Rod whilst he was growing up because as I told you Rod could have a row. I'll always remember the notorious drug lord John McPartland came to see me demanding to know where Rod lived but I said I didn't know! He said, "come on Vince you and he are best pals don't bullshit me". I asked John how would he like it if I gave his address out to somebody looking for trouble which I could tell by John's body language that was the case. Anyway I asked, what's this about? John then told me the pair of them had been in a club the night before and Rod had landed a sneaky one on him before the bouncers broke it up. Now John McPartland was a handy lad and didn't give a fuck about anyone including their Lee. It's been said over the years that Lee and John Mc had had their fights but I can assure you I was friends with both of them and it never happened but if it had done, John Mc wouldn't have bowed to Lee.

Later on that afternoon I went up Hemlington to Rod's house and knocked on the door, I was invited in by Rod's Mrs Jean, who was a lovely woman. Jean was Daren Collins mother and she made me some tea whilst she got Rod out of bed. I asked Rod what had happened and he told me exactly the same as what John McPartland did. I told Rod I didn't want to be involved as they were both my friends but that John was looking for him. I did hear the pair met up a day or two later and had one almighty punch up then became friends. Only in Middlesbrough eh (laughs).

One story he asked me to tell him time and time again from my time in the nick was about a guy from Boro who got six months for shagging his dog. The inmates used to hammer him on a night and call him "humper boy". They'd be dozens of inmates up at their windows on a night all taking the piss out of him barking like a dog or singing 'how much is that doggy in the window'. The same fella used to drink in The Captain Cook over the border, he was one ugly man and completely cock-eyed. Lee loved that story and he'd say to me "Vince I don't know whether to believe you or not but tell me it again" whilst crying with laughter. Lee would tell me off for telling stories because he'd not finished laughing at the first one.

Another lad in Durham I used to tell Lee about was a fella who'd got locked up for shagging a sheep. Well even the judge when sentencing him said to him he'd been a bar bar boy and mutton do that again. Lee used to cry hysterically.

Lee would love all the old jail stories like when I did seven days on bread and water. Lee used to often say to me "ere Vince was there any drugs in jail in the 60s?" I told him there were very few and not like today. I used to tell him about how we used to make marijuana out of bananas in the 60s and he was always like "FUCK OFF VINCE" but I used to say it's true. Every Sunday in Durham everybody used to give me their banana skins and I'd have to put them on the hot plate because I worked in the kitchen. I used to do this little trick and that's how we all got stoned working in the prison kitchen to pass the time away. Anyway, about a week later Lee turned up at my house with four banana skins asking me to do what I told him about the other week. I said fuck off Lee it was about 30 years ago since I even tried but Lee was persistent that I would give it a go for him, so I did. So, I started making this banana cannabis for Lee, after a few hours they were nice and crispy. I then took them out and chopped it all up for him nice and fine, Lee was stood behind me bouncing about all excited like a toddler who'd had too much undiluted Kia-Ora. He was well giddy massaging my shoulders as I was preparing it for him. Lee lit it up making Indian sounds like "HOW" and saying his new name was Chief Lee-Sitting-Bull whilst banging his hand over his mouth on and off like the native Americans did making that ululating war-cry. All of a sudden he started to cough uncontrollably and I asked him what it was like because he'd stopped coughing and he started to look all spaced, I said it must be doing something because he'd stopped barking like a dog. Lee told me it wasn't bad and asked me if I wanted a go but I told him no fucking chance. Lee started mixing it with his blow all night and told me it was his new thing he was going to do from now on but I just laughed at him. I'd like people to know the funny side of Lee and not just the fighting side of him, which is only what people know at the minute.

I first met all the Sayers lot and Manny Burgo with Lee in the Ramsey's blues. Lee thought a lot of them guys, particularly Manny. One night in the blues Lee made me tell them all about the old tales and there wasn't a dry eye in the house. The Sayers told Lee to fetch me to Newcastle with him the next time he was going because they hadn't laughed so much in years. After that night me, Lee, the Sayers and Manny ended up in a flat on top of the Palladium Shops in Grove Hill with one of the Caswell's. A few months after Lee died I saw Manny Burgo in the blues again and I went over and we spoke about Lee all-night. Afterwards three men were starting on Manny and I told him to leave it as he was with a girl. The men had been looking over at Manny and making sly remarks all night because he was from out of town. In the end Manny went outside and I followed him to watch his back but what I was really thinking was 'poor Manny' because he was outnumbered. At first a big tall one went at Manny and Manny dropped him like a bag of sand, then the other two came at him and he flattered the pair of them in one movement. I'd seen Lee fight several men at once but never have I watched anyone so sharp, he was even faster than Lee. Lee would have been proud of him and that display but they wouldn't have even tried it if the Duff had been alive. That was the last time I saw Manny Burgo, when he walked me home to the corner of Princess Road. The three men were sprawled across the road as we headed to my house. After that night somebody told me that Manny Burgo used to be a professional heavyweight boxer so it all made sense.

When Ramsey closed his blues parties down it was me who took it over. Ramsey came to me saying about how he couldn't take anymore with the police raiding him and nicking all his stock/money. He said he was sick of being brought in front of the courts and getting fines. They used to do the same to Terry Dicko when he had The Steam Packet but the little bastard would never give in and would move it to a different building. Another thing Ramsey told me was that after Lee died the blues parties had got too much with people starting trouble in them as usually he had the Duff's backing if anyone got out of hand. At the end of our conversation he agreed that I could take it over and he left. What I did next was spend a few quid on nice tables and chairs and started opening the blues as just a card school. I then told all the riff raff to keep away, this meant that I no longer had to travel all over Britain to play Poker, I now had it on my doorstep. I put my old one-arm bandit in there which I taught the Duff on. Eventually I made it a highly successful illegal gambling house and all the West Indians came back. Lads like Ruddy, Maurice, Dalford, Danny Freeman and Sadu could relax. I went on to run it for several years without one bit of trouble.

I did time with Lee's close pal Jon "Buster" Atkinson and was always winding old Buster up which Lee used to do as well so he'd make me tell him about what we used to do to Buster and he'd laugh some more. Lee used to say, "I can fucking hammer Buster Vince but if anyone else did it I'd kill em". He thought a lot of Buster did Lee.

As much as I was close to Lee he was a bugger and you had to watch him. About six weeks before he died he went on holiday for a few days on every other cunts money with Boothy and their girlfriends. What happened was I'd been getting calls off a few people asking if I'd seen Lee but I hadn't, not for a few days anyway. Not one call but two from different people asking where Lee was and that he'd turned up at their homes and borrowed £300 from each of them on the basis he needed some money for a marijuana deal which was going down, so I sat there in my house thinking what's going on? Only for the Duff and Boothy too turn up at my house with the girls asking if I had £300 to lend them but unbeknown to Lee I'd got wind of what Lee was up to when he pulled this wad of cash out telling me he was £300 short. Well I knew something was happening but I couldn't put my finger on it. I told Lee I was skint and that I'd just come back from Manchester and lost over a grand there for my sins. Even if I did have the money I knew Lee too well to know he wouldn't be doing a deal if he had the girls with him anyroad. Lee wouldn't have put the girls at risk, Boothy yes because he knew Neil would have stood by him and took the rap but not the girls. As I was stood on my front doorstep with them all I noticed the four of them were in this totally clapped out banger of a motor with only one headlight, window wipers not working and it was full of rust. I asked Lee if he'd got it from the scrapyard but he just scoffed and said it'll be ok. Well Lee started the car up and the fucking smoke came out of it that much that I ran in the house and shut the door fast to escape the black cloud of smoke chasing me. I told Lee that he was a mad bastard and that he wanted to watch somebody doesn't phone the fire brigade for driving that and him and Boothy just laughed and drove off beeping the horn with rave music blasting and off they went. It must have been maybe a half hour later when I got a call from Lee and he was telling me he'd only got three miles across the town and the car had given up outside The Fountain pub in Ormesby. I asked him how the fuck had he even got that far and did he get a tow but he just asked me if I could go and collect him, I said I would and told him I'd be there in 20 minutes. When I arrived the lasses were stood there in front of the car and they were giggling shouting "GO ON VINCE, TELL HIM OFF" because I was telling Lee how much of a thick bastard I thought he was. After about ten minutes I realised the car needed a new jump lead putting in and I managed to do this and get Lee's scrap box back to life. Before I went, Lee asked me if I was skint, I told him I was and he gave me £50. He then drove off with the music blaring and smoke following their trail shouting "see ya later Vince you old cunt" and they were off to the Lakes/Blackpool for what must have been around a fortnight because I never heard from Lee or Boothy again for a good while. I did get a few calls from the several people Lee had borrowed £300 off but I couldn't tell them anything. When Lee did turn up and I asked him what he was going to do with all the people he owed the money to, Lee just shrugged his shoulders and said, "relax auld timer, they've got plenty anyway", he just didn't care. I then told him he was bang out of order because he'd tried pulling the very same scam on me but I didn't have it and he just laughed and he told me that even though he did what he did to the others he said he was going to give me mine back and I believed him because he'd never ripped me off ever. I know the others who gave Lee the money but I couldn't tell you in this book because it's too embarrassing for them. Saying that, he did borrow that death trap of a car from Shaun Day.

Not long before he died I went in The Commercial pub with him in South Bank. Lee, I'm not kidding you, must have spent easily over a grand that day and he was giving people money in the pub. There was a lass in there in a wheelchair who'd got covered in petrol when that idiot tried to kill Lee. The Duff went over to her and gave her a cuddle and told her how sorry he was that she'd got covered in petrol. Lee gave her £50 that day also, I saw him give it to her with my own eyes and he didn't do it in front of the whole pub. He pulled her aside and did it on the sneak. Lee did have a good heart and I want people to finally know this. He was a lot more emotional than people give him credit for and I saw Lee Duffy cry a good few times, probably more than some of his family had seen.

One memory I have of seeing Lee cry was over his cousin, little Rodney Jones Junior who'd died in a car crash when he was only young. One day Lee asked me to take him to where it had happened on a country lane. I knew where it was because Lee's uncle Rod had showed me after the funeral. I took Lee to the scene of the accident and told him that Rodney Junior had lost control and had crashed into a tree and that's how he was tragically taken so young. I told Lee that young Rodney used to be his nana and grandad Jones' life and Lee went over to the spot under the tree and knelt and said a prayer whilst breaking down in tears. Lee then got up, wiped his eyes and said, "come on Vince let's go for a drink".

For as familiar as I ever got with Lee I can honestly say he never spoke about himself being bullied at a young age. That was only something I learnt later on through reading about him. It didn't go with his image did it and if he couldn't tell me about it I believe he couldn't have spoken to anyone about it.

"There's no doubt he led a very violent life and we got a lot of intelligence of him assaulting people for various reasons, although few of them came forward giving us information about him, but certainly he was involved in several fights we know about".

Detective Chief Inspector Brian Leonard 1991

INFLUENCES

Everybody knows the story of Lee growing up absolutely idolising Middlesbrough hard case Kevin Duckling but not many people know the closeness of Lee and Ray Duckling.

Lee used to tell anyone who'd listen that Ray Ducko was his second dad and he always loved being in his company.

Lee first met his idol in Rumours Nightclub in the early 80s and was instantly in awe of him.

Before Lee Duffy came along, Ray's son, Kevin Ducko was classed as the main man in the town and Lee would often follow him all over the town like a lost sheep. Kevin Duckling's name in the early to mid-1980s was huge and a few people from back in that era have told me the only reason they'd heard of Lee Duffy's name was because of his association with Ducko. Despite Kevin's best attempts to shake Lee off on nights out, Lee would appear out of nowhere.

Kevin's dad Ray used to go to school with Lee's mother Brenda and Ray and Brenda knew each other very well.

Years later when Lee and Kevin had their fall out before Kev went away to prison, no one could understand why, Ray used to say he could never understand it and even Christine, Ray's widow, doesn't know to this day what happened, some people have surmised it was because Lee thought he'd passed Kev and his reputation but how true that is, we will never really know.

Ray would often talk about Lee and he thought the world of him. When people over the years used to slag Lee Duffy off Ray used to say he always took Lee as he found him and he was always very decent with him. Ray would tell people he couldn't have said a bad word about Lee and the pair would often go out drinking together.

When Ray had his nose bitten off as a young man it was Rod Jones, Lee's uncle, who allegedly threatened to shoot the man who did it. The man in question up and moved that very same night and was never seen again because of the repercussions he was facing from the Duckling family.

Ray Duckling sadly died in May 2018 but when he was alive he did have lots of kind words for Lee's uncle Rod. One night in Rumours Lee was fighting and to quote my source "marmalising this lad" at the bottom of Rumours Nightclub stairs and Molly and Brian Jaffray, and big Mac tried to hold Lee off and he just flung the lot of them away with ease. There was a wildness and a strength that Duffy had that was unnatural. Nobody could stop Duffy from attacking this lad. In fact, Ray's wife Christine still has a scar on her elbow because she accidently got pushed into the pebble-dashed artex that decorated the wall. Ray never held it against Lee because he knew he was in fighting mode and he'd have been mortified if he found out, it was a total accident.

After that incident the police were called because Lee had left a man half dead and it was Ray who put Lee in the boot of his car to escape the scene and drove him past the police.

Another night Ray was out with Lee in The Speak Easy and somebody said something nasty to Ray about his nose, at the time Ray had been a bit of a recluse not leaving the house over his disfigurement and he took this slur badly. In the end Ray dragged him outside and gave him one hell of a beating. Ray then went back in the pub and told Lee "fucking hell I think I've killed him outside, what am I going to do now?" Lee told him "leave it to me, I know just what to do." Lee's then got up and walked to the door and approached the mouthy bloke who was laid out cold and he shouted to Ray, "this is a job for Doctor Duffy", Lee then turned and grabbed a full pint that a bloke stood in the doorway was holding and poured it over the sleeping man on the floor, it instantly woke him up! Lee then turned to old Ray and shouted "NAH, THIS ONE'S NOT DEAD"!!!!

Ray used to say that even though he saw Lee fight a lot he had nothing but love for the lad.

When Lee died in 1991 Ray took it very badly but because he'd just had a car accident he couldn't go to Lee's funeral.

Old Ray did read the Stephen Richards books which I'm told he was never too keen on, saying that those books were very inaccurate.

I'm told that Ray was looking forward to reading 'The Whole of the Moon' but sadly died a few months before its release. One of the people close to Ray told me that even though Ray had cancer behind his eyes and wouldn't be able to read it himself, he had promised Ray that he would read it to him.

Ray passed on May 11th, 2018 and is greatly missed by many people in Middlesbrough that knew him.

It was thanks to old Ray's video collecting that I was able to use the footage of the news bulletin's for the 'Whole of the Moon' documentary. Ray used to tape everything on the news regarding Lee Duffy.

"Lee Duffy was wild and dangerous and he enjoyed the havoc he caused along the way. At the same time Lee was ferociously loyal and protective of his friends. Lee never ever let me down in anything and even though he's been gone 28 years now I'll keep making sure the people of Teesside won't forget him. It's my duty to all the people I've loved in life.

Terry Dicko

KEVIN HILL

Kevin Hill is from Hartlepool and is now 58 years old. Kevin spent time in Durham prison with Lee in 1988. For 3 months of that time Kevin and Lee shared a cell and I was keen to capture just what he thought of Middlesbrough's tornado the Duffer.

Kevin said:-

"I first met Lee Duffy in March 1998 when he had just received his four years for the attack on Martin Clark in The Speak Easy. I'd heard about Lee going back to when he was just a teenager and I was at least five years older than he was. Lee's name was very well known in Hartlepool and I'm sure he used to come through to see a notorious family called the Lancaster's.

Lee and I were padded up together in Durham on B Wing and as soon as Lee walked in my cell my first thoughts on him were that he looked like a pure powerhouse. Lee and I started talking and he told me that he used to be a scaffolder in his younger days before he really started dealing in drugs.

Whenever I was working in Middlesbrough, Lee Duffy's name was mentioned a hell of a lot, I'd sit on my tea breaks listening to all the stories of what he had been up to that particular weekend. I told Lee this when we shared a cell and he thought it was hilarious.

Overall I found Lee to be a bit flamboyant but mostly he was a good lad. He was very proud about telling people he was from Middlesbrough and that he owned the town.

Lee loved to strut out of his cell wearing only white boxer shorts, that was something any other prisoner was never allowed to do. To tell you the truth, Lee liked to wear as little clothes as possible. None of the officers ever told him though when he was walking about with next to nothing on. You couldn't help but notice how muscular Duff was in just his underpants. Lee was forever marching around in just his duds and nothing ever seemed to get done about it. If anybody else did that they'd be banged up so the screws must have given him a little bit of respect in the prison or they chose their battles wisely because I never ever saw anyone else do it.

For as in your face as Duffy could be I never saw him cause any trouble in the jail. At the time there was John Chisolm and Kid Mordey from Sunderland in there and they were known troublemakers but Duffy, surprisingly, never was.

Visually one of the things that were noticeable about Lee was his broken nose. His beak was a total state and I just put that down to him fighting all the time.

Now, I never found Lee to be a bully in the three months I spent with him, he was a character, you never forgot him in a hurry once you'd met him. The only time I ever knew him to have any trouble was with the screws and they took him down the block and he lost seven days, that was the only time I saw his bad side and that was to the officers. You hear the stories of people wanting to kill him because he was overly aggressive but I never saw none of that. When you were in Lee Duffy's company you could see what he could be, I mean he was one big strapping lad. His arms, legs and shoulders were something else but I always found Lee preferred his own company rather than the other lads on the wing. When we were in our cell together Lee was forever doing sit-ups and press-ups. We were banged up 23 hours a day and one hours exercise for Lee was no good for him he used to say.

I felt sad after Lee died because although I heard his name on the radio, papers and telly for bad things I never saw that side of Lee Duffy in three months. He didn't even remotely come across like that in the 14 weeks I knew him. I met far nastier people in prison than Lee Duffy. At least Lee only did his talking with his fists, not like some of the people using blades etc... Lee was one big powerful lad and if you met him it wouldn't have surprised you to know that he went on to smash Brian Cockerill up. The only one he didn't put away was Viv Graham because he was the hide and seek undisputed champion at the time. It's sad the way Lee died in the end. He seemed to have been a target all the way through his brief life really. Although I only knew him for three months it was long enough to know he was very different to how the media have painted him for the last 28 years...

"For as small as a place as Middlesbrough is, it breeds an awful lot of naughty characters. When I used to come here through the 1970s it always reminded me of a mini Liverpool".

Former Liverpool crime lord Delroy Showers 2018

PADDY MOLONEY

Paddy Moloney grew up in Grove Hill and comes from a large well-known family in Middlesbrough and he is now 62 years old. Paddy was very much a man of Lee's era and because I'm working with him on his forthcoming book 'The Altar Boy', it was only too easy for me to gather Paddy's thoughts on Middlesbrough's most infamous son.

Paddy said:-

I first heard the name Lee Duffy when I was working on the doors of The Speak Easy (before The Havana) nightclub and The Trooper (now Camels Hump) in 1982-83 which would have made Lee 17-18 years old. At that time The Speak Easy was mainly a black club and Rumours nightclub was for the white people. Blacks and whites would stay out of each other's clubs I found but Lee used to venture into both.

I first saw Lee when he was a snotty-nosed kid collecting glasses in Master's nightclub (before Rumours) by sight and then I thought he was a quiet kid, dead laid back. I don't think I ever heard Lee swear in my whole life. Middlesbrough's only a small town so you were never far from each other. Soon enough though he would stop collecting glasses and started collecting a reputation for himself instead. He'd spent his time watching what was going on and learning who was who before he emerged as the towns No.1.

When Lee came on the scene, at first I always found that nine times out of ten he would always be on his own and that was the scariest thing about him when he became who he was at his peak in 1990. Today you see lads turning up with baseball bats in gangs, turning up in cars but Lee was never like that whatsoever.

He would always be dressed nice and smart, the iconic image of The Duffer in just his shorts came much later. Lee was a big lad then in the early days before he really started training properly. What I will say is he had a persona about him. There was something about this kid that was different. Even though he wouldn't say much he seemed to stand out. He'd come in, have a drink and he wouldn't bully anyone or threaten anyone. He'd stay for an hour talk to a few of us like Franny Romaine on the door then go back to his own end of the town which was the Rumours end.

In the early 1980s there was a fella named Dave Bishop who was quite handy and Dave kept a lot of the trouble away from The Speak Easy and The Trooper because he was a nice man. Well Lee and Dave became friends over the years and that was when Lee started coming into my places of work more and more through the mid-eighties. Lee would always be seen talking to Mary Price and he was very polite. I think Mary took a shine to him at first.

Lee went from glass collector to bouncer in Rumours first but I never saw him knocking people out like he became notorious for because that was at the other end of the town to us, we would just hear about it. I think Lee used to come up our part of the town to get away from all that to be quite honest.

It was almost overnight around 1985 that Lee grew up and sussed everyone out and became the Lee Duffy we all know now. It was then when he started turning up at places and asking who was in charge, whoever was that night ended up getting knocked out. On his way up boy did Lee ruffle some feathers and he upset a lot of people.

I would say it was around that time that Lee became dead interested in Dave Bishop because he used to have a fantastic reputation and I believe that's why they ended up fighting down the line. Dave was from the same mould as Jonka Teasdale and both were two very hard men in their day. Jonka would keep court around places like Rooney's (now The Oak), The Albert and the Wellington (now Flares) and Dave was up our end and they kept out of each other's way to run their doors as both didn't really see eye to eye.

When Lee got out of prison in around 1985 I would say that's when he became ultra-dangerous. I just found he'd really changed from the quiet kid I once knew to now being on a whole new level. It was like he'd tasted blood.

The memories I have of Lee around then was when he came in The Buccaneer and followed Paul Salter in the toilets and smacked him. Lee was too much for Paul. I know Lee was looking for a reaction but he never got one from Paul.

There used to be a lot of fear factor with Lee Duffy from 1985 onwards and he was an athlete. By that point he'd sussed every doorman out in the town, who were the proper doormen, so he knew how much he could get away with. I don't mean the likes of me, I mean the likes of real hard men like Dave Bishop and Jonka Teasdale and Lee slowly but surely went around the full town of Middlesbrough and knocked them all out.

Many times I would be in a pub and Lee would appear at the door, almost like a ghost and the whole pub would fall silent. He'd stand at the door and scan the full pub for 2-3 minutes. To everyone in the pub it would feel like a lifetime because no-one would move, everyone would sit there trying not to make eye contact with him. Then all of a sudden Lee would put his hand up and wave some poor unfortunate soul out. That's something I saw Lee do dozens of times and whoever had to walk out faced the music whatever it was. As you were walking over everyone in the pub was feeling sorry for you. It was like a death march to meet your fate. Usually it was for a slap or to take something off you or if you were lucky you'd get a warning or you'd have to do him a favour. That's what it was like mid-eighties in Middlesbrough in the Duff's reign. The full pub would get so uneasy because until Lee pointed someone out, no one knew if it was them that he was gonna pull out.

When Lee did that he was always on his own, he never came with an entourage and he did that to some of the hardest men in Middlesbrough and they always went to him and followed orders. I never saw Lee carry a weapon ever, not once in my life. If you lived in that circle and you had a problem with Lee Duffy it was because you were a hard man, a doorman or sold drugs, if you were any sort of criminal or lived in that fraternity in the 80s in Boro then you had a problem with the Duff. If you were Mr Smith sat in the corner with your Mrs minding your own business then all he'd have done to you was probably buy you a pint.

I never ever had many problems with Lee because I was never a threat apart from this one time when I was working as a bouncer and Lee walked in. Looking back it was very comical, although not for me at the time but for you reading this book it is. It must have been around 1985 when I was working in The Trooper. Lee came in one night when it was very quiet and I was next door in the bar playing pool with Tony Boyd. Well the barmaid came through and shouted "Paddy, that Lee Duffy's just come in and he's asking where the bouncer is". I had always been ok with Lee so I never thought anything of it, that was until the barmaid then told me, "he said he's having one drink then he's coming through to knock you clean out asleep". Well I looked at her and I knew she was deadly serious. Tony Boyd then started panicking telling me to do one quick so I told Tony to let me think one moment. I took a deep breath then I came up with a fantastic idea which I put into play. I knew that Lee didn't know the barmaid had told me what he was about to do to me. Looking back It was a sheer stroke of genius considering the pressure I was under. What I did then was to quickly barge through next door to see Lee, before he could react or say anything at all I shouted, "HIYA LEE HOW YOU DOING MY MATE", then before he could respond I said "how's the kids? How's Brenda? How's ya Mrs? You been busy? I looked at the barmaid and said, "Ere love get my best mate Lee a pint on me". I could see Lee was bamboozled and he just looked at me and smiled and said, "yeah yeah everything's alright Pad". And that's how I saved my bacon one night against Lee Duffy. I definitely used up one of my nine lives that evening. I don't think it was anything personal against me other than I was a doormen and that's just what Lee did. Maybe if he'd have seen it was Paddy Moloney he might not have knocked me out but I wasn't planning on finding out and putting it into God's hands. That night in question was a Wednesday if I remember so it was a quiet night in the town. Not many pubs had doormen on a Wednesday so I think it was just Lee perhaps bored walking about looking to knock a doorman out.

Lee in around 1985, befriended my brother-in-law Dale Henderson-Thynne, who was an ex professional middleweight boxer and those two became half decent friends. At the start Dale sort of looked after Lee and tried to steer him in the right direction. In my opinion Dale is a decent fella deep down but at that time he was doing all kind of things in the criminal world and this interested Lee, what interested Lee even more in my opinion was that Dale had had a name in the town of Middlesbrough because he was one hell of a boxer. Dale had some cracking fights at The Marton & Country Club for the old Middlesbrough promotor John Spensley. Around '85 it was when Dale was running the Blaises door for Barry Faulkner and he was doing things with Jonka Teasdale and they'd become partners. You know what happened next don't you! With Dale doing all that he was doing at the time, well this made him a target in the eyes of the young tiger Lee Duffy and the inevitable happened. I don't know how it happened or when it happened but I know Terry Dicko was involved in bringing them two together. To cut a long story short, Lee and Terry went to my sister's house (Dales wife) in Linthorpe and it ended up with Lee and Dale going down the beck near Devil's Bridge for a fight. I remember getting a call from my sister Teresa saying "Paddy, Duffy and Dicko have just turned up at our house for a fight and Duffy's outside with his top off bouncing about hypo". She then said "Paddy he's going to kill him, Duffy's going off it on the front" but what could I do. Well the two went down the beck in Saltersgill and I got told a police car stopped and the two bobbies in the car just watched them fight! One of the neighbours had rang the police and they just sat and watched because it was Lee Duffy, In the end the Duff and Dale agreed to stand up and box, no kicking, no biting just boxing but in the end Lee was far too much for Dale. Dale gave a good account of himself and didn't back down in the slightest and he went all out with the Duff but Lee was too much for any man. I was told the fight lasted a long time. I mean we're talking about an ex professional middleweight boxer here so Dale was no mug but that gives you an example of just how much of an awesome fighting machine Lee Paul Duffy was. Lee might not have been any kind of boxer but he was so special. He was an athlete and whatever he did in the gym he trained so hard and took it seriously.

Terry told me how the fight went and my sister told me the state of what Dale was in after they'd fought. Funnily enough, after Lee had went to fight my brother-in-law Dale I saw him on the same night in The Speak Easy and I told him he was out of order. I don't know where I got the bottle from to speak to Lee like that. I said "Lee, Dale's ya mate he was sticking up for you the other night in your absence". Lee then gives me the eyes and walks towards me and I'm thinking 'oh here we go' but he picked me up, walked me to the bar and when we got to the bar he said, "you're right Paddy I'm sorry, I wished I'd not done it". In my opinion the only true friends Lee Duffy ever had were our Dale and Mark Hartley. Lee became best friends with Neil Booth a little later on but through the 80s I'd say the only two friends Lee had were Dale and Mark.

Now, Mark Hartley himself was a big lad with a terrific KO punch. Mark was a fantastic footballer who played for the Speak Easy team as a strong powerful rough centre-forward with Kevin Hawkins. I worked the Speak Easy door with Mark he could really have a fight. Considering Mark spent a lot of time with Duffy they were very different. Lee was just about thieving and taking what he wanted off people, whereas Mark Hartley always worked in good jobs. Yes Mark did let his hair down from time to time, as we all do, but he was your perfect family man in all other aspects.

Lee and Mark were very close at one point and I think Mark was a good influence for Lee. I've never forgotten my time behind the door and Mark sending me quite a few quid in. He's a good man is Mark Hartley.

A lot of the times when Lee was the man about town as he was post 1985 I would keep out of his way because of what I used to do making a living. In those days in the drug world, there was no cocaine or heroin, it was all rocky, blow, packy black or a bit of whizz. Acids and E's started a couple of years after maybe 1989-1990 then they slowly came in. When Lee was running Middlesbrough doing what I was doing this might sound bonkers but Lee Duffy used to leave me alone to get on with it because I wasn't in anyone's face doing it. Yes I'd worked the doors but I never had some ridiculous name in Middlesbrough as a fighter and I think for that reason, that was enough for Lee to look right past me.

Whenever Lee was locked away for the sentences he served the whole town of Middlesbrough would just go that bit quieter when he was away, then when he was at large the whole of Teesside knew about it alright.

Lee had a great skill in chasing drug dealers to the point where he'd have them grassing on each other, telling him where each other's stashes were. If they didn't tell Lee then they got brayed it was as simple as that and he was untouchable. If you sold drugs or did anything illegal then Lee wanted a piece.

In the late 1980's I was in jail with Kevin Duckling (Ducko). I was in Acklington with him. Funnily enough me and Kevin were transported from Durham prison to Acklington together. Kevin was singing Elvis Presley songs all the way there.

Kevin was inside for manslaughter as he'd punched Paul Dalloway outside of a blues party on Woodlands Road in June 1988, What happened was Allo was having a fight with a guy named "Bigga" and Dalloway came running out looking at what was going on but Ducko thought Dalloway was about to get into him and Kevin's hit him and the kids fell, banged his head and died 15 hours later in the old Middlesbrough General Hospital. Paul Dalloway was black Ossie's son from Sheffield who used to live in Grove Hill, he was a pimp but Dalloway was just a 21-year-old kid in a band. The reason Kevin only got four years was because Dalloway had already had a plate put in his head from a motorbike accident the year before.

Kevin went on the run to London but he gave himself up in the end. Well the closer Kevin was to getting out, the more he used to talk to me because Duffy was sending him messages saying, "As soon as you're out, let's get it on!" I sat with Kevin many times and Kevin would say to me "fucking hell Pad, I don't wanna fight him" but I told him he was gonna have to.

Now Kevin himself had been a bit of a boy in his time and when Lee was growing up he used to idolise Ducko and follow him all-over like a sheep. Lee had first met

170

Ducko in Master's nightclub when he was just 14 years old as a glass collector. Kevin was around 7-8 years older than the young impressionable Duff but back then Lee used to run to Rumours just to be in Ducko's company.

Now the tide had turned and Lee was on a whole new level and Kevin was scared of having to face him. I don't know if Kevin ever faced Lee but Lee was definitely hunting him down.

Another man In Teesside Lee had clashed with was Kirk Garland. Kirk, in his time, was very chewy and he used to pick his mark with people.

Kirk was a good-looking kid and full of himself, always had the best clobber on. Well one day he was in The Trooper and it was disco night when I was working the door. I didn't have much to do with Kirk but I was aware of him because he was chewy and I had to keep my eye on him. Then the next thing I know, I'm stood at the door with Tony Boyd and Dave Bishop and the Duff appeared at the front door like a phantom again without any sound. He walked in, stared about as he did then he said to me "I'm looking for Kirk, Paddy have you seen him?" I said, "yeah he was in a minute ago, why Lee?" Lee never told me why he wanted him and just ignored my question. By now everyone in the pub was mesmerised by Lee's presence and the temperature of the room had gone completely cold. Lee scanned the full room, didn't have a drink and then told me "I'll be back" and walked out. Well I didn't know it then, but Kirk Garland was laid under the table hiding between two women. That was what Lee was like, he would headhunt people like The Terminator and he did that a lot.

It's common knowledge that I've done a few prison sentences for drug-dealing and I'm so happy to say I've changed my ways, but looking back at what I used to get up to through the 80s and early 90s I just thank god that Lee Duffy never had a thing for me because if he did have a thing for you then you were fucked. You got knocked out every time he saw you.

Even when I was a doormen, which is another field that if you were in then you had to be on your guard with the Duff, I wasn't a loud doorman, you'd never hear me threatening anyone, but that 'loud doorman' kind got it from the Duff. I've worked with bouncers who were like that and I know he'd targeted several of them. I considered myself as a good fair doorman and I knew if I let you in then you were my problem. I used to do it all the time with Davey Fields. Many times I'd just say you can't come in Davey and he'd try and push past me. Then he'd be effing and blinding and the threats would come of "I'll get ya in the blues" but I didn't care because I knew it would have been worse for me if I'd have let him in.

Davey has just come out of prison after serving a life sentence for the murder of Peter Homer at Homer's Coulby Newham home in December 1993, but he had a few run ins with Lee in his time.

I couldn't honestly say I saw Lee Duffy fight because yes I'd seen him spark men in the blues but I never saw him struggle with anyone. It was only ever one, maximum two punches and they were gone with Lee Duffy. Most would be out cold or go down because it was Lee Duffy and they were terrified.

Lee was intimidating exactly like Mike Tyson. He was just like a machine. In my opinion, as Lee got older he got even crazier and he started to spread himself further than just Middlesbrough. Lee regularly started moving on to Hartlepool and Newcastle. Lee had gone national and the people in Middlesbrough were just his cannon fodder. Lee was out hunting the big fella's with the big names like Viv Graham and the Lancaster's. This was really the reason why Lee was even in Redcar that day for his fight with Brian Cockerill because Brian lived in Redcar then and Lee was out hunting him.

Talking about Viv Graham, I was in Durham jail with him, I didn't know who he was at first until little Kevin Auer, who was in there, told me who he was although obviously I'd heard the name. Little Kev said, "ere Paddy, that's that Viv Graham there who's supposed to be rock."

I was into my boxing in prison I was never one for five a side and I used to see this big guy on the punchbag in the gym. There was benches like the ones you used to have at school and you'd have to sit and wait your turn then when whoever was finished you'd get the gloves off him and you'd have a go on the bag and that's how I got to know Viv through doing that every day. After the bag Viv would go have a game of five aside and let me tell you what a fast fella he was for a big man! I found Viv an incredibly nice fella who I did a lot of training with.

If I was ever in other parts of the prison Viv would shout "howay then Paddy lad are you alright?"

I just found Viv to be a real gentleman to be around. It wasn't until Lee got out of his last prison sentence in May 1990 that Lee became obsessed with Viv and started hunting him down like a grown-ups version of hide and seek. I saw both men close up, Lee on the streets of Middlesbrough and Viv in the gym and if you want my honest opinion who would have won between those two I'd have to side with Lee. He was just too fast, strong and powerful for his own good! Not to mention he had a big heart and was utterly fearless.

When Lee went to that next level I don't think the people of Middlesbrough were seeing much of him because he was always with the Sayers up in Newcastle and I know Lee was even going up to Leeds around that time too.

When I look back he did do so much in just a short space of time for just a young kid. A lot of the taxi drivers who I knew used to tell me they were petrified of Duffy and the rest of Middlesbrough in 1990/91 were happy that the

Duff was now Newcastle's problem and they'd breathe a huge sigh of relief. I know a couple of drivers that Lee took their cars off them by just telling them "I'm borrowing this for an hour" and then he'd keep the taxi for two days. I mean they knew although it was their livelihood there was nothing they could do and they certainly weren't going to phone the police because even though it was one man and maybe Boro taxi's had 60 drivers all of them together couldn't have beaten the Duff so they just waited until Lee brought it back or he told them they could collect it.

I would say obviously that he was a bully at times but there's not much else I could say negative about the man. If you're talking about taking someone as you find them I don't have anything bad to say about Lee and if I did it was because someone else has told me. I always thought a lot of people used to hang around with Lee for the glory.

I have friends from all over the country i.e. Newcastle, Liverpool, Manchester and Coventry and when Lee was alive so many of them used to talk about Lee and ask me questions about him and they'd never even met him. Without a doubt he'd gone nationwide then and I would say from 1990 that's when he created this image everywhere he went, whether that be a pub, gym, nightclub or blues it was just him in a pair of shorts and trainers.

I think even people like myself who liked Lee kept away from him in the last year of his life. Lee did seem to fall out with a lot of people in his life like Eston man Paul Bryan. Once over they were the best of friends and worked together but that ended up in a huge fallout and Paul being arrested by Cleveland Police for plotting to murder Lee. Paul told me the reason they fell out in the end was that Lee taxed him of a lot of stuff. I know Lee once gave Paul a terrible beating in Brian Charrington's car lot on the Longlands behind the Buccaneer pub. Paul wasn't really a fighter as such but he was a dangerous little man and was a diagnosed schizophrenic. Paul is now doing a life sentence for double murder.

In the Yorkshire Evening Post published on Tuesday 14th 2002 it printed this story with the headlines:

"ASSASSIN SHOT THESE BEST PALS DEAD… WHILE HE WAITED TO BE JAILED"

"Hitman Paul James Bryan was already living in the shadow of a heavy jail sentence when he took on the contract to shoot heavily-in-debt David Nelson – in a hit which also killed Nelson's best pal Joseph Montgomery.

As he stepped into the dock at Leeds Crown accused of double murder, the jury was unaware he had already been snared by police during a major drugs operation in the North-East and knew he faced a long jail sentence.

He had pleaded guilty, along with a number of accomplices including his brother Andrew, to plotting to supply cocaine, amphetamine and cannabis in the North-East.

However, the judge in Teesside ruled that Bryan should not be sentenced for those offences until the outcome of the Leeds double murder trial was reached.

BLASTED

He issued an order, banning publication of details of the court appearance in the North-East, so the Leeds murder trial jury would not be prejudiced against him.

Nor did the jury know that in 1991, Bryan had been accused of plotting to murder a notorious Teesside hard man, Lee Duffy, who was eventually killed in a street fight

175

later the same year. Duffy was blasted at a blues party in Middlesbrough but survived after emergency hospital treatment to a leg wound. However, murder conspiracy charges against Bryan and six others were dropped in June 1991 at a committal hearing.

Bryan was finally caught after National Crime Squad officers bugged his house and car – linking him to major drugs gang operating in the North-East during a major surveillance operation.

To the outside world, Bryan was a second-hand car dealer, running his business from his home in Church Lane, Eston.

RISKY

In reality, he was head of a regional network supplying drugs both on Teesside and as far afield as Leeds and Northampton , always distancing himself from the drugs themselves and leaving the risky work to his couriers.

Detective Chief Inspector Dave Wright, of the National Crime Squad, said: "The listening device evidence proved damning against Paul Bryan as it revealed the true nature of his illegal business – making money from the misery of drugs".

Bryan, born in Middlesbrough in October 1960, was still in short trousers when he first got involved in crime. At the tender age of 10 he was made the subject of a Local Authority supervision order for stealing. The following year, he was placed in the care of Local Authority for carrying out seven burglaries.

Burglary and theft became a way of life and by the age of 15 he found himself in a Detention Centre. Even that failed to put him on the straight and narrow.

At 18 he was sent to Borstal, was later released but then recalled to Borstal for re-offending.

At the age of 21, Paul Bryan was still an unreformed villain and was given his first jail sentence, a total of 18 months, for burglary offences. Shortly after his release he received a prison sentence of 20 days for assaulting two police officers.

In the ensuing years, Bryan continued to commit crime and spend much of his life behind bars. He had amassed a catalogue of convictions for mainly burglary offences, although he did have one conviction for possessing cannabis. He had also been banned for driving while disqualified in 1997.

By the year 2000, Bryan had moved up to what he saw as the big league – drugs.

Yet again he was caught. This time it was the National Crime Squad who targeted and seven others in an operation codenamed 'Casper'.

Unknown to Bryan and his accomplices, Britain's top crime busters had bugged his home with a camera and microphone. They even had a bug in his car.

Bryan was finally arrested in May 2000 but three months later was released on bail, pending a trial at Teesside Crown Court.

It was during his period on bail that he agreed to "sort out" David Nelson, a former rugby league player who had already survived one attempt on his life.

Leeds Crown Court heard evidence that after his arrest over the Wilson Arms shooting, Bryan was heard to claim he was brought in because someone else failed at the earlier attempt. Just three days before he was blasted to death, David Nelson was in the car park of the Wilson Arms when he got involved in an argument with a mystery man. The stranger then pulled a gun and fired. The bullet skimmed Nelson's head but left him otherwise uninjured.

It was that incident which supported the theory that David Nelson had not only gambling debts but also owed money elsewhere.

Rumour was strong that he might have been working for a local drugs dealer but failed to hand over all the money that came into his possession. The murder inquiry had two prime aims – firstly, to track down the gunman and, secondly, to establish who had hired him. Murder squad officers solved the first riddle – but they could never find enough evidence to prove who hired Bryan.

They had their suspicions – but career criminal Paul Bryan, who made wild claims that he was forced to become an informer to help sell drugs by former 'Robocop' Ray Mallon, now Mayor of Middlesbrough, wasn't about to help them.

He had already shown detectives what he thought of them – by smashing a tape recorder during one interview."

When Lee died I was in bed on Homerton Road in Pallister Park and I got a phone call at 5.30am from my brother Billy who lived in the town and I'll never forget that moment, it was almost like a JFK moment when I heard those words "Duffy's dead and there's Bobbies everywhere Pad".

Loads of places in the town started celebrating and having 'The Duff is dead' parties. If you lived through that period in Middlesbrough I don't care what you say, everybody remembers where they were and what they were doing when they received that news. I'm not going to name names but I found more people celebrated than mourned his passing. I even heard people singing a song which is a famous football chant of "Davey Allo is our friend he killed Duffy" which I found shocking. That song originally came from "Hate em all" Harry Roberts who killed those three police officers in Shepherd's Bush, London in 1966 but they just changed the words. (Authors note – I myself heard things of that nature when I started secondary school in September 1991 the month after Lee had died. Kids at school in the playground used to tell a joke, which went "what's Lee Duffy's favourite comedy? Allo Allo". People in bars in Middlesbrough had even invented "The Duff is dead" cocktails back in 1991)

That's what was happening in Middlesbrough at that time back in August of 1991.

David Allison had no part of anything like that, what happened happened and nothing can change that. I've always found David to be a very private person.

When Lee had died Middlesbrough was in a state of shock. The feeling in the town was like some ridiculously famous celebrity had gone. When Lee had gone I don't know what I felt to be truthful. One or two of Lee's close friends were given a hard time after Lee had died. I was there one night about a week after Lee had died and he wasn't even in the ground, I saw a well-known

179

Middlesbrough man slap Lee Harrison telling him, "where is he to help you now?", because normally Lee's close friends were a protected species. That person who did that just wouldn't have gotten away with that had Lee Duffy still been alive take it from me.

Yes, I liked Lee but I was doing a load of graft with certain people in the town and I knew they were absolutely terrified of Lee, I wasn't glad a man had lost his life and the factual reality is even though I was a drug dealer, Lee Duffy had never done anything apart from scare me a little that time in The Trooper. People might read this and say I was blind to what Lee got up to, well people's stories are all very different in this book. This is my piece on Lee Duffy. This is how I perceived him to be but I dearly hope I haven't offended anyone.

"If you were any kind of threat to Lee Duffy's status as top dog in Middlesbrough then you were getting put to sleep by him at some point, it was as simple as that and it wouldn't even be personal. If you had remotely any kind of name in Teesside then it was in the small print that it was going to happen".

Lee's close associate

CRAZY TIMES WITH BOOTHY

The one person I would have loved to have included in this book was Lee's faithful and maybe just as nutty sidekick Neil Booth. When you meet Neil Booth and spend a bit of time in his company you quickly learn why him and Duffy bounced off each other. I've got to know Neil quite well in the last year and my thoughts on him are, if he's this bonkers at 49, what was he like running about with the Duffer when he was 21 because even now there seems to be very few boundaries with him. It's something that is scary to grasp. Even now, approaching 50, he's still a bit of a "lad".

Neil himself didn't have the best starts in life. He was brought up in children's homes. Neil was a "lone wolf" just like the Duffer was and when the two joined forces they became a pack, like family.

There's no doubt about it that Neil Booth was Lee's most trusted ally in the last two years of his life. Whether they were out pulling birds (and there were a lot), doing deals, taking drugs, fighting, pulling scams, ramraiding shops or just winding people up in general.

I've met Neil several times and I must say I liked him instantly. He has a good energy about him and you quickly realise he's very forthright and someone you can trust.

For all the digging I've done on Duffy and all the people I've spoken with I've never come across anyone that doesn't like Neil Booth in Middlesbrough yet. Although one of his close friends told me about him, "I love Boothy and he's one of my best mates but he's half a doyle." (laughs) I myself really like Neil and he's become someone I count to be in my close circle of friends in the last year but I would have to acknowledge that's a fair assessment of the former original Boro hellraiser.

Even today the women love him but he doesn't seem to want to settle down and would rather go around the world backpacking and getting himself locked up in Thailand for a few months as he did only this year. Neil told me for personal reasons he couldn't have any part in this book the same as his friend Mark Hartley and I've had to respect that. The bits I have found out I've researched from others.

I'm told how they met was from a drugs deal and Boothy just happened to be in the house, well the young Neil saw it was the Duff coming around to talk business so he was about to say I'll leave you to it, but for some reason Lee told Boothy to sit back down and that he was ok to listen. Lee had basically come around to tax the third party but ended up going 50/50 which is not usually a thing that Duffy did. I'm told by the third party who was there that day that the Duffer and Boothy had an instant connection and from that day onwards wouldn't leave each other's sides unless Lee was in jail. In fact, for the last 16 months of Lee's life Lee would go and stay with Boothy whenever he would have a falling out with Lisa. In those 16 months, the only time those two weren't together was when Lee did a couple of weeks on remand in the April of 1991 or when they fell out for four days. That brief falling out happened because Lee nearly accidently shot at Boothy whilst messing about with a loaded gun at the rear of South Bank Football club. Boothy then sulked, as you would when someone could have killed you, and didn't speak with Lee for four days.

If you've met Neil Booth like I have and you knew anything of Lee's personality then you'll understand why those two got on so well. Neil didn't even get his first proper job until he was 28 so that gives you an idea of how bonkers he really was and the things he was up to.

Boothy when he was young would get into anything such as ram raids, stealing safes, jewellery robberies along with his trusted friends Andrew Delve and Mark Sayer (now deceased). I'm told by Neil's close friends around him that he didn't calm down until he was 30 and he lived everyday 100mph just like Lee. The bond those two had was like brothers and I dare say maybe the young Neil who was five years Duffy's junior was probably the only man in the town (barring Terry Dicko and Vince Agar) who could shout back at Lee and live to tell the tale.

What Lee and Neil got up to well only Neil truly knows and right now he feels it's not right for him to speak about it in any books, but I know from speaking with others that what those two did together isn't normally what lads in their twenties usually got up to.

At times when Lee was at war with (Beefy) Kevin O'Keefe, Peter Corner, Shaun "Nippa" Harrison and lifed off double murderer Paul Bryan from Eston young Boothy's life was in danger. Not really because of anything personally that Boothy did, but because nobody could do anything to Duffy without a gun, so there was no better way to hurt Lee Duffy more than hurting one of the people in the world he loved the most, one of those being Neil Booth.

At times when Neil lived with Lee the pair couldn't sleep at the same time. One would get a few hours' sleep on the settee whilst the other watched out the windows in case the house was sprayed with bullets. Their lives really were at that level of craziness, particularly in 1991. At times the pair would stay up for three days going back and forth to Newcastle. One minute everything·was fine and they'd be partying away, the next minute one of them would be cabbaged in the corner and unable to speak from too many ecstasy tablets. Doves were usually the pairs favourite and back in those days E's were E's so I'm told!

If the Duff wasn't in jail then Boothy was by his side, from drinking in The Commercial (where that famous pic of Neil and Lee in the rugby top was taken) to holidaying in the lakes where that photo of Duffy, Boothy and both girlfriends in the jacuzzi was taken.

The most iconic of all Lee Duffy pictures was taken in the Lakes by Neil Booth. The one where you see Lee looking at his most awesome and sat on the blue Ford Escort's bonnet in just trainers and a pair of blue shorts. That snap was taken just six weeks before he died. If you look closely at his left knee in that snap you can see the mark of a bullet wound. The actual photo I used on the back of the first book 'The Whole of the Moon' of Neil Booth, Lee Duffy and Lee Harrison was taken in The Havana doorway in the summer of 1990. The full picture showed Lee in a pair of red Fila boots to go with his shorts but we cropped it to fit the book.

Trouble was never far away when the Duff and Boothy were together and when they left the Boro for Newcastle and then went on to the Lake District to travel over to Blackpool for the weekend they ended up getting into a mass brawl outside Cloud Nightclub on Blackpool seafront. This ended with Boothy getting hit over the head with a hammer and the Duff putting four men away in one go outside the club.

In April 1991 when Lee was on remand it was Neil's 21st birthday party upstairs in The Albion and even though Lee was locked up he made an appearance at Neil's birthday celebrations even if it was only his voice. Lee was allowed to call his best mate from the governor's office in Durham nick at 9pm and it was put on loudspeaker to hear, "now then now then Boothy". Usually you're not allowed out of your cell after 8pm but they made an exception for Lee to do that. Lee was released a week later. The whole of South Bank were there at Boothy's party as well as Lee's full family so everybody was falling about laughing when they heard Lee's unmistakable Teesside twang on loudspeaker.

There were many times when obscenities used to be sprayed all over the A19 and A66 about Lee Duffy and the pair would have to drive, sometimes at 4am in the morning to pull over on the motorway with the car still running and the music blaring so they could cover over it.

Lee was a bit of a maniac when driving he used to drive home at literally 130mph all the way home from Newcastle, sometimes even making joints at the steering wheel. Quite often than not the pair would be pulled by the police when the pair had kilos of blow and guns in the car, anybody else would be searched but when the police officers saw it was Lee Duffy they'd say, "oh I didn't know it was you Lee" and they'd be sent on their way without being questioned.

One of the funniest stories I've heard about the pair has to be the one where young Boothster ended up on top of The Havana roof like King-Kong being chased by all the aeroplanes in the film. What happened was Boothy was in The Havana on Linthorpe Road when he was asked to do someone a favour and to nip round Ramsey's blues to get someone some cannabis, Boothy said yes no bother and got a taxi to Ramsey's which was about half a mile away then back. Back in 1991 it was only £1.20 to get a taxi on the meter so the whole journey shouldn't have come to more than £2 tops, I'm told Boothy was completely off his napper and the taxi driver obviously was trying to take a liberty with Boothy by asking for £8. This resulted in Neil telling the taxi driver to go fuck himself and said he wasn't getting a penny now for being a cheeky cunt then the pair of them exchanged blows. The taxi driver reversed into the alleyway at the rear of The Havana trapping Boothy in the car, only for Boothy to kick the sunroof out. Then he climbed on the roof of the car and onto the wall joining the roof of the club. Now the taxi drivers radioed into every taxi driver in Middlesbrough for backup as well as the police. Neil's climbed up the Havana building like King-Kong and when he was on top of the roof he's then started pulling slates off the roof to throw at the taxi drivers. You don't have to be Einstein to know what happened next! Of course Neil was causing a scene and with scenes come along crowds of nosey people watching. There was that many watching Boothy going 'off it' that people even started buying cheeseburgers from the nearby burger van to throw up to the young rebel in support and chants of "GO ON BOOTHY LAD" could be heard all around Linthorpe Road in the early hours. It didn't take long before the boys in blue turned up, largely because of the owners of the club being not too happy with the state of the roof. After 20 minutes of the police trying to reason with Neil and not getting anywhere, the Middlesbrough police knew exactly what they had to do. They knew he wasn't going to come down for them because every time they used a megaphone to try and talk Neil down, the cops were told to "FUCK OFF". The old Bill knew Boothy was only going to listen to one man because the police had enough intelligence on Lee Duffy to know who his best mates were. It turns out that at that exact time, around 1am, which is when this whole episode was happening, Lee Duffy was only around the corner in Ramsey's blues on Princess Road. The police first went to Vince Agar's looking for Duffy but he directed them to the blues, so the only thing for it was for the police to go find Lee at Ramsey's and tell him the full story of what was happening. To cut a long story short the police did find Duffy and the full situation was explained in detail. Lee, I'm told, when the police found him was in the blues dancing in just a pair of shorts and trainers covered in sweat from dancing so much. As it was a cold Winters night in 1990 the police gave Lee one of their huge illuminous police jackets to put on and they put him in the van and took him to the scene where Boothy was still going bananas and the crowd had now grown.

One man who was there told me that all of a sudden the police van came spinning round the corner with the sirens on then stopped, that was when Duffy jumped out of

187

the back of the wagon shouting "NOW THEN NOW THEN" as if, don't worry the king of Teesside has arrived. Lee Duffy did love a grand entrance so much so that even the DJ's in The Havana used to shout on the mic "LEE DUFFY IS IN THE BUILDING" and whenever Lee was leaving any club it was known that the residence DJ would shout, "LEE DUFFY IS LEAVING THE BUILDING"! Many times you knew that Duffy was in a club without seeing him because all of a sudden it would lose hundreds of customers within minutes. Also if you heard 'The Whole of the Moon' people knew that Duffy was in before they'd even clapped eyes on him.

Going back to the situation with Neil Booth, Lee then walked up so he was standing directly below Boothy and shouted, "WHAT THE FUCK HAVE YOU BEEN DOING?" Boothy stopped throwing tiles for a moment and the pair started talking. An eyewitness who was there told me Boothy's body language changed as soon as he realised it was Lee who'd turned up. After a couple of minutes of them talking Neil Booth agreed to come down. Before Boothy was handed over to the police I'm told Lee grabbed hold of the biggest police officer there and told him "If anything happens to him (Boothy), I'm going to hold you personally responsible and come looking for you." Apparently at that time Middlesbrough police were known, its alleged, for being overly aggressive and known to give one or two a kicking once they'd gotten them in the cells. The end of the matter was Lee gave Neil a kiss and hug before handing him over to the police and off he went to the cells and Lee went back to party. I'm told that Middlesbrough police didn't lay a finger on Neil Booth for the time he remained in their custody suite down at the old Middlesbrough police station on Dunning Road.

Another thing Lee couldn't grasp was that he had to pay for things. It was almost like Lee lived in another era when people would barter for things and people didn't deal with money except he thought everything should be free. He had no concept of money and that you had to pay for things. When Lee did have money in his pocket he was a weekend millionaire and would just waste it and give it away. When him and Boothy were out and about he just stopped paying for things like petrol and he would drive off, or Lee would go into John McGee's designer Menswear shop 'Changes' and they'd get free rig outs before going to The Havana. It really was crazy times for two crazy lads back then.

Lee himself was a bit of a kleptomaniac and would steal anything, from ridiculous things like chocolate bars to big hauls of drugs from hardened criminals. Although Lee was involved in the selling of narcotics (mainly cannabis) I'm told he was useless at it and couldn't run a bath. Yes he was good at braying drug dealers or taxing them but to run it as a business he just couldn't do it.

Lee didn't care what he stole. One man told me that after Lee died he went into a former girlfriend's home and she showed him a load of Lee's belongings she was now treasuring, only they weren't Lee's but belonged to the man who was shown them and Lee had stolen them off him. Things like belts and rings Lee had just stolen over the years. The same source told me that Lee would tell silly lies about anything. He would tell all kind of lies and after every sentence if he was with Neil he would say "didn't he Boothy" and Boothy would have to nod and when he confirmed Lee's lies that would sort of make it ok. Lee Duffy didn't need to lie that was the funny thing. If Lee told people in Teesside that he walked on water they would have believed it.

Lee I'm told believed a lot of his own lies but they were always silly things like telling people they were at a certain place or time, that sort of thing. Lee Duffy wasn't really the type of man who needed to lie about the important things in life because he was a man who talked the talk and most certainly could walk the walk better than anyone else.

The last eight months of Lee Duffy's life really took its toll on him. People like his close friend Jon 'Buster' Atkinson have told me about the first time he was shot outside Ramsey's blues on December 27th, 1990. Lee was inside Ramsey's blues when a man knocked on the door and asked if Lee Duffy was in there, "Joof" who was on the door went looking upstairs and when he found Lee he told him "ya mate wants you outside Lee", when Lee went out he saw the gunman and charged at him but was shot in the knee. It's said the gunman then got in a waiting car on Waverley Street and headed off back to Blyth.

Authors note – The Evening Gazette printed a story with the headline: *"MAN SHOT IN STREET" December 28th.*

"A man is recovering in hospital today after a mystery knee-capping shooting in Cleveland. Victim Lee Duffy 25 is "fairly comfortable" in Middlesbrough General Hospital. The South Bank man was found yesterday in Princess Road, Middlesbrough, with gun wounds to the leg.

Detectives have questioned him at the hospital but are still searching for a motive for the early-morning incident.

"The circumstances of the shooting are still unclear," said Detective Inspector Dave Lumb. "We are treating it as an isolated incident."

Police believe it happened at the junction of Princess Road and Bow Street at about 2.25am.

Mr Duffy underwent an operation on his left knee but is not expected to suffer any permanent injury.

Anyone with information is urged to contact police on Middlesbrough 326326."

One Middlesbrough detective said after he arrested the three Blyth men for attempted murder, "If the chap had been a good shot it would have been murder." Over 70 pellets were removed from Duffy's shattered left knee the same day by surgeons at Middlesbrough General Hospital. Good old Buster (aka car 43) even told me "you could see it in his face he wasn't the same lad, he was living on his nerves".

Only a few days after Lee was shot that first time he was outside the Empire pub on Linthorpe Road and it was the Chinese New Year. At the time over the road from the Empire there used to be a Chinese restaurant and when they let off firecrackers to celebrate Lee dived under a car thinking he was under threat once again. It was no life to live for a twenty-five-year-old Boro lad.

That last year of his life Lee spoke about his death to anyone who'd listen, he knew he'd reached the point of no return and there was no going back.

Lee was a proud Smoggie but it didn't matter where he went because everybody was out to get him. In the last year of his life he spoke about moving away, he had several offers from the Sayers family in Newcastle, having met Stephen Sayers a few times I can see why Lee and Stephen were so close. Stephen's a funny wacky character himself and he loves a night out and has a cracking dark sense of humour. At one-point Brenda even asked his childhood friend Lorna Lancaster if she would put him up in Sheffield but it was never going to happen. He just loved being in Middlesbrough too much. Lee used to say that what he missed the most whilst being incarcerated was that he missed The Havana and he couldn't wait to be back out on the dance floor being the talk of the town once again.

Lee Harrison, Lee's close friend, was always teasing Lee in his letters about how good the club was when he was locked up. He'd tell Lee about the birds he pulled and it would do Lee's head in. Even when Lee was in London for a brief spell the person who he was there with told me he would pine for Teesside like a puppy being taken away from its mother. My source told me he would tell him "for god sake Lee we're in the capital we can get up to all sorts" but it didn't make any difference to Lee. Lee used to say the hairs on his neck stood on end whenever he came back to Middlesbrough and he would clap eyes on the Transporter Bridge.

I've been told by a couple of people that Neil Booth, out of them all, was close to the Duffer more than anyone. One guy I did speak with who had a bit of a rep in Middlesbrough did tell me about the time he had an altercation with Duffy and it was over Neil Booth, although it wasn't quite Boothy's fault. What happened was the man in question was in the toilets and he told me Boothy had asked him a simple question but the man was talking to someone who he hadn't seen for quite a while, Neil asked the man a question and rather than ignore Boothy he simply turned to him and said "two minutes mate I'm busy", with that the man told me he just seen a giant right hand come over from behind Neil Booth and smack him on the jaw. Of course that huge right hand was from the Duffer because he thought this man was being funny with his best pal Boothy and nobody takes a liberty with Boothy whilst the Duff's about. Maybe Lee was out of order or he just got that one wrong but for me it shows the level of protectiveness Lee had over young Boothy.

It's a shame that Neil Booth won't put his side across but I've had to respect his decision. Maybe one day he will and I for one would drop everything I was doing to write his account.

"The people who didn't know Lee Duffy would all move out of the way if they saw him. Them people only knew of his reputation and not the man. Lee would always greet his friends with a loving warm smile".

Terry Dicko

BARNEY FREWIN

Barney Frewin and his wife Ann were the landlords of The Commercial public house from 1988 – 1991. Although this was the scene where Lee had the petrol poured over him by David Tapping it was also the local pub which Lee frequented the most. The Commercial bar was on South Bank High Street just around the corner from the Duffy family home. I spoke with Barney for obvious reasons and I was interested in finding out his thoughts on the man he would go on to know so well.

Barney said: –

I'm 75 years old now and grew up in Skelton just near Saltburn. I took over The Commercial pub, South Bank in 1988 when Lee Duffy was doing his four-year sentence. Before I took over the place everybody was warning me not to take it because I'd have Lee Duffy and others going in causing me all kinds of bother. I'd never met Lee at that point so I wasn't going to listen to gossip and what was said about him until I met him in person, so me and the wife took the place over. Before I saw Lee in the flesh, many of the lads in the pub used to talk about him, several even showed me pictures of him which I thought by looking at him he didn't look that scary because on them he just looked like a big tall skinny youth.

When I finally managed to meet Lee in the flesh in the May of 1990, by god, what a difference in size to the one I'd seen in those pictures for the last couple of years. Lee had obviously been weight training in jail and my first thoughts were that he'd put on about four stone from the lad I'd seen in the photos.

Lee came over and introduced himself very politely and me and the wife took an instant liking to him from day one. Not only Lee, but I also used to get his younger brother in and his parents Brenda and Lawrie Senior. His mam and dad were smashing with me and I never got any bother

194

from them ever. His brother tried to play people a few times, what I mean by that is he used his brother's name like 'buy a pint or I'll tell our Lee' but Lee Duffy himself I never had one bit of bother with in all the times he was in my place. I got him in regularly as well with me being in South Bank. In those days I got them all, Anthony and Peter Hoe, the Venis family and the McAvaney's but Lee was the quietest and most respectful of them all believe it or not. The only time I ever saw Lee Duffy slightly annoyed was when he was sticking up for me. What happened was that I'd had a little bit of bother during the day with Jimmy Douglas mouthing off at me and Lee had got to hear about it. A few days later Lee asked my wife Ann, "what's the matter with your lad he's been quiet for days?", in the end Ann told him what had went on and the same night Lee went to pay Jimmy a visit and told him "anymore bother from you with Barney and I'll knock your head clean off its shoulders". From that day onwards Jimmy Douglas never even looked at me.

When Lee used to come in my pub he'd love to sit with all the old men and play dominoes with them, he was very calm and peaceful.

One night I was in the bar and a flash car pulled up outside and six lads came walking in, "is Lee in?" one of them asked as I was stood at the bar with Davey Birstow, I told him he wasn't and he only comes in on an evening. "Are you Barney?" he asked and I told him I was, then he said, "Lee's told me you're sound so can you give him this?" which was a box all taped up and away they all went. Anyway, Lee came in on the night and I gave him it and told him some gang had left him it this afternoon. Lee then took the parcel and asked me to ring him a taxi to the town which I did and he was off, I thought no more of it. Anyway I got a call from the local firm of taxi's which I'd called for Lee and it said, "do us a favour Barney, don't ring us no more!" I asked him whatever was the matter and he told me, "well that box you gave Lee, he opened it up in my taxi and there was a little handgun inside of it." I told the driver I had no idea and it wasn't my fault but he seemed to be having none of it. He went on to tell me that all the way through the journey Lee was in the back of his cab pulling the empty trigger at his head from behind shouting "BANG BANG YOU'RE DEAD, BANG BANG" like a 7-year old kid playing Cowboys and Indians. Whatever Lee went and did with that in the town I don't know but I never saw that side of him.

My ex-wife Ann got on smashing with Lee and she thought the world of him. The only time she ever had to tell him off was when he was getting over excited doing this Russian dancing on the tables after he'd been shot in the foot and she told him to get down. In fact she shouted at him "OI LEE GET DOWN" and straight away he jumped down shouting "I'm sorry Ann I'm sorry Ann" and she just started laughing at him and he smiled back. Ann found it impossible to ever be mad at Lee.

When I read the other book by Stephen Richards and people were in it saying, "Lee was punching people every other day", well that to me was a different Lee Duffy than the one I knew. I never ever saw anything like that from Lee so I was surprised to read that.

I left the Commercial about a month after Lee had the petrol poured over him and I was out when that happened so I never saw that.

When I heard Lee had died me and my wife were devastated because we thought the world of him. In the couple of years I got to know Lee I can only speak good of him.

"If I have one memory, it's of how much love he had to give".

Brenda Duffy speaking on her son after his death.

LEE DUFFY AT LARGE

In the May of 1990 the whole of England were waiting with eager anticipation for the World Cup Italia 90. The Boro had just been beaten in their first ever trip to Wembley in The Zenith Data System Final due to a free kick from Chelsea's Tony Dorigo, Bernie "The Wolfman" Slaven's name was chanted at the Holgate end of Ayresome Park, Adamski's Killer was the sound to the summer and Jack Hatfields Sports was the main shop in the town of Boro. Also at that exact time the whole of Teesside were bracing themselves for the hurricane that was about to come. Except this wasn't any normal hurricane which was about to hit Middlesbrough, this was the tornado that was Lee Duffy who'd been pacing like a hungry caged lion in Walton prison ready to wreak havoc on his beloved town of Middlesbrough once again. The King was coming home for the final time to take everything in it that he saw as his.

I often refer to Lee Duffy's life as several stages, you all know about the timid mouse who was scared of his own shadow hiding behind Lorna Lancaster like a duckling aged 6-12yrs. Then you've got the tough South Bank kid who had no choice but to toughen up or be beaten up which went from 13 to 17yrs, then you've got the Duffer who worked his way up the ladder knocking out all new comers to build his awesome reputation at 18 – 24yrs and then 25-26yrs was when he took everything to a whole new level, he even surpassed himself and the whole town of the Boro fastened their seatbelts for one final bumpy, gruesome ride, and what a journey that last 16 months of his life was. In that time Lee Duffy was the undisputed ruler of Teesside and there was no higher he could go. He'd reached his Everest and left a trail of broken jaws and stories embedded in Middlesbrough folklore to last several generations.

Lee was released from Walton nick a month short of his 25ᵗʰ birthday and he did not have time to waste, that was when Lee had put his tremendous statue-like physique in tip-top condition over the last 26 months of his incarceration.

When Lee was released I'm told he weighed seventeen and a half stone which is quite incredible considering he'd managed that on a prison diet over two years. Now all the hard work had been done and now he was going to reap the rewards of what he saw as rightly his. Every blues party, hard man, drug dealer, doorman, criminal or anyone with the hint of a name in the North was going to answer to Lee Duffy's call and nobody else's.

When Lee got out he went straight to Ibiza and partied hard, it's not like today where if you finish a big sentence of four years you're not allowed out of the country and even if it was he wouldn't have cared. Lee went and partied hard with his friend Lee Harrison and when he was back he thought, 'right I'm having this town and everything in it' and that's just what he did. Middlesbrough was there for the taking. This was the exact time when he was at his most dangerous and most volatile. He was a celebrity before celebrities were about. I myself personally have sat and looked through the Northern Echo and Evening Gazette archives for hours and have seen just how much Lee used to be in the papers. Even stories where the Middlesbrough paper never named Lee Duffy, everybody in the town knew who it was referring to.

Although I never saw him I'd heard of him and saw his pictures in the papers a lot in 1990/91, I felt like I was sort of familiar with him from all the things I would often hear about him on a weekly basis. In fact around 1991 there was an actor in the Australian soap Home & Away called Tristan Bancks, he played the local bad boy in Summer Bay Peter "Tug" O'Neale and that guy used to be the spit of the Duff (Google it). I would see Lee in the papers and think 'ooh Tugs in the papers again', in my young mind I'd just link Lee to this Home & Away fictional character. On Google it says that "Tug" got his part in Home & Away from 1992 but he was used from early '91 in the show before he got the part as a main character, before anybody points out that the dates are wrong. I actually spoke with Tristan Bancks via Twitter and he even told me that he thought Lee Duffy looked a lot like him.

It's been said that Lee Duffy himself got an acting part featuring as a bouncer briefly in the BBC1 cop series Spender, starring Jimmy Nail. I've sat and watched the episode of series one, episode 5 called 'iced' on YouTube several times and I don't think it's Lee and neither do any of the people I've spoken with. I don't know where the Gazette got that story from but they printed it in February 1993.

Everybody knew of this man named The Duff back in the day, even primary school kids in Berwick Hills like me who still believed in Santa Claus!

Lee Duffy knew when people were afraid of you then you could do exactly what you wanted to and he did just that.

One incident from Lee Duffy's life illustrates his arrogance, during a one on one drugs deal he refused to stump up all the cash and owed the supplier £1,800 and in an effort to pay off part of the debt he robbed a Boro dealer of a pistol and £800 in forged notes. He then tried to fob off the supplier with forged notes. Its things like that which rapidly made Lee a marked man on Teesside and to say he was hated by some was an understatement.

Not only did Lee take his fighting to another level, to quote John Butchworth in our first book "this is when Lee literally went around and kicked the shit out of everyone in the whole town" but also Lee took his drug taking across new boundaries. Lee was well into having crack pipes on a morning and I believe this was the explanation as to why he ended up becoming as bonkers as he did.

Today in 2019 people in Teesside have tried to emulate Lee Duffy's antics and failed. Society today has changed so much that even Lee Duffy wouldn't have been allowed to do the things he did back in 1990 in 2019. There's far more camera's and Middlesbrough council along with Cleveland police haven't tolerated it when others have tried to follow Lee's suit. These people have been pushed right out of town, put on pub watch or house arrest with electronic tags. These days if Lee Duffy was carrying guns then it's a five-year sentence before a ball is kicked, even without any bullets, never mind firing shots through taxi drivers roofs for the craic and shooting holes in the Brambles Farm Hotel ceiling like he did.

If you look at the last 16 months of Lee's life it was literally impossible for him to have even made 30 because normal people just don't do what he did. I asked someone who knew Lee extremely well and he told me something very fitting if you look at Lee's life, he said "he was totally fearless, far more fearless than was necessary and that was what got him killed in the end". When you look back at the overall statistics in 1990/91, I'd say only 50% of the population even had a landline, there wasn't any internet so that makes it truly remarkable that people in Essex/London were talking about some young kid from Middlesbrough! People like Lee you'll only ever read about in books on social history like this one. From May 1990 until August 1991 Middlesbrough had a wild untamed lion on the prowl and he sought out and devoured.

Once as a little boy he was the hunted and targeted, now in the final year of his life he was the hunter and yes, still a target! Lee went to a level of utter craziness that there wasn't a return ticket from, it was only ever going to end one way and it did just that on Marton Road, Middlesbrough. Lee Duffy literally went around the whole of Middlesbrough and kicked the shit out of everybody, then he died. That legacy he cemented in Middlesbrough folklore, the ones your grandkids will talk about in twenty years' time was 80% all made in the last year of his life. In fact all the attempts on Lee's life were all inside the last 8 months of his life, from the first being December 27[th, 1990] to the fatal one being August 25th, 1991, it really is quite incredible. Like Arnold Schwarzenegger who played the indestructible Terminator in the new T2 film which was released only a month before Lee was killed in July 1991, even Arnie dies in the film and as hard as Lee Duffy was, there was no way he was getting out of 1991 alive. Sometimes even Teesside Terminators have to die. Although it's on record that Lee had the three serious attempts on his life there was a further gang of men waiting with baseball bats and that happened on August 11th, 1991, I know from my research and have spoken to the people responsible that there were other attempts waiting in the wings had he turned up at certain places.

Jim Morrison once said "none of us are getting out alive" referring to life in general and in Lee Paul Duffy's case this was so true but prematurely so.

In the final month of his life he knew he was on borrowed time. A lot gets spoken of about regarding the two shootings Lee was victim of and of him being doused in petrol, but for me, another serious attempt on Lee's life as I've just told you above was made only two weeks before he died when he had his skull beaten with a crowbar by a gang of men. These men hadn't come to mess around they'd come to batter Duffy to death but that encounter is seldomly mentioned. Astonishingly in regards to that failed attempt, Lee escaped rather unharmed but I know he "copped a few cracks" which he managed to shake off with ease. It was down to Lee's fitness levels and his South Bank teak toughness that enabled him to do things like that compared to your average man on the street.

As invincible as The Duffer seemed though, even he couldn't prevent his time running out.

"Death is the beginning of immortality".

Maximilien Robespierre

MARK DEBRICK

Mark Debrick is now 57 and grew up on the Hemlington estate of Middlesbrough. Mark and his brother Paul Debrick (sadly passed in August 2007 and author of The Brick) were both very well known in the Middlesbrough area for being "handy lads" and "big bruisers". These days Mark's very much changed his lifestyle from when he lead a very different life which saw him up on kidnap charges and had people plotting to shoot him, at Mark's heaviest he got to over twenty-two stone. Mark told me he didn't mind talking to me about the past as he's now "long out of that game".

Mark told me: –

I first met Lee Duffy when he was around 14 years old in Middlesbrough town centre. Now I used to knock about with a lad called Tony Legg and Tony had a fight with Lee in the town one Saturday morning about 1979. It ended with me and another lad splitting Lee and Tony up. That's how I first met Lee through him fighting one of my mates when he was just a kid. Tony was classed as one of the "kiddie's" in Boro and him and Lee kicked off behind where Binns was (now House of Fraser) on Corporation Road. Lee had a grey Lonsdale top on and was bouncing about like a boxer, to give Tony his due he stood his ground with Lee but that was well before he became what he went on to become.

I used to work for his uncle Rod Jones. I used to run Rod's boarding houses in Hemlington and that's how I would go on to properly know Lee well. I was actually a chef in there for Rod making everyone's food and the young Lee used to come in for his breakfast most mornings. I lived in Hemlington and so did Lee for a couple of years when he went to live with Rod at 12 Faygate Court.

A couple of years later after Lee had been in prison and I got into what I got into well that's when I got to know Lee on a different level once again.

It was only after about 1985 that Lee became the force he did. He was fucking deadly. There's a lot of hard lads in Middlesbrough that never got mentioned but he was what he was. Lee could walk into any pub from 1985 onwards and clear the full pub and I've seen it. Lee put everyone on edge and even though I knew him and had been around him from him being young, you could never trust him not to give you a sly dig.

Although this might sound crazy, Lee wasn't actually a nasty man and I never had any issue with him. Maybe that's because the main thing I dealt in was steroids and he didn't see that as appealing if you like. Whereas my younger brother Paul was into the other things but it never went off with them two. There was always a lot of talk in the town that Duffy and Paul Debrick would eventually come to blows but I can tell you now nothing like that ever happened with Lee and our Paul. In fact, Lee had taken a shine to our Paul in the end before he got killed. Lee regularly used to go in Wickers World just to sit with him when Paul was on the door.

The night Lee broke Peter Wilson's neck I was working there but it was my night off so our Paul was head doorman for the night. If you want me to be truthful it was a bit of a shit trick when Lee did that to Peter. What our Paul told me was that Peter Wilson was at the top of the stairs and Lee had ripped his dicky-bow off him and chucked it down the stairs, then Peter turned away to go get his dicky-bow and Lee smacked him on the back of his neck with a can of Red Stripe lager. It was our Paul who set the deal up afterwards for Lee to pay Peter off with £10,000. (Author's note – I told Mark that the sum of money was only £2,500 which was offered to Peter Wilson and he started to laugh. He said his brother Paul was

206

making money on that deal by adding a few quid more than what was said). It was our Paul who told me that he was going to one of Lee's close friends to set the deal up and I told him I couldn't make it so our Paul must have been fleecing the lot of them.

I say our Paul and Lee never had any trouble but there was almost an altercation between the pair. Paul took the door over at Just Ji's in South Bank as well as Wickers World and one of Lee's ex-girlfriends took a shine to our Paul and Lee had found out. He also found out that our Paul had took over the door which obviously caused a bit of friction. So one night our Paul asked me and a few lads to work on the door this night because he was expecting trouble from Duffy. I can't go into it but also at the time I'd had a bit of trouble with one of Lee's best mates which ended in some yardies shooting my front door off and Lee's mate was behind it all. I got in touch with John Black and he smoothed it out, but this was around the time Lee was just about to get out of prison in May 1990. Our Paul knew that when Duffy got out the first place he was going to turn up was Wickers World door. What we did then was get a little firm of me, our Paul, little Gunnar and another three men who I'd rather not name ready for Duffy to come. We knew it wouldn't be long and as soon as we saw the white Golf go past we all thought here we go. Our kid told us all to get ready and sure enough Lee's mate come round the corner all cocky as if, 'what you gonna do now, I'm with the Duff' but it backfired on him in the end. At that moment all six of us were all tooled up because we all knew what might have happened. We were all prepared for the worst especially when the Duffer comes to your door. I'll never forget Lee came walking from under the bridge behind his gobby mate in a big white sweatshirt on and pair of jeans and his usual swag that the Duffer had and he came up to me and Paul and said, "now then now then lads how ya doing?" then a load of small talk started which isn't what Lee's mate was expecting. Lee then started talking about the old days when I knew him from Hemlington and he gave me a cuddle. Lee's mates face was just a picture because he thought we were all going to war. I know he'd brought Lee there with the intention of blood being shed in the first place.

Not long after that I was in the blues with Tony Walker and I saw Lee lay a lad clean out in there. I don't know what it was over but it was just outside Ramsey's toilets and he chinned him and he went down like a bag of shite, he had some punch on him I'll tell you that now. I think that was Lee just being Lee in the blues. He was a fucking nightmare in there and sometimes it was because he didn't like the look of some people.

Lee should have been a rich man if he'd have put his head together and done things properly. On the other hand whenever I saw Lee he just wanted to party all the time, like literally every day.

Regarding my brother Paul Debrick, I shit myself when he told me he was bringing his book out (The Brick) in 2005 because there were things me and him did which can't ever be told and I thought he was going to put them in. Luckily he left them out but if our Paul had have put them in the book we'd have both been going to jail for a long time. In the book itself, Paul only put a few things in that he'd done. He stayed on the football hooligan side of things. His book overall did brilliantly and sold huge numbers although I've never read it even to this day. The one thing that not many people know about our Paul was that he was a paranoid schizophrenic which is the exact same condition that Ronnie Kray had. He should have had more help with his condition in life than he got.

I'll never forget one day I'd come out of the gym with Brian Cockerill and Paul rang me asking me to go see him at his home. When I asked him why he wouldn't tell me other than he had something to show me when I got there.

Bearing in mind I had our Luke, my son with me who was only four at the time, Paul told me to leave Luke in the car and to go straight round to his back garden. When I got to the back of Paul's house I seen our Paul with his training partner and I saw what can only be described as a man crucified to his back-garden fence with four-inch nails. Paul had told me he'd caught this guy trying to pinch his motorbike. Paul was then punching him and caving his ribs in and I grabbed him and said, "WHAT THE FUCK YOU PLAYING AT PAUL, HE'S GOING INTO SHOCK YOU'LL KILL HIM", and I let the kid go. As I was untying him the kid was shouting, "I didn't know it was your house Debrick", but our Paul would have murdered him had I not turned up. Paul warned the lad not to go to the police before he let him go or that he'd come and find him. Paul has chopped people's fingers off with garden shears when he hasn't been well. At periods of our Pauls life he ruined himself with drugs but when he was clean and wearing all his gold the women used to be obsessed with him. More often than not though our Paul always had to have something in his system. I didn't know he'd got on the crack cocaine and it was only when we were on The Hairy Lemon door when I found out. I said to our Paul, "fucking hell you're losing loads of weight you", but he just told me he'd been dieting. It wasn't until my mate and Middlesbrough doorman Jay Duffy told me, "he's on the fucking pipe Mark" that I knew.

I'm happy to say I got out of all that shit over 20 years ago now and I should have been killed three or four times easy. I've been glassed I've been stabbed and I just woke up one morning and thought I needed to change. I'd been out with Leo Auer (Kev's brother) and we used to get that bad I'd forget where I lived. It was after that day I had a word with myself because I knew I was going to be killed or end up doing a life sentence so I walked away from it all. I packed in drinking and haven't drank booze in over 15 years.

Going back to the Duff he was a lovable character like Terry Dicko and he certainly never did me any harm. I showed respect to him and he showed it back to me and our Paul which was a good thing in those days. To be quite truthful, that story I told you about earlier on Wickers World door in 1990, if it had went the other way he would have been killed because the six of us were all tooled up with hammers and other things. Luckily enough fate decided against it although Lee knew about the rift between me and his best mate at the time. After that night me and Lee were like best mates and never had a crossed word. Years later I made up with Lee's mate who started it all and we used to talk about it saying they were daft stupid days which could have ended up with someone needlessly getting killed. Lee always had my respect and when he died people will always make the worst of people and unfortunately it's happened to him.

There's no getting away from it though back in the 1980s Middlesbrough could quite possibly have been the most violent place in England. Middlesbrough was an evil place and there was so many times looking back I could have ended up being killed. For instance, one Sunday morning I was in a pub called The Newmarket in Parkend which Rudy X from Leeds used to have. The next thing I know some fella's ran in and sprayed the bar with a machine gun and me, Kev Auer, Kev Hawkins and a few others all dived for safety.

The day I heard Lee Duffy had been killed is a day I'll never forget along with everyone else in Middlesbrough. I'd just walked out my flat in Hemlington when I saw a group of chav's in tracksuit and baseball caps and they'd shouted, "HAVE YOU HEARD ABOUT THE DUFFER MARK?" I replied no, then the gang of lads told me he'd been killed and that they'd heard it was Anthony Hoe that had killed him. I ran back in the house and made a few calls and I found out it wasn't Anthony Hoe at all it was Davey Allo. To be honest at that time the town was rife with all kinds of stories on who did it and why it happened which were all untrue. What I do remember is just sitting back on my settee on my own and becoming quite emotional about it. At the end of the day even though he was what he was you don't like to see a friend die in that manner. I haven't made many enemies in my life but I still wouldn't like them to die the way Lee did. Everybody talks about the parties people were having celebrating the death of the Duff but I can tell you now that in Middlesbrough there was a lot of people like me who were gutted. Lee, as I said earlier was a loveable character and now he's a legend and he'll go down in Middlesbrough's history for a long long time. You've got all these kids in Middlesbrough in the last twenty odd years coming up but nobody and I repeat NOBODY will be like Lee Duffy was again. He was a fucking nightmare sometimes but he was a true one off.

One story I'll tell you about Lee Duffy was when he went water-skiing to the Lakes on holiday with my brother Paul, Dale and Ian Henderson-Thynne and another little lad named Robbie who was a boxer. Our Paul told me that all of them walked into this little country pub and got a drink, Lee wanted a game of pool so he went over and put his 20p coin on the table to play next. Well there was four lads all sat in the pool area playing and one of them turned and said to Lee, "ere mate we're on this all night so you're gonna be waiting a while", our Paul said Lee then just knocked the four of them out in the space of literally three seconds like BOOM-BOOM-BOOM-BOOM. Paul told me that was on the first day of the holiday and he couldn't fucking believe it. That's what I mean when I said Lee was a nightmare because things like that used to happen all the time if he was about. I've told you my brother Paul suffered with a mental illness and I think that Lee was the same. For me, I don't think Lee had any kind of guilty conscience if he did something and our Paul was the same. Another thing was Lee had that look in the eyes and I've seen the same in Peter Hoe, Peter used to have a look in his eyes and it was like fucking death. I used to say when I looked into Lee's eyes I could see he was a walking life sentence if he'd have lived. Another thing I found out about Lee was when they did an autopsy on his body they found abnormalities. When doctors had a look at the back of Lee's neck in a part which led to the brain they found it was like an apes. I'll never forget I was talking to a man called Harry who was a paramedic and one who'd tried to save Lee's life and he told me that from his autopsy the Middlesbrough General Hospital team found that the back of his neck in the muscle department was abnormal and the same as a Silverback gorilla and bigger than a normal humans. (Authors note – another factual thing I found out whilst researching Lee Duffy was when his autopsy was done they found that his heart was also abnormal and much larger than it should have been. Maybe that was due to the drugs he was on, only a medical profession will know the answer.)

One thing I'll never forget regarding Lee Duffy was his needle with Scotch Bri (Brian Cockerill) before they became mates. Before Lee and Bri had their scuffle in Redcar there was a fight arranged between Duffy and Cockerill outside of Wickers World. I was stood on the door with little Gunnar and our Paul at the time when Cockerill turned up. Little Gunnar at that time was Brian's best mate and used to train with Brian. How the arranged fight happened was Brian asked Gunnar if it was ok to arrange a fight with him and Duffy at the back of Wickers World and he said yes. Brian then came down at 7.30pm on Tuesday on his own like a raging fucking bull. At the time Brian must have been over twenty-two stone and he was being a complete nutter whilst waiting for Duffy. The next thing that happens, and I'll never forget it was this brown Cavalier car pulled up on the corner outside what used to be Henry's and I could see it was Duffy inside. As soon as Brian saw it was Lee he ran over the road like a screaming lunatic and he hit the back of the fucking car with his arm that hard he actually lifted the front end of the car. As soon as Brian's hit the car its skidded off and fucked off. I don't know who Lee was in the car with but it was definitely Lee inside and they were off. If that was me and I had seen Brian running over the road and hit the car that hard it lifted it I'd have fucked off as well. In fact, I'd have been on a flight to Barbados. Brian then came lumbering back over to where me, little Gunnar and our Paul were stood and he said, "the fucking shithouse... I'll fucking get him." Brian then shook mine and Pauls hand and said, "I'll see you later Debricks" and went on his merry way but that wasn't hearsay because I watched that with my own two eyes.

Brian in his time could really have a do with anyone and I mean ANYONE! One time I was in The Blue Monkey with Stevie Small from Stockton, Jay Pearce and Elvis Thomo and we were all at the bar but Brian was running the door in The Blue Monkey. I could tell there was trouble brewing and Brian was on his own when he came up to me and my friends saying that he wanted a load of lads out who'd been causing trouble. These lads who'd been causing the chew weren't ravers, they were all big blokes, all beer monsters. By the time we'd told Brian we'd assist him he'd gone and he was in the middle of about seven of them knocking them down like skittles. I'll never forget Smally and Elvis looked at me as if to say, just leave him he's doing ok and we just sat there drinking. Elvis Thomo in his time used to have just the most fantastic physique you'd ever seen. God did he used to get the girls, he had the best hairstyle you'd ever seen and he could fight for fun. If

I remember rightly, Elvis and Lee Duffy used to get on very well.

Me and our Paul went to Lee's funeral to pay our respects when he died. My brother himself died in 2007 but what is quite surreal is that our Paul is only maybe seven or eight plots away from Lee in Eston cemetery. As I've said earlier people always thought it was gonna kick off between our Paul and Lee but it never ever happened. I think both had big respect for each other. Both were big strapping lads who ended up in early graves. Like I said I've never ever read our Paul's book but I'm told he doesn't mention Lee Duffy's name once which really surprises me because he knew him so well. What many people don't know was there was plans to make 'The Brick a hooligan's story' published by Milo Books a film! Guy Ritchie, Matt Goss and Nigel Benn had talks about it. I didn't believe him at first when he told me but Paul's author called him when he was on the rig and told him. The next thing Matt Goss rang Paul and told him who he was and our Paul said, "ERE FUCK OFF" and put the phone down. Our Paul thought it was an actual wind up and when his author told him it wasn't and they really wanted to do a film on Paul's life he just couldn't believe it. When Paul got time off from work he was asked to go to Newcastle to pick up some other football hooligan and then go down to London to talk about making 'The Brick movie'. I know the film producers were planning on making Curtis "Cocky" Warren's film at the same time. The most tragic thing is eight days after that call our Paul died so it was never to be. It would have been quite interesting to see what would have come of that wouldn't it?

"He must have been walking about looking over his shoulder all the time. He certainly had a lot of enemies from the drug scene in the Cleveland area. In a way we knew that some form of incident would take place involving serious injuries but we didn't expect it to result in death and Lee Paul Duffy was very unfortunate but he led a life of violence and intimidated a lot of people and unfortunately in this case he received more violence than he dished out".

Detective Chief Inspector Brian Leonard speaking after Lee Duffy's death 1991

TONY SAYERS

Tony Sayers is from Elswick and now 53 years old. Tony is one of the rather large and infamous family members from the Sayers family. Tony told me being the full cousin of John, Stephen and Michael Sayers isn't always easy as sometimes you're judged before people even get to know you. Tony told me that most people in Newcastle know of Newcastle's most well-known crime family and like them, but in the case of Tyneside police's eyes he's a bad guy before a balls been kicked purely through "being a Sayers".

I met Tony when filming 'The Whole of the Moon documentary' and although Tony has always been a "straight goer" involved in the families fruit & veg market business and not been like his older cousins, I couldn't help but notice Tony's distinctive almost Soprano's look with his dark hair slicked back, dark glasses and immaculately dressed all in black. He fitted the part of an Italian mobster. I found him to be very warm, polite and couldn't have been more helpful for this interview. Tony is very familiar with some of the Teesside lot having been friends with Terry Dicko for a number of years. I sat down with the guy with the film star looks and Tony told me all about when he first met The Duffer,

Tony said :-

I first met Lee Duffy through running about with our Michael. It was our Michael who received four years for a fight he had in Bentleys Nightclub and funny enough he was sentenced the same day at court when Duffy received his four-year sentence in March 1988. Up until then Lee had only been familiar with our Stephen and John but both had told our Michael to keep their eyes open for The Duffer because he'd become good pals with them both. Our Michael is a bit crackers and one day he saw Lee being served his dinner in the canteen so he followed him.

Lee had picked his food up and walked back to a table and with that our Michael walked up behind Duffy and slapped him across the back of his head. Lee immediately turned around ready to kill whoever it was who'd just slapped him when he saw our Michael stood there laughing. Straight away Lee's said, "you're Michael Sayers aren't ya?" and they hit it off straight away and became best friends. I can understand having spent so much time in Lee's company why him and our Michael gelled because our Michael's got this crazy sense of humour. Michael and Lee were always playing practical jokes and winding people up.

Michael and Stephen are the double of each other so Lee knew not to lay Michael out when he slapped him on the back of the head. The Newcastle police call Stephen and Michael the Mitchell brothers from Eastenders because they say they look like Phil (Steve McFadden) and Grant (Ross Kemp). In 1989 also our John got his 15-year sentence and was in and out of jail most of his life so that's where our John came across The Duffer also.

Our Michael got out before Lee in 1990 because of Lee's extra time he was given for fighting with the screws, Lee assaulted a prison officer and did an extra few months if my memory serves me correctly. When the time came for the Duff to get out in May 1990 it was our Stephen who sent me and our Michael down to Teesside with £1500 to give him. I'd never heard of Lee Duffy before because he'd always been in the nick. I'd heard of Brian Cockerill though and of course Viv Graham because he was from my manor but not Lee Duffy, although I was to quickly learn all about him. Boy you don't forget Lee if you'd ever come across him I can promise you.

The day Lee came out me and our Michael were in our Stephen's little flat in the West End of Newcastle. He asked us both to do him a favour and go down to Boro and give Lee this "starter" which had money in it. Me and our Michael went down to meet Lee in a boozer called The

Brambles Farm Hotel and had a craic with him whilst we all had a couple of halves of lager with a few spliffs in the bar. The pub was empty because it was during the day, apart from one incident when three big fella's all rowdy came bursting in. Straight away Lee's stood up and told the three to get back out because he was talking, funny enough the three fella's walked back out and even said, "sorry Lee". Another one or two tried to come in but Lee chased them as well which made me think, 'who's this geezer here does he own the town or something?' We sat in the Brambles Farm for a good few hours just on our own then Lee took us to a nightclub opposite the Middlesbrough Town Hall called Blaises. As we were walking in I noticed a horde of doormen, which I found strange because it was such a small nightclub. I'm not kidding you there must have been double figures in bouncers. I noticed Lee talking to a few as he pulled them to one side, when I asked Lee what was up he told me, "nothing I've just had a chat with them", but it turned out that three of them sacked themselves that night and left the premises. I think, when I look back that the reason there were so many doorman was because Lee had just got out that very day and they must have been getting ready for his return to the town.

Me, our Michael and Lee spent the night in Blaises and before the night ended one of Lee's close friends Craig Howard turned up and give us all a lift back to his for a smoke. It wasn't just a smoke there was cocaine out and Lee wasn't even using lines he was just putting it on the table in a pile and sniffing it in huge amounts like you see Al Pacino do in the movie Scarface. I was looking at our Michael and Craig thinking how the fucks he still alive! Anyway, it all finally caught up with Lee because he took "a whitie" and he went to throw up in the toilets. He was hyperventilating at one point. After he'd been sick he managed to pull himself back around and he was alright and back with us laughing about it. When I was sat in Craig Howards house in Eston I was looking at Lee dancing about with his music blasting. I'd only just met him that very same day but I felt like I'd known him twenty years. Another thing about him I remember was he was one big fucking man you know in the flesh! Lee just reminded me of Ivan Drago (Dolph Lundgren) from Rocky 4 as he had his hair spiked exactly the same. I remember thinking at the time how much of a fresh face Lee had and there wasn't an ounce of fat on him.

I came down a few times and met all of Lee's close friends like Lee Harrison and Boothy and we'd go drinking in The Commercial in South Bank. People often ask me when I'm in Newcastle what was Duffy really like and I just say he was a lovely lad. I never felt threatened around him, even times when we'd had a few joints and a few pints and I'd put my head on his shoulder or he'd have his on mine and we'd just sit and talk a complete load of shite to each other. I'm not going to lie to you though I have seen Lee being that way. One particular memory I have of Lee was when I was in line waiting for a payphone with him and a lad was being cheeky with him. Lee didn't knock him out like he could have done but he slapped the guy ridiculously fast for his lip then said, "You've just met the Duffer". It was our Stephen that christened him The Duffer you know and it stuck.

When Lee was laid in his coffin at 6, Durham Road in Eston I did go in to see him before they buried him. Me and my uncle John went to see his mother Brenda before and I gave her a cuddle and told her how sorry I was. I'm not just saying this but it was the most emotional day I've ever known in my life. The only funeral I've ever seen bigger than that was on YouTube when you watch Ronnie Kray's.

His face was all bruised and it was just heart breaking to see such a young vibrant lad at only 26 years old laid there like that. Our Stephen was one of the six pallbearers that day who carried Lee's coffin.

Two 56-seater coaches that were full and several cars came from The Bay Horse Inn in Newcastle to pay their respects to Lee. It wasn't only from the Bay Horse they came, it was from a few pubs which are still there today. It was when Lee was on his toes that he came to stay in Newcastle with John Brooks who was also very close to Lee so he wasn't only close to our family in Newcastle there was a load of Geordies who loved Lee for just being Lee.

Where I live now in the West End of Newcastle The Bay Horse Inn was at the top of my street but its long gone now. These days it's a motorbike shop. Another pub that Lee used to use around here was the Dodgers Arms which got burnt down in the riots. The Balmoral pub was another he regularly frequented but it's now a Best Western Hotel. The Mill Inn was another Lee was always in because our Stephen used to run it. Then there's the Bigg Market which is where Lee came up on his own looking for Viv Graham. Before it all started with Lee knocking Viv's doormen out I knew it was about to "go off" because our Stephen phoned me up and told me Lee was in town hunting him. Lee didn't need any backup but I know a few of the boys who I'd rather not name were there to keep an eye on Lee. These lads were more "pirates" or "proper cut throats" so I'll give that one a miss. I told our Stephen I'd just had my twins being born so I kept away as I didn't want the bother. To cut a long story short on the night Lee went and biffed three doormen in one place then straight away went and put another two away on another door literally twenty minutes later. I can assure you that with Lee doing things like that on his own, news like that travelled fast around the city centre. All that chaos was caused by Lee on one drunken night and if I remember right it was a Sunday.

I don't think Viv was scared but he definitely didn't want anything to do with Duffy. Viv was a proper businessman and he was happy getting what he was getting. Viv Graham represented good and in his era it was forbidden to smoke a joint in a bar. Many times lads would smoke joints in Newcastle and when the landlords told them to pack it in they'd be told to "fuck off" and they couldn't do anything. That was when Viv Graham came into play and the landlord would go to see Viv and say, right I've got these right radgies in my bar' and Viv would put a stop to it for maybe £50 or £100 a week depending what their takings were. I know that Viv had so many boozers he was looking after in the East End of Newcastle and he ruled them all. Not so much the West End mind, that was nicknamed "The Wild West" for obvious reasons. To be honest Viv couldn't come into the West End and start taming it like everywhere else because it was just full of "pirates" and "cut throats" who'd think nothing of glassing you or stabbing you. Viv knew it as well and that's where the conflict came from with Viv and anyone from the West End. The attitude of most West Enders was Viv was, "a grass who works with bizzies", and that's where the bad blood started. I personally think there was an element of truth in those accusations. I myself was turned away by Viv's crew one night and when I asked what for, they said, "You're Westenders". I wasn't having it as I didn't think I'd done anything wrong so I told them to go get Viv. Viv came down and I asked him what the craic was, then he just came out with "you're from the Westend" and as he said that I could see his face getting a bit red as if he was about to lose his temper. Then he told me that everyone in the Westend calls him "a copper" and I wasn't getting in. I told Viv that I hadn't called him anything because I hadn't. Viv just shrugged his shoulders and said maybe so, but then told me if he let one West Ender in he'd have to let them all in so I couldn't come in.

I'd say the difference between Duffy and Graham was that Lee was anti-establishment and he hated any kind of authority. I think in Lee's mind it was just because they were there and he loved a challenge. Lee Duffy enjoyed being the rebel. A lot of the time Lee would say things to me like, "do you think I could do him" and so on, that's what Duffy was like. Lee was a thorn in Cleveland police's side whereas Viv was a rose only helping them if you like. Viv more or less did their job for them and in all honestly he wasn't like Duffy because he hated any kind of drugs. That was the difference and I knew them both very well.

The one thing about Duffy though was he had a wicked sense of humour. Whenever him and Lee Harrison or Boothy got together they would just bounce off each other and end up doing crazy things.

You could tell Lee Duffy was recovering after he'd been shot as often the people in Middlesbrough would see Lee being driven around in Lee Harrisons white Golf GTI with the music blasting and the roof down shouting, "THE DUFF IS BACK".

At the end of 1990 my Mrs had twin boys and Lee's girlfriend Lisa at the time wasn't far off expecting their baby. I think she was born only a couple of months after my lads. One day I was sat outside the Bay Horse Inn with my lads in the double buggy and Lee came over and picked both my lads up and was telling me all about his baby daughter who's just been born. It was quite funny watching someone as big, hard and full of tattoos as Lee was cooing over these little babies. It was only about a week or so after that Lee was killed.

I'll never forget I had a phone call off our Stephen telling me that Lee had been murdered and I was inconsolable for hours. What's bizarre is that particular night Lee died I should have been with him. The night Lee died there was a load of Newcastle lads out with him like

Tom Brayson and other roughtie-toughty Elswick lads who were all pirates.

Today in 2019 Lee's still spoken of so much up here in Tyneside. All the time in fact among our family. Over the years I've often heard members of my family saying, "ooh he was the size of the Duff", almost like a ruler to measure someone by. Lee never suffered a fool mind. If someone was in our company and they was just poncing drinks all day he wouldn't tolerate that.

"Anyone can stop a man's life, but no one his death a thousand doors open on to it".

Phoenissae

RAY MORTON

Now, retired Detective Sergeant Ray Morton is a name I never ever thought I'd get to put in this book. I spoke with two retired former top Cleveland police officers last year for 'The Whole of the Moon' book and both declined to speak with me in regards to chapters although both gave me certain bits of information to use if I wanted to.

Ray spent time hunting Duffy down and it was actually Ray and others who put together the case report for David Allison's trial at Teesside Crown Court.

Ray is originally from Jarrow, Tyneside and is now 65 years old. Ray's been retired from being a top rank Detective nine years now but remembers Lee Duffy very well.

I met up with Ray one morning in Billingham for a coffee and this is what he told me.

Ray said :–

I originally qualified as a PE teacher and was working at a school in Peterlee before I joined the police force. A few of my mates at the time had joined Northumbria police and that's what gave me the idea I suppose. It was a big decision for me to join the police but after three years at university, five years teaching P.E and after training at RAF Dishforth I was stationed at Billingham in 1980.

Within three years of joining the force I had worked my way up and landed a detective's job in Stockton. I was doing that for six years until I was promoted within the C.I.D at 35 years old to Detective Sergeant and moved to Middlesbrough CID in 1989.

It was very soon after being moved to Middlesbrough that Lee's name was becoming extremely predominant within the station.

I started working on the Lee Duffy cases after the Dr David Birkett murder case which I'd been on. A lot of cases at that time seemed to lead back to Duffy.

The things I'd heard from my colleagues about Lee before I met him was that he was a hardman who was involved with, what is loosely called, 'organised crime'. I think he was looked up to by a lot of people in Middlesbrough. Lee was usually somewhere in the background when it came to crime in Teesside in 1990/91.

Back when I was a Detective Sergeant I was ridiculously busy when it came to locking 'bad guys' up. I always used to say in the 90s, when I was acting head of the drug squad, that Middlesbrough was the busiest place for crime compared to what some of my friends on the force in the Yorkshire, Durham, Northumbria and Tyneside areas were dealing with. Their forces weren't anywhere near as busy as my unit for general crime. I know a few of my senior managers didn't like that being said because it was a bad reflection on them but it was very true. In those days police intelligence was dealt with in Middlesbrough and it wasn't as it is now, now it's all done away from the area.

From the summer of 1990 it was obvious to us that there was a hell of a lot of incidents going on that pointed back to Lee Duffy. I don't think anyone on our police force could get a grip of what Duffy's effect was on the numbers. I'd say it took quite a bit of time for the intelligence to get the full picture of what he was about. At that point in time an incident in South Bank might not be linked to an incident in Middlesbrough because it was a different police division, the force intelligence worked to bring things together between forces. These days it's very different and everything's linked nationwide but back then it wasn't. So, Lee could break someone's jaw in one area and it technically wouldn't get linked to something else going on a few miles away because we were different divisions and forces.

When I eventually got involved with Lee Duffy I would say the amount of violence he was linked to was of a great concern to our team. One of the greatest struggles we had as a team was knowing that Duffy was involved in an incident but not having tangible evidence that he was involved. Things have come a long way since the early 90s.

In 1990/91 I would say that Duffy went through a period in his life where he was just a loose cannon. He was still getting his hands dirty regarding the crimes he was committing when he didn't need to, he had enough power by that time to have someone do it all for him if he had wanted that. In my opinion though, he just couldn't stop himself, it was part of who he was. That was Duffy's biggest mistake and we knew sooner or later it was going to catch up with him and of course it did.

I was part of a small team led by an experienced D.I. who was given the task of tracking down the people responsible for the second shooting of Lee at a wedding boutique shop on Hartington Road in Middlesbrough town centre. The next day I went to see Lee in his hospital bed in the old Middlesbrough General Hospital but he didn't want to know, he wasn't interested in the slightest. I told Lee that he was very lucky to be alive but his reaction was to tell me he wasn't going to give a statement and he didn't want to know. Lee told me that if we caught up with them then good luck to us but that he wasn't supporting us with any method of prosecution. I told Lee that because of the serious nature of the crime we had a duty to investigate the incident even without him. I also told Lee that this wasn't a warning, they'd come from Aston in Birmingham to murder him.

When me and the team went down to Birmingham to arrest the culprits it was a full firearms team job to arrest them because they were considered to be that dangerous. The team I was part of led the chase by busting them in the early hours but stayed behind the gun team for safety. The men, who had been linked with several armed robberies, were extremely dangerous and the West Midlands Police would only go and arrest them if the professionally trained firearms team was present. When we brought them back to Teesside one of them got put on remand in Durham prison because he was already wanted for the robbery of a hotel in Birmingham.

The people who were there who witnessed the shooting just wouldn't speak to us about what they saw. It would be a lie if I told you it was an easy task but me and the team slowly put together what had happened.

It brought it home to me when I was in Birmingham just how dangerous a life Lee Duffy was living at that time.

The stories that Cleveland police wanted Lee Duffy dead and just stuck him outside with a target on his head are ludicrous. The police had done their job by putting him before the courts. If Lee then got bail that wasn't the police's fault. What the courts do is up to them. It was frustrating for us that Duffy kept getting out and kept being given bail. At the end of the day at that time we had this person going around the Middlesbrough area intimidating everyone. Now it was our responsibility to get him off the streets.

Every single time I ever saw Lee Duffy was crime related until the unfortunate day I saw him lying in the mortuary.

My main investigations regarding Duffy was the Hartington Road shooting and when I investigated his murder. I can tell you what was true and wasn't just hearsay, we always kept a close eye on Lee Duffy before he died. I know before he died Lee was taken off the local C.I.D, which is what we were, he was being monitored by the regional crime squad instead. Dealing with Duffy, towards the end of his life had been taken up the chain by command and what the next steps would be to deal with him was no longer a decision for local C.I.D, in the eyes of Cleveland Police, he had reached the big time.

On August the 25th it was a warm Sunday morning and I know exactly where I was when I got the call saying that Lee Duffy had just been murdered. I would say I got the call to go down to the station ASAP at maybe 4.30 – 5.00am. That day I was on Detective Sergeant cover and I still remember to this day that feeling of just thinking, 'WOOOOW' as I sat up in my bed still half asleep. I then turned to my wife and said, "Lee Duffy's just been killed." Although she had never met Duffy she felt like she knew him because of my involvement in dealing with his fall out for so long. My wife knew the reason I went to Birmingham for 3-4 days was because of Lee Duffy. I think even she was in a state of shock to tell you the truth. This was the biggest thing to happen during my career up to that date and I was in a daze.

You're reading my side of the story 28 years on but what I've yet to get across to you, without dramatising it, is that this guy, Lee Paul Duffy, was a real problem for us as police generally.

I got myself ready then I then got down to the old Middlesbrough police station on Dunning Street and it was my Detective Inspector John Kelly who'd briefed us all at 6am and told us that on the front of the Afro-Caribbean centre on Marton Road was now a murder scene and it had all been cordoned off with police tape for the forensics. A few of us Middlesbrough CID who'd dealt with Duffy in the past and had knowledge of Lee were told what we needed to do and how to do it. At that point I was only Detective Sergeant so I wasn't a senior officer but I was made head of a small team none the less so, there was a hell of a lot of pressure put on me.

One of the last but very important jobs for me that morning was to secure Lee's body at the hospital morgue which is what was done. It was difficult talking to eyewitnesses because of course they had been at an illegal bar, most of them taking illegal substances and they were still under the effects of whatever it was they had taken. That very morning it was my job to go down to the hospital for the post-mortem on Lee and to interview the medical experts. Sat here now in 2019 when I look back my biggest memories coming back to me are of seeing Lee laid on the hospital morgue table. He had nothing at all on, only something like a towel which kept his dignity intact. When I was looking at this young lad on the table I thought of all the times I'd interviewed him, now he was laid there naked and had probably been dead at that point for 7-8 hours. Another thing I remember when I was looking at Lee that morning was that he was a big man and I mean one really big man, tattoos and broad shoulders. Apart from the injury under his arm there was no other injuries that I could see. Lee looked like he didn't have a mark on him, certainly facial-wise. There were a couple of stab wounds on his leg and hip which were covered by his towel and the one to his back of course I couldn't see because he was laid on his back. When I looked at Lee's lifeless body that morning what came over to me was that although Lee had been killed, he wasn't involved in much of a fist fight. After interviewing the pathologist that morning, whose job it was to look closely at the injuries, we got an account from him and I'll never forget the words he said to me that morning, he said, "he's been dead unlucky you know", and then I asked him in what way and he told me, "because of the injury he had if he'd have stood still and held his left arm close to his left side, he would have still been alive!" He said that all Lee had to do was stand still and by the time the ambulance had got there he wouldn't have lost a great deal of blood. What was fatal for Lee was that he ran off down Marton Road screaming frantically.

The next day the car that Lee was put in was classed as a crime scene also and we had to go out to find it and bring it in for the forensic team to go over. When we made the file for the case to go to the Crown the file said that the pathologist said this man should still be alive today. I always thought that was going to be hard for the Duffy family to hear, because in that report it said that in some ways Lee Duffy had almost caused his own death by running. He should have stood still but as you can imagine Lee was never the type to stand still and he'd have been after getting back at David Allison.

Around eight hours after Lee's death we quickly identified three suspects who we had down for possibly killing Lee and teams were sent out to bring the chief suspects in . An hour later David Allison handed himself in for the murder of Lee Paul Duffy which was good news for us because it meant that we didn't need to work at 100mph anymore. Once you've got someone in police custody you can then slow things down a bit. After we got Allison into our station the next thing we went on to do was try to find eyewitnesses again but in my opinion this was never going to happen because a lot of them wouldn't talk to police in Middlesbrough anyway as its seen as, "grassing."

One big breakthrough we had was when we found the three-and-a-half-inch lock knife which was used to stab Lee, we recovered that, it was stuck down a drain on Grange Road in the town and that was exhibit A used in the trial. I can still see the knife now in my mind with its 3 ½ inch blade. From finding the deadly weapon we quickly established next that it was Lee King who provided the knife. You could say that without Lee King, Lee Duffy wouldn't have died that night. People will always say that he would have died prematurely anyway somewhere down the line but those were the facts that we found out on that fatal morning of August 25th in 1991.

We found out that it was David Allison that stabbed Lee Duffy in a moment of fear. It wasn't as if he was hanging around with a knife somewhere waiting for Lee.

As I've said earlier we put that trial together to be presented to the Crown Court in February 1993. I was at court for every one of the eight days it lasted. I don't think Middlesbrough has seen such a hugely media-based trial before or since. Regarding the actual trial itself my memories were that I was absolutely astounded that David Allison got a NOT GUILTY verdict. ASTOUNDED. The team thought the least he would have been found guilty of was Manslaughter to be honest. Allison was saying self-defence but how had he ended up with a knife if it was self-defence? I know his brief was 50/50 as to whether they were going to play the manslaughter card or not. Us as a police force would have been happy with a manslaughter charge, not murder but manslaughter. Me and my team would have accepted the manslaughter tag on David Allison.

I can remember me and Brian Leonard (who was the senior investigating officer) talking about it, wanting David Allison to face a manslaughter charge and not the murder charge which is what he faced but David and his legal team headed by Jimmy Watson were offered the manslaughter charge but refused. David took a risk by turning it down and he ended up being faced with a murder charge which potentially brought with it a life sentence if he was found guilty. I'm telling you before that not guilty verdict came back it was completely hanging in the balance and could have gone either way. Allison must have been sitting in the dock thinking, hang on a minute, I could get found guilty of murder here! If David was found guilty he'd have been looking at 15-20 year easy. If he'd have been sent down for manslaughter it would have been maybe 2-4 years but of course he refused to even entertain the thought of it which was a very brave and bold move indeed on the chess board and one that could have quite easily ended in disaster. Out of the people who were in the dock that day David Allison, Lee King and Richy

Neal, the only person who was found guilty and did 18 months was Richy Neal for perverting the course of justice.

When it had all finished I was astounded for days, if not weeks that it had all ended the way it had. Lee's death was an end of an era for many people in Teesside. Lee was a major problem to us police, he was a nightmare to the other criminals and drug dealers in the area and it had all ended so quickly which was bizarre.

Without dramatising it, Lee was the No.1 criminal in that era. I stand by everything I said about Lee Duffy back in the early 90s.

During the last 16 months of his life us police had over 90 separate complaints about Lee Duffy. Some of them were serious and others minor, but if that's not a one-man crimewave I don't know what is! The way Lee Duffy was he was never going to last forever. He'd got past the point of no return.

After Lee's death I went and spent three years in the National Criminal Intelligence Service which was looking at major criminals in the North-East and countrywide. Later on in 2003 I ended up as Chief Inspector of the Regional Drugs Intelligence Unit, that covered all North East forces, and I can say quite confidently that there wasn't anybody I met who caused us as many problems as that one-man Lee Duffy did just on his own. In my thirty years on the police force Lee Duffy was the most profound criminal I ever met. I can say that nobody of Lee Duffy's magnitude came in the ten years after he died either.

Regarding Lee's funeral, I didn't go, the police wanted to be respectful by not putting too many officers there so Brian Leonard attended to make sure it went smoothly because we thought it may have ended up in chaos.

I did have quite a bit to do with his Mam Brenda through the liaison work I did with her and his girlfriend. When the trial and liaison was over it was time to move on and start hunting other bad guys to arrest and bring before the courts.

It's been such a long time ago since Lee Duffy died. Today in 2019 policing has moved on locally and nationally in a more sophisticated manner. Back in Lee's day what worked for him was brute force and you wouldn't have been allowed to have done what he did back then today. Even moving on just a short time to 1995 four years later things were so much better with D.N.A technology and other things.

Even when I moved on to monitoring the big boys in 1993, although much cuter there was nobody like him.

Lee was a bad guy but he was respectful in the manner that he didn't give me any grief. Yes he wouldn't answer questions and I understood the reasons why but he was never ever aggressive to our team. He knew what I had to do and he knew why I had to do it. I would say it was a shock that Lee was the way he was because we'd all heard about this animal of a man who looked the way he did but he certainly wasn't ever on my case like some of the criminals I've had to endure. In many ways Lee Duffy was old school like when you see all these old villain characters from the East End who live by this strong code and never break it, especially by talking to the police. Even when I was trying to help him by catching the culprits who'd just shot him, only hours later he still had these old school morals and wouldn't talk.

"We are pleased to have brought this episode to a conclusion. Hopefully everything will now return to normal. I don't think Middlesbrough will see the likes of Lee Duffy again for a very long time".

Detective Chief Inspector Brian Leonard speaking after David Allison's not guilty verdict.

STEVE WRAITH

Where do I start with Newcastle's Steve Wraith for a title? Doormen, Actor, Author, Filmmaker, Boxing manager, BBBofC promotor and probably several other things I've missed out that Steve's been involved in over the years.

I first came across Steve in a Channel Five three-part documentary called 'An Empire Behind Bars' which was about his close involvement with Ronnie and Reggie Kray. Steve first became intrigued with their story as a 10-year-old boy after having seen both middle-aged men on the news when they were on day release from prison to attend the funeral of their mother Violet Kray in 1982. Steve told me he can still remember sitting with his mam and dad having his tea and this two "oldish" geezers got out of that green prison van and Steve's parents were saying to each other, "eeh I remember when those two were about" and "haven't they aged" etc...

Steve has gone on to become involved in all kinds of true crime projects and has done very well from it but Steve told me it was that day in 1982 that sparked his interest and he knew what a gangster looked like. Fast forward five years to when Steve was 15 and about to take his exams, Steve realised he didn't have the best education and in his own words was, "two years behind everybody else" so Steve's parents took him out and put him into private school. It was then Steve's teacher told him that if he wanted to improve his English then he should read a lot about something that he was interested in and use it to work on his coursework so Steve chose the 1972 cult classic book 'Profession of Violence' written by John Pearson which Steve bought from Newcastle's Quayside market for only 15p and the rest is history.

Steve passed all his exams with flying colours and has been involved with many projects such as books about Freddie Foreman, Paul Ferris, The Kray Twins, Stephen

Sayers and Charles Bronson among several others. The book I wrote before this one was 'Roy Shaw – Mean Machine', which told the story of the infamous legendary East End hardman. As I'm writing this Hereford Films are making the film on Roy Shaw and Steve is also technical director on that movie so there's not much in the British crime world that goes on without Steve's involvement.

Predominately the reason I included Steve in this book was because he's a Geordie, a former Newcastle bouncer and Stephen Sayers PR manager. I wanted a Geordies view on what it was like in Newcastle when a lad from Boro went into one of the biggest cities in Britain looking for their hardest fighter in just a pair of shorts.

Steve told me:-

I'm 47 years old now and I grew up in Felling, Newcastle. I used to work on the doors, mostly down the Quayside which was an all-night rave that used to go on until 4am. You see things and pick things up quite quickly working the doors, you had to! I also worked in Ibiza and in London for over 18 years.

From working the Quayside I was then asked by Billy Robinson to work with his son Jamie and another well-known doorman in the city named Hassan to work in Red Skins and that's when I started to hear the stories about Lee Duffy. Working for Billy Robinson was a great way to be introduced to door work but you quickly learnt that you had to be able to cope with the demands that are put on you, like having all kinds of situations put on you that you would have to make split decisions about. Some situations could literally be a matter of life or death. When you work on the door you're told who to watch for regarding who would be more likely to be trying to bring weapons into the club or who would more often than not have drugs on them. You'd be forewarned on who was who or who had connections with what family and so on. These names then became faces when they'd then turn up at your door.

The stories of Lee Duffy turning up in Newcastle would often be told. The stories of this big man going round knocking all Viv's doormen out have been imbedded into Tyneside folklore too like tales of Robin Hood if you like. Lee Duffy became a bit of a legend for his antics when he used to visit Newcastle.

I know from people who were there that Lee went into a bar which used to be called Macey's and he flattened several of Viv's bouncers. When I talk to Stephen Sayers he tells me it was between eight and ten, others who were there have said it was only five. What I will say is that club in the early 90s was the busiest in Newcastle and I never saw it with less than four doormen on the front door and four inside because it was a two-level bar. At that time in Newcastle to be a bouncer on Macey's you had to be some of the   hardest of door staff anywhere in the city possibly even the country as it was all about steroids back then. All the door staff on Macey's were like something you'd see on the World's Strongest Man programmes and were complete colossal units. The ones I know who Lee chinned were like 19 stone and bench pressing like 400lbs plus so for   Lee to have done what he did to those doormen was crazy but it was all very true. Even if it wasn't eight doormen but four that is still some good going when you take into account just how big these men were. Before Lee left a trail of bodies on the floor I was told he said, "go tell Viv you've just met The Duffer". That was a hell of a statement for anybody to make.

When I started doing the doors in the early nighties Viv Graham was at the peak of his powers if you like, it was around 18 months before Viv was murdered. Not many people know this but it was Middlesbrough that was the first place to put licensed doormen on their foyers and Newcastle quickly followed in the late 1990's.

I've been involved in true crime all my adult life and now the Lee Duffy story has catapulted in the last year because of Jamie Boyle's book. People enjoy reading about people like Lee. The true crime bookshelves are full of people like Lee Duffy although I don't think I've heard of anyone who caused as much mayhem as he did and died so so young.

Twenty years ago London had the monopoly on these kind of characters like Lenny McLean, Roy Shaw and Charlie Richardson, they were all from down South. Books by those type of characters were a big thing in the early millennium because I know a lot of these names were pestering their publishers to keep their names alive with all these books and the publishers knew it was an easy way to make money. That era of true crime books has died now with Amazon selling books for 99p so it's very hard for writers to make a living off it these days like you once could.

Even though Lee Duffy's been dead for so long they hasn't really been a lot on him until Jamie Boyle came along and now the public's appetite, especially in the north hasn't diminished and people more than ever want to read about this young kid from Middlesbrough. There's been previous books which have touched on Lee which haven't done him justice until now in 2019.

I said in 'The Whole of the Moon' documentary that I realised how important Lee Duffy's story was to Middlesbrough when we started getting ridiculous amounts of orders from Middlesbrough Waterstones for Stephen Sayers book Tried and Tested. It wasn't only one order it went on for some time and I believe that was purely because of Lee's involvement in the book.

I have been asked by people who knew Lee on several occasions over the years to write a book on Lee Duffy but I just didn't feel it was right for me to do one having not known the area. It's the same with Ernie Bewick from Sunderland who's a massive name but it's not where I'm from.

It looks like Stephen Sayers' book 'Tried and Tested' is going to be the subject of a film. At the moment it's at the planning stages and that's everybody's goal because when you write books you do it with one eye on getting it dramatized, as an author that's your goal.

These days I'm multi-tasking as I'm also an actor and a producer, so I'm on both sides of the camera now.

When the Stephen Sayers film happens I can tell you now that Lee Duffy will be featured in it because Stephen will be involved in writing the script. Me and Stephen have spoken about it actually and I think we both know the scene we'll be pushing for with Lee Duffy when it happens. Lee Duffy's life is a tragic one there's no doubt though.

When we were filming in Middlesbrough at the locations for the documentary and I walked the streets where he walked for the first time, seeing where he was killed and also being at his grave it was all quite emotional. The thing that always amazes me with the Lee Duffy story was that he was just so young and now it's been 28 years since he died it almost makes Lee Duffy seem older but he wasn't. He was actually only 26 which is no age at all. He was a man who had so much potential. Lee certainly knew how to use his hands and as a professional boxing promotor myself it's a crying shame that he never went on to become a proper contender as he was quick and powerful you know but that wasn't the path which was laid out for him.

Lee was loved on Tyneside and from what I've been told by the people who knew him best in Newcastle was that he was very genuine. Up here he associated with all the "right people" i.e. the Sayers family. Lee was involved with the Sayers when they were on the up and coming into prominence in the city. All the Sayers love a night out and Lee was the same. All liked the high life and lived on the edge. Lee and the Sayers came from the same type of background so birds of a feather flock together is a fitting way to describe their friendship.

Geordies and Smoggies always get on whereas as a whole we can't usually abide the Mackems.

If you'd like to get in touch with Steve about any of his projects you can follow him via Twitter @stevewraith

"London normally gets all the glamour in the criminal world, if there is such a thing, but the further up North you go, the harder the men are".

Dave Courtney

STEWART LEE

Stewart Lee is now 55 years of age and is from Durham. Back through the 1980s Stewart ended up doing several big sentences in Durham Jail for firearms and robbery offences. Stewart told me he's not proud of it but he's travelled through the prison system that long that he has spent nearly 18 years of his life locked up.

Stewart told me –

I first met Lee in Durham jail in 1986 but before that his name seemed to be everywhere in any wing in any prison I went in. When I actually met Lee in person he was very different from the person I was expecting to meet. I was expecting to meet this fierce Lion but he couldn't have been anything further from what I'd heard on the prison grapevine.

In Durham Lee just wanted to keep his head down but he was not allowed to because the screws were trying to goad him 24/7. Most of the time I was in Durham with Lee the screws just kept him down the block or when he was out and he had put his name down to use the punch bag in the gym they'd put a notice on the punch bag room saying, "out of use". In fact they closed the boxing room down and when Duffy got shifted it opened back up the very next day.

It happened time and time again and that's when Lee got it into his head that the Durham screws had it in for him, because they did.

When Lee clipped someone in Durham that was the end of him in there and he was off to another prison. It was too much of unpaid overtime having the likes of Fred the head, Sykesy and Duffy all in the same prison at the same time so they got rid of them all slowly but surely and sent them off in different directions. Saying that, my memories of Fred the head and Lee were that they got on fantastic. Every time Lee saw Fred he had a smile on his face whereas he hated Sykes. Paul Sykes did a few tours of Durham when I was in there. Back then though it wasn't only those three men who could have it as the "Tamsies", the Abadom's and the Conroy's were all equally as naughty and each had their own reputations.

I also spent a little time with Lee in Acklington (HMP Northumberland). In my time in Acklington I got a job as a reception orderly which is for the good lads. Well because I had this job, which was a position of trust if you like, I got a list a week in advance of who was being transferred to Acklington. I saw Lee Duffy's name on that list the week before he arrived but I never said a word to the others on the wing. The reason I didn't was because there was a load of lads from Boro who were talking about Duffy on a daily basis. About what they'd done to him, how they'd told him straight or what they were going to do with him first chance they set eyes on him blah blah blah... I think I must have been the only con in the jail that knew that Duffy was on his way up but I never said a word. I know a few of the screws who I worked with in the reception said to me, "watch what happens to all these gobshites on Monday when Duffy turns up!" Well rightly enough that Monday came and the bombshell arrived and it soon got around the prison that the Duffer had landed and I'm not kidding you, because I was one of the first lags to see Lee arrive with me working in the reception, but when Lee arrived all the pretend hard men got up from sitting in association and walked behind their door and closed it behind them.

With me having a job of trust it also meant that I would get extra gymnasium. Normally you only got a load of gym if you were a red band (trusted con) but Duffy had it every single night in Acklington when I was there just to keep him quiet. In Acklington gym they used to be a punchbag and a ring and when you wanted to use it you had to book it in for maybe 10 mins a spot and he used to get his turn more than any other con hammering away at this giant brown Everlast leather bag. One thing I did witness with my own eyes was just how much of an awesome trainer Lee Duffy was in the gym. Powerlifting, free-weights bag-work you name it he could do it. He was just the complete athlete compared to your average con who lived on a diet full of shite. Lee used to demand extra food on the servery if it was the good food, you know the steaks or sausages. He'd make you give his mates more as well, he was never a greedy lad wasn't Lee. Even with bits of dope he was always giving bits away to the people he liked and he loved carrying a spliff behind both ears and the screws wouldn't do a thing.

Lee would make a habit of only demanding good food and that's what he got. I think the reason he got "ghosted" (moved away in the middle of the night) was to break any bonds that he had made and to break his spirit so that he couldn't influence any other prisoners, being 'ghosted' was usually reserved for Cat A prisoners though. Lee was moved on and a black prison van came and moved him in the night. I just remember the inmates were all saying that Duffy had been "ghosted" off to Armley. I knew Lee was sent to Leeds nick because Lee wrote me a letter telling me that when he'd been "ghosted" in the night it was by 12 prison guards all tooled up in riot gear or mufti squad as we used to call them. They just sprung it on Lee at the last minute. There was that many because they was expecting Lee to kick off but he went quietly. He said it was in the middle of the night and he was that tired he couldn't be bothered anyway he said, "alright lads, lead the way" and he was off. I got letters from Lee for months until I was released.

When I first heard the news that a Middlesbrough man had been murdered my first thoughts were that it was either Lee or Cockerill (Brian) that's the honest truth. When I found out it was Lee my stomach churned. A young lads life snuffed out like that at 26 years old it's fucking terrible.

Every time I'm ever in Stockton these days I think of Lee because that's where we used to meet doing business when we were out.

The story that makes me laugh the most when I think about Lee Duffy was the story he himself told me. Lee told me he got in his car one day in just a pair of shorts and trainers and drove all the way up to Tyneside. When he got there Lee told me he went to Viv's busiest door which was ran by Stuey Watson. Lee said he demanded to know where Viv Graham was but the bouncer didn't know. The doorman said he'll call Viv now on the condition that he doesn't belt him. When I asked Lee what happened he said, "the lad rang Viv but Viv's phone was off". I mean, when was Viv Graham's phone ever turned off? If you knew him you'd know what I mean. Lee told me he didn't lay the doorman out as he'd done in the past because he wanted him to give him a message which must have been a frightening experience for Viv. Lee told me it was a Sunday and that he was just bored in his house so he'd gone up to Newcastle to make a statement. For me Viv didn't want nothing to do with Duffy and that said it that day when his phone was turned off. I was told that Viv was expecting bother that day and left his phone off all night but Viv was a businessman, Lee was all about being a pure caveman.

"I wondered, I guessed and I tried… You just knew".

Mike Scott

ANONYMOUS

Whether you loved or despised Stephen Richards books which had Lee Duffy in them they certainly put Lee Duffy in the public eye. Over the years Mr Richards has come in for a lot of criticism from people not happy with the contents of his books. I myself have been a victim of Mr Richards past projects as several times when I've asked people to speak with me, I've been met with the answer of, "I won't speak with you because of what you put in the other books about Lee". This was before I'd even done the first one, meaning they'd got me mixed up with Stephen Richards. Another source told me he wouldn't speak with me because of what I put in the Tax Man, Brian Cockerill's book in 2005, that wasn't me either, that was also Stephen Richards.

On speaking to Viv Graham's wife recently it was very nice for me to hear that although she's never read last year's Lee Duffy book, she was told that my book wasn't like the others and was far more accurate and very fair which was always my aim. Although I agree with Lee's uncle Rod in 'The Whole of the Moon' that the fight to the death between Duffy and Graham was a ploy to sell books, I have no doubt the beef between them was very real. I spoke with an eyewitness near the end of this book to confirm exactly my thoughts.

He said: –

I'm 57 years old now and I grew up in Newcastle. I hadn't heard of Lee Duffy until the night I saw him chasing Viv's bouncers around cars. The lad who I was out with at the time who'd done a lot of work through Middlesbrough told me all about this man who'd come into our town looking for the hardest Geordie of them all Viv Graham.

Looking back on that time I can remember it clearly like it was yesterday. I was on Shields Road in Byker drinking and I heard there was a fella from Boro that had come on his own looking for Viv. Me being a young and inquisitive lad decided with my mate to have a walk over to the town and have a nosey and see if what we'd heard was true. When me and my mate got to the Beehive, I'll never forget one worried looking doormen telling me and my pal, "here you two get in the bar quickly, Duffy's in town and on a mission." You'd have thought Newcastle was being taken over by King-Kong the way he was going on and the fear written all-over his face. Like I said I hadn't heard of Duffy until that night but what Lee was doing was walking up and down the streets of Newcastle and flattening any bouncer stupid enough not to be inside. All the doormen in the Beehive were panicking when we were in the bar that sunny Sunday evening. If I told you the whole of Newcastle city centre was on lockdown because of one man then I wouldn't be lying.

After a drink or so I'd got bored so me and my pal decided to stick our necks outside the door to have a butchers. I knew that me and my pal would be safe because by that time everyone knew that Duffy was looking for Viv Graham and any bouncers not civilians like us. As I've been out for maybe three or four minutes I saw this big lump of a lad marching up the road looking totally focused. He looked like he was a man with a job to do and that job was to seek and destroy on sight any of Viv's doormen. I'll never forget it as long as I live that when I saw Duffy he had a red t-shirt on, shorts and a pair of red Fila boots. As I followed this huge man he walked straight up the Bigg Market several times, as well as stopping outside of the old Macey's Nightclub too. I personally knew one of the doormen Lee set about that night. A few days after it I asked him what happened and he told me the only thing Duffy said to him before he punched his lights out was, "give Graham this", then BANG and the next thing he knew he was being put in the recovery position by a barmaid and she was calling an ambulance for him. One

249

of the things I did see personally was Duffy chasing a bouncer around a car like a game of cat and mouse but Lee didn't manage to get him. I'm well aware that these sound like made up stories but they aren't I was there and I was an eyewitness and when I saw Duffy that evening he was completely on his own.

A little while later me and my pal ventured further up the town and none of the bars had so much as one doorman on. When I asked the barman why there was nobody on because I knew Sunday was a busy night I was told, "both have had to go to hospital from fighting with that fella from Boro earlier".

Today when you see the S.I.A doormen you see doormen 5ft fuck-all with specs who look like the Milky Bar Kid. Back then in the places that Duffy wiped out they were all big men I'm telling you. I knew a few of them and they were all big bodybuilders. Not only did Lee bash all Viv's men up but he was taunting them when he was doing it. Even when I saw Lee chasing that bouncer around the car he was psychologically breaking him down. Telling him things like he was the Duffer and he just wanted to give him a message to go back and give to Viv.

"I'm absolutely delighted at the verdict. David Allison was always an innocent man. He had to fight for his life in August 1991, he's had to speak for his life in that trial and I'm just glad the jury have given him his life back again. We were expecting this verdict. David Allison was an innocent man who did no more than what was expected of him to defend himself."

James Watson, David Allison's solicitor speaking after court in February 1993

ANONYMOUS –
CLEVELAND POLICE FIGURE

Ray Morton wasn't the only figure I was lucky to get for this book. In July 2019 I was lucky enough to pick the brains of another former top-ranking Cleveland police figure through one or two of my friends pulling a few strings on the basis that I wouldn't include his name. The former elite, top of the tree officer granted me an hour of his time one Saturday afternoon in one of Middlesbrough's plushest pubs so that I could ask him about a man he was very familiar with once upon a time.

He said: –

I would first hear Duffy's name around the early 1980s. The very first time I clapped eyes on Duffy it was because he was being dragged into the station by a lot of officers. Duffy was marked up because they'd had to give him a bit of his own medicine just to keep him at bay because he was that much of a handful.

We all got to know him down the old Dunning Street Station over a period of about eight years. Although anytime we had Lee in our custody office he was very respectful apart from during interviews when he would just give us a load of, "no reply's" as answers. Lee would never entertain any kind of interaction with us during questioning.

Overall when I look back at that generation of hard man in Middlesbrough, the likes of Allo, Dale Henderson-Thynne or Jonka Teasdale were all very respectful, not like it is today when they'll just tell you to fuck off and the rest of it. To give you an example, I once saw Kevin Duckling in the town when I was out myself drinking. I liked Kevin but one of his mates started mouthing off at me calling me a "pig" that kind of thing. Kevin turned round and knocked his mate out cold because he was embarrassed at what he was shouting over to me.

The things that Duffy used to be brought into our custody suite for was usually for chinning people. There were a few other bits and bobs like receiving stolen goods or drugs offences but Lee always seemed to be able to get off i.e. charges dropped or witnesses not turning up at court that type of thing.

One of my officers tried to arrest Lee once on Normanby Road and he went up to Duffy and told him to get on the floor, Lee then shouted back, "FUCK GETTING ON THE FLOOR, I'M GETTING ON NO FLOOR"! Lee told the officer that if he tried to put the cuffs on him that he was going to break his jaw and the officer wouldn't go near him and Lee walked.

From around the mid-eighties I saw Lee Duffy's rise to the top. I saw him turn into a monster and become the top of Teesside. Lee was the No.1 name in Boro I suppose in a fighting sense then there were the other names like I mentioned earlier along with Ducko and Cockerill.

I know many of my officers used to say it wasn't Duffy who was the name in the town it was Ducko over Duffy and maybe for a time that was true. Kevin was a real character and anytime he was in our station he just never stopped singing.

Before Duffy had a fight with Brian Cockerill, many of us in the Middlesbrough C.I.D knew that was going to happen.

It wasn't just the criminals who were different back then, through the 1980s policing was very different also. Officers tended to get away with far more. Back in those days, even though officers used to police the tough streets of Boro, they could then go drinking in The Bongo, The Madison or La Roche's and they wouldn't be approached by the villains they'd been chasing during the day because there was a line of respect that wouldn't be crossed. I've known officers who were on shift but were boozing in nightclubs and then when they've been called in they've had to interview a suspect whilst steaming drunk, then they'd go back to the club and get fixed up before they went home to their wives!

Although Duffy was a thorn in our side, many officers at Cleveland police believed there was bigger fish to fry, such as armed robbers like Keith McQuade or faces behind international drug cartels like Brian Charrington, what Duffy was doing compared to men like that was only small-time.

He was what he was but he wasn't burgling houses every day, that was the type I couldn't stomach, the utter scum like that. When I was a serving officer I went out of my way to get them off the streets at any cost and I viewed them as being far more beneficial for us to get in than Duffy ever was. They're just my views personally though.

Cleveland police knew exactly what Lee was up to when he wasn't locked up.

In the last year of Lee's life he went to another level with the assaults and some other things he was up to. We had the intelligence on him about a lot of it but we couldn't get the people to stand up in court and testify against him. We had the same problems with Peter Hoe from Eston after Lee had died. He had that same aura of badness about him that Lee had.

I'll never forget being outside Duffy's home in a disguised van when we had him under surveillance in December 1990. We'd been waiting for him for ages but he must have been tipped off because he never went near his bungalow on Durham Road in Eston. We did find out later that Duffy had been just around the corner partying.

Some of the officers working on Duffy's cases used to work like fourteen-hour days just to try and get him nailed down on some of the things he was up to.

When Lee was shot for the second time it was me with a team (including Ray Morton) that went to Aston in

Birmingham and brought the suspected culprits back to Teesside.

On the way back one of them told us everything and I do mean everything off the record. They were telling us about all the "blags" they were doing at the time. These were dangerous dangerous men. One officer asked him, "How the fuck did you miss Duffy?" He then told us that he played for Aston Villa as a youth but failed to go any further because of his poor eyesight. He also told us that before he shot Duffy, he put his balaclava on but failed to put his glasses back on and that was the reason he didn't fatally wound Duffy that night.

When Lee Duffy died a lot of the top bosses of Cleveland police were glad. Some of them were top brass too and they viewed Lee as being too much to deal with. I wasn't glad personally because I don't like to see anyone die. I know a few though whose only thought was "thank fuck that's all over!" Even the ones like me who weren't nasty about Lee were relieved his reign was over, but still I didn't want him dead!

Back in the era of chasing Duffy we were all made to earn our wages the hard way. If I look back at that time in Middlesbrough and the people we were pursuing I'd say that 98% were all mouth, Duffy was the 2% that wasn't.

In today's society Duffy wouldn't have lasted as long as he did. If he hadn't of died in 1991, he'd have been shot a dozen times over by now and killed or if not that he'd have spent the majority of his life in prison.

For all the bad guys I've locked up in my career and believe me there's a lot, Lee was up there for me in standing out in his own unique way. He'd have been a major problem in any of the biggest cities in Britain believe me.

"Disgusting, there is no justice is there! They brought too much of Lee's past up and not his (David Allison) and the only consolation is my son would have wanted it this way. My son would not have sent that man to jail so that's all that's keeping me going. Lee wasn't a man who would have took anyone to court".

Lee's mother Brenda speaking outside of court at the end of the eight-day trial. Brenda went on to say that she now wanted a full investigation into cases of violence against her son.

FAMILY, FRIENDS & ENEMIES
– as told to the press

LAWRIE DUFFY SENIOR – FATHER

"Our son was a hoodlum" the frank words of Lawrie Duffy – father of South Bank hardman Lee Duffy. In a remarkable admission the loving father revealed how his son – stabbed to death in a street fight – ran a number of illegal rackets in South Bank and Middlesbrough. "But he was not a member of a gang" said Lawrie, who was given money by his son.

He admitted he was doing things illegally and was making money. He told me what he was doing. He said, "I make money out of what I'm doing and other people are making things illegally, I stop them doing it and I do it," he said.

Lawrie and his wife Brenda are a typical Teesside couple. They live on a typical South Bank council estate. There is nothing special or exciting about them. They live a normal life except one thing, their son Lee was a notorious criminal. But his death in a street fight has left them devastated and unable to cope. Even today (1993) they are still haunted by the memories of their son. After his death the hardest thing they have faced is the trials of the men accused of trying to kill Lee. They knew their son was a criminal with a fearsome reputation for violence. But they cannot accept why or how they were let down by a criminal justice system. They think their son was written off by lawyers and judges appointed to protect everyday people. There were three savage attacks on their son – he was shot twice by hired hitmen and petrol was hurled over him in a bizarre execution bid. But all the men accused of the attacks were set free by the courts when witnesses refused to testify or the Crown offered no evidence. There were rumours of bribes being offered and threats of violence. A violence that pervaded the shadow world walked by Lee Duffy

BRENDA DUFFY – MOTHER

"He was no monster", were the words from Brenda Duffy. Days after being stabbed to death a national Sunday newspaper painted Lee Duffy as a brutal drug dealing thug. Grief-stricken mum Brenda was horrified when she read the damning story. "Yes he was a hard man but he was not a monster" she said at her family home in Keir Hardie Crescent, South Bank.

The mum of four still remembers the antics Lee got up to as a child – falling off the roof of a South Bank club, teaching himself to swim in six weeks and then swimming a mile. "He was always a mischievous child but was always a soft kid and loving," she said.

His first real taste of violence came at 14 when he was attacked and knocked unconscious in a fight with a mob of thugs. Young Lee Duffy was awarded £80 compensation. "He never got hard or stuck up for himself until then," said Mrs Duffy. After the battering the youngster decided to take up boxing to protect himself. "I am proud of my son. He was a legend and there was only one Lee Duffy," she said. "He used to come round every day and he was my life. He was the hardest man walking and knew people were frightened of him, but Lee was a target. I am absolutely disgusted about what people said about Lee. He was never charged with drug offences. He was never up for shoplifting and never demanded money with menaces," she added. She says her son was never afraid to show love and often kissed her and her husband Lawrie in the local workingmen's club. "That was the sign of a hardman. He was not afraid to show his love in public," She said.

LORNA LANCASTER – THE FRIEND

The grim lesson of the boot. Lee Duffy was often beaten up as a child, and the beatings, often handed out by older youths, affected him badly according to a close friend. Judo champion Lorna Lancaster says she was like a sister to young Lee. When he was only 6, 19 and 20-year olds used to stick the boot in. I think that had an effect on him," said Lorna. People should know what he went through as a child. He had lots of hassle at school. There were people who got him when he was young that he wanted to get back," she added.

The British judo international carried Lee on her shoulders when she went on training runs. She took him swimming, to judo and boxing lessons. She feels he could have been a top sportsman if his energies had been routed in the right direction. "He'd have made a great PE teacher," said Lorna, a born-again Christian now living in Sheffield. Lorna also took Lee to Christian meetings from time to time. "He was always well behaved," she said. He was a mischievous kid but we all were. He used to go all over with me and tell people I was his sister, that he was called Lee Lancaster!"

Lorna first met Lee when he was six years-old and took him to judo lessons at The Budokan in North Ormesby and boxing at Grangetown Boy's Club, but it was really in the swimming pool where Lee really excelled, said Lorna. "He could have swum the English Channel. I'm a lifeguard and he was a far better swimmer than me."

Lorna left Teesside more than ten years ago (write up was from 1993) but kept close links with Lee's mum Brenda. "Lee got a lot of love and attention from his mother" said Lorna. "She always wanted the best for her kids.

When I turned to the church, I wanted kids to see the good in life. I used to be a street fighter, but I went to church and changed gradually." But Lee never knew any other way than stealing and fighting, all his friends were into fighting and stealing. Lorna has no reservations : "There was a lot of good in Lee Duffy," she said.

THE MENTOR

Its commonly known in Teesside that Lee was being used by people above who were pulling his strings for various criminal activities. In an interview the Gazette printed on Friday, February 19th, 1993 a well-known Cleveland criminal gave an interview and he said -

"I introduced Lee to the hard world of working the doors of clubs and pubs in the town. He was there to stop trouble. He was the best on the doors and people knew not to cause trouble if he was working. Lee was as good as gold. I am sick of the lies said about the lad. The people who said he took drugs off them should stand up and be counted. Lee was not what they said and they have just jumped on the bandwagon. He has been painted as a monster but he was a good-hearted lad and was a caring person to people who knew him. Lee gave you what you gave him. Give him love and he gave you it back. Give him respect and he gave you respect."

RIA MARIA NASIR - THE ENEMY

Ria Maria Nasir was described in the Gazette as a former prostitute and drug dealer who hired a gunmen to shoot Lee outside a blues party on Princess Road in Middlesbrough after a series of run-ins with the South Bank born hard man. Regarding that shooting Lee was very lucky because most of the pellets hit the car as he somehow managed to jump out of the way at the last second, almost cat-like.

"It was a warning," she said. The first shooting had been set up after Lee Duffy quarrelled with a North-east drug dealer. The Teesside woman had known Duffy for many years and they rarely tangled until she started dealing cannabis from her home. She was the key witness in the second shooting trial involving the 25-year bouncer. She refused to give evidence as seven men stood trial on conspiracy to cause grievous bodily harm.

The trial collapsed dramatically at Teesside Crown Court in October 1992. This is an example of just one of the long list of trials that fell to bits involving the attempts on Duffy's life.

Trouble was brewing for many months as Duffy made her sell his supplies. Lee Duffy wasn't used to men even bigger than him standing up to him so when this slightly built woman told Lee no, she began to receive threats herself, as well as her family and there were a series of sinister attacks on her home. "Lee Duffy did not frighten me and even if he did he would have been the last to know," she said. "He was just a bully and did not have the guts to face me on his todd.

I started dealing a couple of ounces of cannabis but did not go onto his patch. The people who came to me did not want the rubbish he was selling," she said. Other dealers working from South Bank were being threatened and several gathered to arrange the hit. The woman first became involved in the drug scene when she worked as a prostitute dealing in cannabis-based drugs in the blues party scene. Then over the years the drugs market became more competitive and increasingly violent with the arrival of the Duffer. Duffy was to start figuring in the brutal drugs underworld and tried to take over long-established blues parties. For months he supplied all the drugs at these terraced street gatherings and it was at one of the parties where the woman's gunmen tracked him down. At the parties Duffy would walk around "taxing" dealers who refused to sell his gear. It would never just be a "taxing", beatings, loss of money and drugs would always follow to send a message out there to other dealers. I'm told though that Lee would always give them a choice first to work for him or take what was coming. Maria told the Gazette in 1993 the final straw came when her front room window had a brick thrown through it. The woman claims at least twenty dealers wanted Duffy out of action and it was only then that she made the call to the men who would go on to shoot Lee. When the men burst through the door into that party on Hartington Road they were all heavily under the influence of cocaine and had spent the night looking for Duffy through the streets of Middlesbrough. "Guns were brought up and it went haywire. The man with the gun aimed to kill Duffy and the other man pulled the gun down. If he had not done that Lee Duffy would have been in a wooden box there and then," she said.

"One day someone will come and write a book about me."

Lee Duffy

THE FINAL WORD

Now my work is done with the Lee Duffy projects and I can walk away from it for good. If ever I'm in pubs in Middlesbrough these days all people want to talk to me about is Lee Duffy, he has again captured everyone's imagination.

During these last 18 months I've discovered so much about the life of the original Boro bad boy. As I said in the first book I grew up on a council estate in Berwick Hills, Middlesbrough and I was very familiar with who Lee Duffy was from the age of eight. For most of my youth I spent a lot of that time in various boxing gyms in Middlesbrough and his name was often spoken of among the fighting men on Teesside because boxing attracts that type doesn't it?!

What I didn't realise was the full extent of Lee's life and what he got up to until these last months from researching for the books & documentary. Even though I'd been brought up on the council estates and I've been close to the Lee Duffy story like everyone else in Middlesbrough, there's been so much more to it that I've learnt since studying Duffy that was hidden.

Middlesbrough is a rough place to grow up so it helps you to have your wits about you so I'd say its second nature to know who's who when approaching people. Even now as I write this in July 2019 and this book is about ready to be sent off to the publishers, I'm about to walk away from the Lee Duffy projects for life, there's still some things I've discovered about Lee Duffy which will remain unknown to the wider public forever because it would take a very brave man to print some of the things I've discovered and I'd say only a handful of people close to Lee will know what I'm talking about. Some have told me in the strictest of confidence and not for the book so of course I've honoured the word that I gave them and have left some details out. Others I've recorded with their permission to print what was said but it wouldn't have been right for me to put some of those details in out of respect for the remaining Duffy family.

I've even met with one of the two brothers in person who were offered £100,000 by a wealthy businessman to shoot Lee Duffy in 1991 for allegedly doing something really bad but they declined the offer. That wasn't hearsay for me, I heard that from one of the brothers' mouths.

Lee used to make the hardest of hard men disappear into walls when he was about. One very big man even told me that when Lee ever came into The Havana, he would literally try to spread himself into the leather settees to appear as small as he could so Lee didn't see him as the 6ft 5 man he was. That's a crazy tale but it's true.

Yes we all know by now what Lee Duffy was but I've also heard of people misunderstanding Lee. Quite recently I spoke to Middlesbrough's most successful ever professional boxer, Grangetown's Cornelius Carr. Cornelius told me how he once saw Lee "eyeballing" him all night in Bennetts Nightclub. Now you can't blame Cornelius for just thinking 'oh that's Lee Duffy wanting to fight me because I'm a boxer', when in actual fact, when Cornelius' sister pulled Lee a couple of days later and asked him why was he staring her brother out all night was he wanting to fight him? Lee responded totally innocently saying, "I was wanting to speak with him about his boxing honestly but I didn't know how to approach him".

Over the last year when I've had some of the unpleasantries sent to me one of the things I've heard several times is "ooh I hope the curse of Lee Duffy is going to get you eventually Jamie". It's a saying that's been said over the last quarter of a century in Middlesbrough because several of those involved with Lee Duffy's demise in one way or another have eventually faced their own karma and are no longer here. I did cover this in the first book but since I brought 'The Whole of the Moon' out the lady Ria Maria Nasir who put the second contract out on Lee with the Birmingham men died suddenly on October 23rd, 2018 aged 66 but I was told by a family member of hers that she read the first book before she died.

Also a story I've been made aware of since the last book was after Lee's grave was smashed up on one of the four occasions that I'm aware of, a man who was responsible in carrying out such an evil unforgivable act on the authority of others actually ended up taking his own life because he was that worried about the repercussions of his actions. The man hung himself even after Brenda Duffy, Lee's mother, caught up with the man and told him she forgave him for what he was made to do by others. The circumstances that occur around people associated with these stories just carry on.

Maybe the saddest story of all I've heard was when I went to the studios of BBC TEES whilst doing some PR for this final book, I was invited onto the very likeable Scott Makin's morning show and he played our chat in two parts, only separating the show to play The Whole of the Moon. When I announced that myself, Steve Wraith and Neil Jackson's company Media Arts were doing the Whole of the Moon documentary I was approached by two BBC members only for them to both come back to me and tell me that although it was a huge mega story in the Teesside area, their boss had told them to stay away from the Lee Duffy story because it upsets listeners which I can understand. To be honest when I went in to see Priestfield born lad Scott Makin he told me he wasn't even sure if he'd be allowed to air such a highly controversial subject like Lee Duffy but he asked me in and he was going to push for it. In the end Scott got his way and the interview was aired in April 2019.

Scott told me that back in 1993 he was working for Big Mac's Talk In and his job was to take the calls for Big Mac before handing them over to him live on air. Scott told me that he got a call from a woman named 'Brenda' and that she just wanted to talk about her son who'd died not long back. Of course Scott agreed and he told me the show didn't have any idea who she was or what it was about until she dropped the bombshell of "my son was Lee Duffy" live on air. Scott said he'll never forget the words the broken Brenda said on the show and its stayed with him for over a quarter of a century when Brenda said, "I always knew I would lose him one day but I thought he'd have at least made thirty". Brenda said she knew Lee was a "wrong un" but even she just didn't even realise more than half of the stuff Lee had got up too until well after his death.

I know somebody very close to Lee told me that his younger sister and closest sibling Louise told Brenda so much after Lee's death and only then did she discover the full picture of what he had been getting up to.   I imagine we could all say the same for our own parents though couldn't we?!

One story which did make me smile was the story Scott Makin told me before we went on air. Scott told me that only two weeks before Lee Duffy died his best friend "big Marty" had a kinda altercation with Lee that he'd never forget. Scott told me exactly what happened, he said "my mate big Marty was driving on Marton Road just up near Stewarts Park in Middlesbrough when a car collided with his. Now Marty was a big guy of maybe 6ft 3 but wasn't what you would call a fighter. He said when he got out of the car he saw the giant of a man with spiked hair get out of the other car who then came walking over to him saying ' OOOOOOHH... NOW THEN NOW THEN... NAUGHTY NAUGHTY and tutting as you would to a naughty child! Well it was Lee Duffy. What the funniest thing at that time was that it was August 1991 and big Marty must have been one of the only people in Teesside who didn't know who Lee Duffy was, so when Lee asked him "do you know who I am?" Big Marty just said "nooor mate who are ya" In a slightly embarrassed stage whisper! Marty even asked him if he'd gone to school with him or was he a celebrity?! Marty said Lee looked at bit amazed that he didn't know who he was then he seemed annoyed thinking that Marty was taking the piss, I mean, big Marty would have normally been cannon fodder for Duffy because he was a big guy and Lee was forever knocking big men like Marty out. In the end Lee said to him 'what, so you're telling me you really don't know who I am'? and Marty apologised and I think the penny dropped for Lee that Marty was telling the truth. Before he left he said that he'd been shot twice and had petrol poured over him and that he was Lee Duffy and maybe he should start reading the papers, then Lee got back in his car and drove off. Big Marty then saw his face in the papers a few weeks later and realised just how lucky he'd been. I think his own stupidity was his own saving grace on that day".

I was also on Hartlepool radio doing an interview that was aired and afterwards the show's producer Paul Suggitt told me that the listeners ratings had shot up because we were speaking about Duffy and I was even invited back to speak about the aftermath of this book. Paul told me that even though he grew up in Hartlepool he was always hearing about what this crazy guy in Boro was up to across the water. One of the Radio stations even told me they'd played The Waterboys song much more than usual since my book about Lee came out last year in 2018.

Today in 2019 the population of the whole of Teesside is said to be over 376,000 and I bet over a big percentage of them remember the name Lee Duffy.

Whether people like to admit it or not, in August 1991 after Lee Duffy's death it was the end of an era for Middlesbrough. So many people have come up to me since they have read the first book and have spoken to me about one of the end chapters in the book, 'The Day the End Came' and said, "Jamie that chapter alone moved me to tears because it was that hard hitting and revealing".

I've done a hell of a lot of research myself into the fatal injury which ultimately cost Lee his life. It was his main artery in the top of his left arm just under the armpit. If you put your right arm across your left and feel inside you'll feel almost like a wire, that's the one that was cleanly severed completely. The experts say when that happens a human will die with 5 - 60 minutes maximum and then they've had it. The hospital medics told me for Lee to survive such an horrendous cut he'd had to literally be on hospital grounds to survive and have been operated on within 6-7 minutes of it first happening.

It goes without saying that the amount of drugs Lee was on at the time didn't help his cause and it thinned his blood it is also possibly why his heart was enlarged at the time of his autopsy too.

From my intensive research Lee was stabbed around 3.20am but was pronounced dead at 3.55am although he was clinically dead thirty seconds to one minute before that so I'd say he died around 35 minutes after the stab wound was inflicted and he slipped into unconsciousness maybe twelve to fifteen minutes after he was fatally wounded.

The one man who shouldn't be forgotten about in all this was Lee's friend until the end Mark Hartley. Although Mark declined to speak with me. Mark told me that after Lee Duffy's murder trial in February 1993 he never looked back and changed his life from then onwards. Mark told me all he concentrated on was his family and business and the reason why was that the list of casualties from his era and amongst his close friends was staggering. Mark told me a list of some of the former associates he was once close to during various periods of his life.

Davey Allo killed Lee Duffy 1991,Keith McQuade allegedly killed Lee King in 2000 who was only aged 32, Anthony Allan (Ano) died tragically aged just 42 in the Parkend pub 2010, Kevin Auer hung himself at his home in Thorntree aged 36 1998, Paul Debrick was found dead in his home at Teesville aged just 42 in 2007 and is now buried very close to Lee's plot, Boola (Hassan George Farah) killed Speedy and got a life sentence then died inside, "Wogo" Watson killed himself in 2001 but had also been accused of murder, David Fields received a life sentence for blasting Peter Homer with a sawn-off and then stole his car in 1993, drugs king pin John McPartland died in Frankland prison in 2002 whilst serving a 12 year sentence for dealing heroin, Teesside drug baron John McCormick aged 47 was found shot dead outside of his flat in Denmark by a 9mm handgun in 2002, Richy Neal who was the only man to receive a conviction in the Lee Duffy murder trial in 1993 died in 2011 aged just 38. I've been told from good sources that although Richy Neal received an 18-month sentence for perverting the course of justice it wasn't even him. He was allegedly taking the rap for his friend Lee King who'd only recently stabbed a police officer beforehand and was going to be going down for some serious time if Richy Neal hadn't of taken the wrap, Redcar hardman Kevin "Rico" Richardson who was part of the 1990 Strangeways riots was gunned down outside the Parkend Community Centre in January 1993 age just 29, allegedly shot by Keith McQuade, Keith McQuade himself died in Hull prison age 54 while serving a life sentence in 2009. Keith McQuade the Middlesbrough villain was once at the heart of the extraordinary "cash for guns" affair, Micky Salter was stabbed to death at a family barbeque in Saltersgill in May 2001 which ended in a neighbour doing a life sentence, Eston's Paul Bryan went on to shoot three people, killing two of them in Leeds in 2000. Paul Bryan received a double life sentence, Tommy

Hoe lost his life, Peter Hoe was murdered in his own Eston home with a samurai sword aged just 43 in 2006, Robbie Hoe died in February 2019, Stephen Johnson killed Jed Heinz in my old local The Eagle pub in Berwick Hills, Paul Dalloway was killed by Kevin Duckling in June 1988 outside a blues party and Lee Harrison was found dead in April 2016 in Lebanon under suspicious circumstances. The overall view in Teesside and by the Harrison family was that Lee Harrison was murdered.

Mark told me all of the above were good lads in their own way before drugs & violence took over as the main focus in their lives. When Mark was talking to me and explaining his reasons for not wanting to be involved with this book I couldn't help but notice that there was an eerie feeling to all these facts and the full picture for me was beginning to build up. Afterall, all the names from above all came from within a four-mile radius of each other. Every one of them knew or was very familiar with each other, whether that was going to football matches together or growing up in the youth clubs as kids in "Boro". There's many more names Mark told me who were close friends of his that I wasn't allowed to mention, names close around Mark who'd been shot, stabbed or attacked with baseball bats. Mark told me that in his generation among his friends life was cheap.

That generation from around 1980 until after Lee's murder trial in 1993 was in my opinion the craziest of Middlesbrough's almost 200-year-old history and will never be repeated. In my opinion the death of Lee Duffy has had a deep traumatic effect on Mark Hartley and it's one thing he doesn't like thinking about so I'm grateful that he spoke to me about it at all. I think when Lee Duffy died in his arms Mark lost a huge chunk of himself that night.

One of the sad things is that over the years fully grown adults have made up lies to Mark saying that they were there, one even telling him that Lee died in his arms! The same man goes around telling people he picked Lee up from the hospital when he was shot. It takes all kinds in life doesn't it?! I fully understand Mark Hartley's reluctance to speak about that awful time in his life and I've respected his wishes. It wasn't Mark but the countless by standers who were there that night who told me what happened and how Mark ran to his friends aid and cradled him in his arms in front of Fife street next to the gold drain that still bore Lee's blood the day after. Telling the dying Duffy to stay with him and reminding him to think of his loved ones. I told you in the first book about how not one but two taxi's turned around when they saw who it was dying on the floor.

In actual fact it wasn't a taxi that took Lee, Mark Hartley, Peo and a 3rd man whose name I know but who will remain unnamed. This unnamed man still to this day has the very shirt he had on that night still covered in Lee's blood in a bag. The man who drove the four of them to the old Middlesbrough General Hospital, was a man named John Smith (that's his actual name). John raced through every red light in record time up Borough Road, left onto Linthorpe Road which took Lee passed his favourite place in the world The Havana one final time and right onto Ayresome Street and into the hospital grounds and into the A&E entrance after Lee gave out the death rattle in Mark Hartley's cradling arms. Mark had had all his fingers over the deep wound all the way but it was to no avail. It didn't seem to stem the blood flow, it kept on coming regardless of Mark's efforts. His large heart had stopped because of the lack of blood being pumped through his system.

The one thing I will say though and I've heard it over and over again is that the hospital staff were incredible in trying to save Lee's life. As soon as they ran out to treat Lee they all were around him and around different parts of his body like busy bee's trying to save Lee's life but it was to no avail, even after they'd shocked him with the paddles lifting Lee's body a foot in the air It was too late and I'm told that no hospital in the world would have managed to save him. Lee was gone. I was told that even though Lee had been there only minutes the full hospital corridor was like a scene from a horror film, it really was that gruesome. I have actually spoken with one of the St John's ambulance staff that was on duty that night and he told me even when Lee was laying in the morgue that some other members of staff were saying terrible things about Lee. He told me that Lee had often kept them busy over the years in the A&E department that's for sure. Although the man I spoke with from Saltburn remained respectful when talking to me about Duffy he did tell me that one of the most used questions in A&E to patients when they'd come in with all kinds of injuries i.e. broken jaws on a Saturday night was, "did Lee Duffy do this to you"? Usually many were too scared to say but some did acknowledge it but tell staff please don't say anything. He told me he certainly provided a lot of overtime for the paid staff in Middlesbrough General Hospital over the years, more so during the last year of his life.

It did seem though that Lee had an awful lot of bad luck to his left side himself in general, having been shot in his left knee, left foot and then fatally wounded in his left arm just under his left armpit in just eight months.

Now today in 2019 through my books and documentary people are curious once again. Some that weren't even born before Lee died.

Who really was this young kid who instilled absolute terror into the hardest men in Teesside? Did he really do it all on his own? Some of Lee's closest friends I've spoken to have even told me they couldn't speak with me even if they wanted to because now their grandkids are asking questions about who this Lee Duffy was and grandad can't be seen as being associated with such a villain.

The bottom line is the tornado that was Lee Duffy happened and now in death his name is bigger than it ever was because Teesside just can't get enough of the towns favourite bad guy. Although I'm done and I've enjoyed researching such a character I don't think it will be the end of Lee Duffy. Don't be surprised in the next few years to see film companies coming along to bring to life the Lee Paul Duffy story and take it to the big screen like the Paul Sykes books I've done. Work starts on the Sykes film in late 2020.

Before Lee's death in 1991 he wasn't only causing men like Viv Graham in Newcastle nightmares, he was even giving international drug lords like Toxteth's Curtis "Cocky" Warren sleepless nights and that came from Warren's mouth in 2017. A very good friend of mine goes into prison almost on a daily basis with his registered charity trying to help criminals reform. My friend is asked to go visit the worst of the worst like Lee Rigby's killers and other monsters in the most secure prisons in England.

How Curtis got on the subject of Lee was when my friend was stood up giving a talk and Curtis asked him where his accent was from? "Middlesbrough" was the reply, then Curtis asked him if he knew Lee Duffy which my friend told him he once did, very well in fact. Curtis told him that although he never actually met Duffy in person, Lee had caused him big issues as Lee had been taxing the people that he employed. That was Curtis Warren talking who went on to make millions with the Columbian cartel.

Over the last twelve months and because of the work I do now writing books about criminals amongst other subjects, I've spoken to several people regarding Lee Duffy such as former Kray gang member Chris Lambrianou, ex London gangster Dave Courtney, bareknuckle boxer Decca Heggie and one half of the Richardson torture gang Eddie Richardson who've all asked me questions in regards to this young upstart from South Bank. Everybody knows his name and is intrigued in his story.

I haven't always used the people I've spoken to during my research for these Lee Duffy projects for various reasons. Even my harshest of critics who've been against me doing these books who knew Lee very well have admitted that Lee would be loving all this attention and being spoken about almost 30 years on. Some have given me interviews then changed their minds and ask me to delete it, more than once, others have just become far too difficult and even though they were big names in the Lee Duffy story it's been better to give them a swerve.

There's some stories though which have really been powerful and thought provoking, like stories that Lee has visited them in death. One man told me he saw Lee sat on his bedroom chair where Lee's shirt has been folded over for the last 20 odd years. Another has told me that a few weeks after Lee died he heard Lee's unmistakable voice clearly from behind him saying the words "pray for me" and he fell to his knees in tears praying for Lee. I couldn't help but notice just how emotional this very religious man was getting when he was telling me this.

I think it's ironic that I must have walked past the West Afro & Caribbean club for a good 25 years without even giving it a second glance once in that quarter of a century. Then when I finally decided to write the books on Lee it was bulldozed completely down not long before. It would have been interesting to have been allowed in to see where it all happened.

What doesn't get spoken of much though was that Lee had a side to him just like me and you. However small that side of him was, Lee adored his one and only true love Lisa. The people close to Lee have told me just exactly how much of a loving boyfriend he was to her and a loving father to their baby daughter who was only 6 months old when Lee died. Lee loved nothing more than bathing his tiny baby girl and dressing her. I've been told that he was a very loving father to all of his children.

As much as he had that ferocious hardman streak in him there was also a gentle, soft side which only a handful of people close to Lee Duffy ever saw. I know from speaking to certain people that the stories of Lee being in tears and saying that he wanted to change only 3 weeks before he was killed are very true. Lee knew deep down that at only 26, because of what he'd done over the last 8 years there was a no going back policy.

It's so terribly sad that at such a young age this kid thought he was doomed and just had to carry on being The Duffer, the Teesside Terminator, the seek and destroyer, the bounty hunter of Boro which he'd turned into, especially when you see the amount of hardmen who've went and turned their lives around at a much older age, men I know on a personal level like ex lifer and former Kray gang member Chris Lambrianou and ex street tramp Gram Seed. Then you've got the dozens of others who I don't know but I've read their books. Men like Bobby Cummines, Noel "Razor" Smith and Jimmy Boyle who all turned their lives around and were released, even after being sentenced with life sentences. I find it so sad that Lee spoke like a terminally ill man of 86 at only 26 and that he knew he was going to die. Like there was just no way out and that he was doomed and that he just accepted his fate and continued to batter people.

I believe his full story, life and crazy times have only just begun to be told. Remember when you judge that evil vicious brute named Lee Duffy, his life was snuffed out before he even reached his prime. He never had the chance to change his ways in his thirties like you and me. He'll be forever young and forever causing mixed emotions in the town he knew so well for many many decades to come yet and all your grandchildren will know the name of Lee Duffy, even in twenty years to come. Through his death though maybe he achieved exactly what he wanted and that was a lifetime of immortality in death. Brenda Duffy once gave an interview in The Sun paper in 1993 and she said, "if Lee could have had his life again I don't think he'd have changed a thing" so maybe he did in life what he wanted to achieve and got to the top and died there. Brenda was very public in defending her son after his death. Threatening several papers saying that she'd like it in writing that Lee was a drug dealer because he was never convicted.

Even the very first name you automatically think of regarding Lee Duffy said to me 'Lee Duffy' was a one off and you'll never see his like again. In fact, I'd go as far to say That Lee Duffy has almost put Middlesbrough on the map because who else has been a bigger splash than him in the true crime element?

In my humble opinion and as somebody who's studied true crime for almost 30 years nobody comes close to the level of notoriety that man caused from just a small town in the North East. Lee Duffy was the ultimate at everything that he did. One man described Lee to me as a gunslinger who was born in the wrong era. He said he'd have been far better suited to being like Billy the Kid fighting men every day. There's no getting away from it as far as violence went, Lee Duffy was an absolute Neanderthal/caveman who once even broke his own brothers jaw allegedly.

Lee would often mix his dark humour with his violent side, like the time after he'd had his scuffle with Brian Cockerill. One man told me that when Lee rang him and the man told Lee that he was with big Bri, Lee then before slamming the phone down and said, "wait there I'll be five minutes. The man on the phone thought great, I'm dead here. The man thought that Duffy was gonna run in and dust Cockerill then batter him for just being in Brian's company. What Lee failed to mention on the phone was he'd already made his peace with Brian the day before but didn't tell him. Lee wanted him to panic and believe me that's just what that man did for the next five minutes. Only for Lee to walk in and barge over to Cockerill as if he was about to fight him but at the last second start cuddling Brian and then laugh at the incredibly worried man. Lee thought that was hilarious.

One of Lee's most used saying was, "I have no scruples when it comes to violence" and he most certainly didn't. For all the fights Duffy had in his life and I mean certainly after the ages of 18 he hardly took much punishment back. Nothing seemed to faze him. Even situations like when four big men came from Sunderland went to The Miners Arms in Eston. Him and Kevin Duckling went through the lot of them with ease.

Another similar true tale was when four men from out of town went into The Havana looking for Lee to beat him up. Just before they came, Lee asked my uncle Michael Parsons if he'd back him up, well the truth is he didn't need backing up because Lee ended up giving the four men all a hiding on his own.

In all the fights that Lee was involved with from 18 to 26 I've never discovered anything about any 50/50 battles during my extensive research, where he was hanging on for dear life and I put that down to two things. One, he had the equalizer in both hands and two, most people were beaten like all of Mike Tyson's opponents through the 80s before it started. Nobody wanted to go and meet Duffy in a field for a one on one and if they did they just did it to save face and they were a beaten man before the blows were traded like one man in the town I won't name. This guy had a huge name around the Speak Easy door but I'm told didn't even put a fight up against Duffy and just stood and took his medicine. To give you an example of just how terrified people were of Duffy I spoke to one cannabis dealer. He told me that when Lee was hunting him down he literally lived in his attic. He told me he was that scared of even the front door buzzer going off so he stayed in the roof space for over a week living like a rat.

A true freak of nature in every sense of the word who should have channelled his aggression and skills into much more positive ways than of the ones you're reading now.

I don't think even Lee could have seen just how crazy his life was to become back in 1982 when he was the young upstart seeking a name.

Although his life was brief his life was just one journey to reach the top of the criminal world which he was only at the top for a year or so.

Today in 2019, 26-year-old men are living at home with their parents getting tucked in off their Mams, not running Walton prison or owning the tough town of Middlesbrough and that's what makes the Lee Duffy story so hard to believe.

Lee used to laugh and say that many people's favourite saying when they were in his company was that they had to get in for their tea. Lee used to say if he had a pound for every time people told him that he'd be a rich man.

For the people who think I've written these books to glorify the life of Lee Paul Duffy are sadly mistaken. What could be glamorous about a young man who could have had it all but died before he'd even reached his prime! If that's not a powerful message for any young wannabe Lee Duffy's then I don't know what is.

He would have been 54 years old now which is still not old is it? He should have been here being a grandfather talking about all the old crazy things that he got up to, featuring in documentaries, writing books or going into schools telling the youth of today it's all just not worth it but instead he's in Eston cemetery pushing up flowers. There's nothing glamourous about that only tragedy, heartache and a waste of potential. Maybe the most ironic thing is that over 30 years ago Lee Duffy wrote letters to people from his prison cell predicting like Nostradamus that one day they'd be books written about him. I've even seen them with my own eyes... well here are those books! I don't glorify Lee in any way but the truth is nobody will come along and do what that man did in such a short space of time ever again on this planet and that is why people are fascinated with him.

R.I.P Middlesbrough's very own Lee Paul Duffy 1965 - 1991 hated by many, loved by few... Feared by all

I saw the crescent, you saw the whole of the moon, the whole of the moon...

DURHAM
by Terry Dicko

Back to Durham from courtroom to cell, having to serve
time in this Victorian dungeon of hell,

in and out of reception was quick and brief, but down in
the isolation block was waiting the chief,

Sykesy was separated far away from Lee, a fight was
brewing the screws did not want to see,

now Sykesy and Fred the head Mills had had their war but
Lee the Duffer just wanted to settle the score,

who was the prison daddy he wanted all to see, Lee even
said Fred the head could be the referee,

through the prison grapevine it was all a big fuss, but not
for the grasses and nonces getting off the prison bus,

meeting in reception Lee give them all a clip, and I can
assure you not one set up his lip,

as nonces and grasses get their just desserts, and a big
slap off the Duffer that really hurts,

so don't run to the governor to settle the score, because if
the Duff finds out he will hit you some more.

Charlie Thomas - Flying Jacket

Born on the south of the Tees
Walked the streets with memories
Sweet feelings of revenge
The wilderness and what it meant

Every man that you saw
Potentially a broken jaw
Destroy and you will be free
The Dragonora and the Princess Road
You took the money and the blow
From the crescent to the sea

Tripping like a light switch
In your head you heard a click
You got the love I need to see me through
I remember you in The Havana
Standing in your flying jacket
City lights, the whole of the moon

Live and die by the sword
Let it sweat from every pore
A t-shirt to wipe your brow
You walked well through the fire
You really couldn't get much higher
There is no fear of dying now

They locked you up and made you lame
A wild horse no one could tame
From the victim to the rave
Through the fog by the bridge
I think of you a little kid
From the prison to the grave

Also available

The Sayers:
Tried and Tested at the Highest Level
ISBN: 978-1-9114820-5-5

Coming from a huge close-knit family of street traders long before it was legalised, Stephen Sayers spent his early years on the barrows, witnessing constant brushes with the law. Aunties and uncles were frequently incarcerated and a hatred and distrust of authority swelled within the younger members of the family. The scene was set. Standing alongside his brothers and cousins in vicious street fights and feuds with rival gangs, they've been linked to multi-million pound armed robberies, extortion, unsolved gangland murders and protection rackets. Those links made them a formidable force in the criminal underworld. Stephen gives us a first-hand account of growing up as a Sayers and living up to the reputation the name carries. He didn't just carve out a criminal career, he wrote it in blood on the streets. If you've heard the rumours... if you believe them... the Sayers run Newcastle. Check out **www.thesayers.co.uk**

Lee Duffy: The Whole of the Moon
by Jamie Boyle
ISBN: 978-1-9125430-7-6

A book which has taken over 25 years to arrive. The definitive story of the man who held an eight year reign of terror over the town of Middlesbrough. Containing many first hand and previously unheard accounts from some of Duffy's closest friends and associates.

Lee Duffy 'The Whole of the Moon' Documentary DVD

From Media Arts

August 25th 1991 at 3.55am saw the inevitable end to Lee Duffy's life. Everyone knew Lee's existence on this planet would be brief, including Lee and his Mother but the news Teesside was waking up to that gloriously sunny morning would rock it to its foundations. Lee has been gone now more years than he was alive although he is still spoken of as if he was here yesterday. Lee Duffy was arguably Teesside's most prolific criminal but where did his violent side stem from? Was he a figure of evil or misunderstood?

Coming Soon from Warcry Press

Terry Dicko: The Madness Continues

What's it about? Well the clues in the name... More bonkers tales of the funny man from Teesside coming this Halloween. The eagerly anticipated follow up to Laughter, Madness & Mayhem.

Paddy Moloney – The Altar Boy

Tales from the estates of Middlesbrough over the last 50 years.

Matty Turner – From Boys to Champs

Marty has given 42 years his life to grass roots amateur boxing on Middlesbrough